CURRENT ISSUES IN AUDITING

Second Ed

D1099110

Edited by

MICHAEL SHERER

M.A. (Econ.), F.C.A.
Royal London Professor of Finance, University of Essex

and

STUART TURLEY

M.A. (Econ.), C.A.
Peat Marwick McLintock Senior Lecturer in Accounting,
University of Manchester

P·C·P
Paul Chapman
Publishing Ltd

Paul Chapman Publishing Ltd
144 Liverpool Road
London
N1 1LA

British Library Cataloguing in Publication Data
Current issues in auditing. -2nd. ed.
  1. Auditing
  I. Sherer, Michael   II. Turley, Stuart
  657.45

  ISBN 1-85396-090-X

Typeset by Best-set Typesetter Ltd., Hong Kong
Printed by St Edmundsbury Press, Bury St Edmunds
Bound by W.H. Ware, Clevedon

Contents

Preface

When we edited *Current Issues in Auditing* in 1984 we expected, and even hoped, that a new edition would be required about five years later. We could not, however, have anticipated just how much auditing practice, the auditing profession and the regulatory framework would change during that time. Many of the current issues of today were not even on the agenda in 1984. Consequently, the second edition is not so much a revision or update of the original, but an almost completely new book.

The new regulatory framework for auditing is reflected in separate new chapters on audit expectations, fraud, regulation and the financial services sector. We have also commissioned original contributions on audit risk, computer audits, analytical review and statistical sampling in recognition of the recent developments in audit practice and methodology. All the remaining chapters, which have the same or similar titles as in the first edition, have been revised and updated to take account of changes and innovations since 1984.

In keeping with the first edition some of the chapters are written by practitioners and some by academics. In this way we hope we have maintained a sensible balance between theory and practice. This balance also reflects our intention that *Current Issues in Auditing* should be valuable reading for students on accounting degree schemes or taking professional examinations in auditing, as well as the busy practitioner in search of a lively and readable discussion of issues of the moment.

We are very grateful to everyone who took the time to give us their comments on the first edition and to suggest where changes might be made. Many of these suggestions have been incorporated into the second edition. We would also like to thank Marianne Lagrange and Catherine Blishen of Paul Chapman Publishing for the encouragement and support they gave us when preparing the first edition, and the patience and sensitivity they showed us when we kept missing the deadlines for the second. Finally, we could not have completed the second edition without the efforts of our contributors and we are very much in their debt. We only hope that they are as pleased and thrilled with the completed book as we are.

MJS
WST
August 1990

Part I
Credibility

1
Audit Expectations

Christopher Humphrey

In the first edition of *Current Issues in Auditing*, Sherer (1985, p. 1) wrote that auditors had 'come out of the closet'. Perceptions of auditing as dull and boring had, accordingly, been shattered. Auditing now had a new public image and was facing an exciting, if sometimes controversial, future ahead (p. 12). Whilst the days of attacks on the mundanity of the accountancy profession certainly seem to belong to a distant age, auditors' emergence from the closet does not mean that auditing has become a more visible and clearly understood activity. Indeed, the 1970s and 1980s have seen a growing literature on audit expectations, with doubts and uncertainties being expressed about the role of auditing, about what is expected of auditors. In particular, the professional accountancy press provides witness to an increased concern with the notion of an 'audit expectations gap', a debate fuelled intermittently by major financial scandals (such as, most recently, Barlow Clowes, Ferranti and British & Commonwealth) which place the audit function under the public microscope. The purpose of this chapter is to try to cast some light on this very matter. By offering an overview of the literature on audit expectations and analysing the issues which have been the major focus of debate, the chapter seeks to facilitate understanding of what remains a frequently misunderstood, or misrepresented, function.

STATEMENTS OF COMPANY AUDIT OBJECTIVES

Concern that the fundamentals of the rationale for auditing were misunderstood has led numerous writers over the years to call for the publication of better defined and clearly communicated statements of audit objectives. If such statements were available and had the acknowledged approval of interested parties, they would certainly provide a solid basis for answering any expectations gap problem. What can be gleaned from an analysis of contemporary professional statements on the limited company external audit function (i.e. auditing standards and guidelines published by the Auditing Practices Committee) is that the audit is primarily being portrayed as a process designed to assess the credibility of information contained in a company's financial statements. Auditing is not regarded as an exact science, designed to specify to 100 per cent accuracy the information contained in the financial statements. It is more a process of judgement, concerned to ensure that the information is reasonably accurate, true and fair, not true and correct, sufficient rather than absolute.

Christopher Humphrey, M.A.(Econ.), B.Com., A.C.A., is a lecturer in auditing and public sector accounting at the University of Manchester.

However, the heavy reliance in such professional statements, and also in any statutory declarations on auditing, on subjective terms such as reasonable, materiality, adequacy, reliability, relevance and judgement tends to cloud the audit process with a large degree of uncertainty. In particular, there remains one question (fundamental to any analysis of audit expectations) which is largely left unanswered: 'Why audit?' Why is an audit needed? What are the reasons justifying its existence and particular form and content? The obvious, but rather unhelpful, response is to say that audits are performed because statutes require them. But why was such a requirement invoked in the first place? The question remains the same. Interestingly, in this respect it is worth noting the findings of Turley's (1989) investigation of the audit methodologies of twenty-one large UK accountancy firms. A quarter of the firms' audit manuals (the closest one can get to an ABC approach of how to audit) did not contain any definition of auditing activity and, generally, very few of the manuals gave any significant discussion to explaining conceptual factors such as the need for independence, the benefits of an assessment of the credibility of the financial statements, etc. Turley concurred with the view of Mautz and Sharaf (1961, p. 1) that auditors prefer to view the audit in procedural terms: 'to them, auditing is a series of practices and procedures, methods and techniques, a way of doing with little need for the explanations, descriptions, reconciliations and arguments so frequently lumped together as theory'.

Given this, it does seen rather ironic that the cover illustration for the published version of one firm's audit manual at one stage comprised solely the dictionary definition of the verb 'to think' (Thornton Baker, 1983)!

The concepts of auditing

Any attempt to enhance understanding of audit expectations and the nature of any audit expectations gap is severely restricted if it only adopts a procedural perspective. Perhaps the resolution of the expectations gap rests in the employment of a deeper, theoretical perspective: a perspective that goes direct to the underlying concepts of auditing, to the bases on which the audit function is constructed. Indeed, if auditors are currently following procedures based on unclearly specified theoretical principles, it is not hard to see why an expectations gap exists. As Lee (1970) noted, 'if auditors do not fully comprehend their auditing role in society, then how can non-accountants be expected to understand it?'

Shifting from procedures to concepts unfortunately makes redundant a whole number of auditing texts. In the auditing literature the conceptual approach has tended to be dwarfed by the number of writers seeking to provide practical, technical guides as to how to perform an audit. Nevertheless, some auditing texts (see, for example, Mautz and Sharaf, 1961; Lee, 1986; Flint, 1988; Sherer and Kent, 1988) have explicitly sought to address the philosophical basis of auditing. As Flint argues, there has to be

> an explanation of why auditors do what they do, what they believe they achieve, and what the public believes they achieve. There has to be an explanation of the nature, purpose, possibilities and limitations of auditing so that members of society who seek to draw benefit from the function can understand what they can expect to obtain.
>
> (Flint, 1988, p. 4)

Starting from such a premiss, the general approach of these writers has been to identify a number of basic concepts and postulates about the audit function. Lee (1986), for instance, identified justifying, behavioural and functional postulates, stressing (among other things) the importance of credibility assessment to investment decisions and stewardship functions, auditor independence and accountability and the ability to obtain audit evidence in a cost-effective manner. Whilst providing a representation of the assumptions underlying the present statutory audit requirement for limited companies, however, such approaches tend to fall short on philosophical analysis. The emphasis is more on the way that auditors should behave than on exploring the reasons why auditors may behave differently and why their performance may not live up to expectations. In particular, they fail to give appropriate' consideration to alternative perspectives on the nature of professionalism. As such the views of Flint (1988, pp. 14–15) that auditing is wholly utilitarian, and Mautz and Sharaf (1961) that 'a profession exists . . . to serve society' sit uneasily with Collin's opinion (quoted in Haskell, 1984, p. 181) that 'professionals are wolves in sheep's clothing, monopolists who live by the rule of caveat emptor, but lack the integrity to admit it', or with Turley's (1989) finding that the benefits stressed by the methodologies of major audit terms are not expressed in terms of any societal role of auditing, but as a commerical service to the management of the company they are auditing.

Market-based approaches

In response to the conflicting views over the nature of, or existence of, professionalism, market-based approaches to auditing have argued that the persistence of audits through time in unregulated environments (where auditing is not a mandatory statutory requirement) provides evidence that auditing services are valued by their consumers. If auditing was not providing the necessary benefits, in a free market, the resources currently expended on auditing would be switched to more preferred products (Wallace, 1980). In examining why audits have been demanded and the valued characteristics of the audit service, then, such approaches have developed a number of hypotheses and propositions about auditing which are seen as expanding the basic concepts ingrained in the above-mentioned 'philosophical' texts. Wallace (1980), for example, identified three hypotheses in explaining the demand for auditing: the stewardship (monitoring) hypothesis; the information hypothesis; and the insurance hypothesis. The added insight provided by such hypotheses is nicely illustrated by the use of agency theory in explaining the stewardship hypothesis. According to agency theory, the demand for auditing can be generated by the agent rather than the principal (by the directors rather than the shareholders or other users contractually related to the company). The rationale for this argument is that principals are basically indifferent to the use of monitoring activities because they always have the ability to protect themselves from the risk of loss (incurred by agents spending the company's resources on personally related items, e.g. a holiday or other unsanctioned perquisites) by paying lower wages/salaries for the services of the agent. Thus, agency theory purports to establish that agents have an incentive to subject their stewardship of the principal's resources to external monitoring if the benefits of monitoring (in terms of avoiding or minimizing wage reductions through the guarantee/protection provided by the monitoring to the principal) are greater than the costs (in terms of monitoring/audit fees). Again, with the insurance hypothesis, Wallace (1980) provides additional insights on the rationales for auditing. She notes the 'deep pockets' of auditors relative to ailing or bankrupt corporations (the victims of undetected fraud) and concludes that auditors can provide some protection from an otherwise uninsurable business risk.

This consideration of the economics of information can also be used to examine the type of monitoring applied to the activities of the agent. Wallace (1980) concluded that principals (and agents) will prefer attestation of financial statements by independent, external auditors if the cost of such work is less than the accumulated cost of each principal individually undertaking the monitoring activities him- or herself. The application of cost-benefit analysis to the role and functioning of external auditing has also been utilized by Moizer (1985 and Chapter 3) in considering the likelihood of auditor cheating. He sought to analyse whether a rational economic person could be expected to 'tell the truth' – whether it would be in such an auditor's economic interests to report detected errors and omissions of management. Drawing on the work of DeAngelo (1981), Moizer concluded that such an auditor would have to weigh up the expected value of the economic interest that will be lost (if he or she is dispensed with by management for disclosing a breach) against the reduction of future net auditing revenues that will occur as a result of the loss of reputation suffered by the auditor if the misconduct (of not reporting a detected breach) is made public. The benefit of this approach is that it helps to address the aforementioned conflict between the alternative perspectives of auditors acting as altruistic, ethical professionals and profit-seeking monopolists. Moizer concluded that, even in the extreme case of an auditor acting purely on grounds of economic self-interest, there are many occasions when such an individual would choose to act in an independent manner. Interestingly, though, in a later article, Moizer (1988) presents a gloomier picture with regard to the auditor's choice of audit quality, when concluding that auditors really have an economic incentive to ensure only that the quality of audit work does not fall below the minimum specified by the law (and endorsed by the auditing profession). The relative unobservability of higher quality audit work was seen as such that it would have little impact on the reputation, and hence earning power, of the audit firm. Thus, instead of expecting auditors independently to improve the quality of their audit work, Moizer saw the stronger economic incentive being to improve their image with company management and with users of financial statements through public relations activities, etc. In a similar fashion, Kaplan (1987) has questioned market-based presumptions of auditor independence by highlighting the apparent immunity of audit firm reputations to any 'fall-out' following a publicized audit failure.

By necessity, the review above of theoretical studies of the nature of auditing has been able to provide only a broad insight on the key concepts and issues. However, what is striking is the contrasting theoretical stances with regard to expectations of the purpose and operation of the audit function. Most notable is the distinction between views of auditing as a socially orientated function (in which auditors are portrayed as ethical, socially responsible individuals) and the views of auditing as a monopolistic business (with auditors hiding behind the profitable mystique of professional judgement). Some reconciliation of this conflict can be provided through reference to theories of information economics and market-based approaches to auditing but even here there are divergent views, with some academics providing rather gloomy prescriptions of the benefits of a self-regulating audit function. Given such diversity and conflicts in theoretical perceptions, it is not surprising to find that discussions about audit expectations have become concerned with or focused on the existence of an 'expectations gap'.

The remainder of this chapter attempts to summarize the major strands of the debate on the expectations gap, including some examination of the strategies that have been put forward or implemented in order to close the gap, and the relative degree of success or impact such strategies have had. The chapter concludes with a consideration of where the debate will move in the 1990s and the likelihood of the gap being closed.

THE AUDIT EXPECTATIONS GAP

Defining the expectations gap
As might be expected from the diversity of views about the audit function, described above, a variety of definitions has been provided for the audit expectations gap. Some have seen it purely as a role-perception gap, leading to comparisons of the views of shareholders (and/or other users of audited financial statements and/or the general public) regarding the role of the audit with a predetermined, sometimes legalistic notion of what can reasonably be expected of auditors (or with what auditors believe should be expected of them). This has led to talk of an 'ignorance gap' – a gap that can be closed by the professional auditing bodies educating the recipients of audit services (and in some cases the auditors) as to what can reasonably be expected from an audit. Others have sought to broaden the definition of an expectations gap by incorporating a service delivery element – specifically considering whether auditors are performing, or are perceived to be performing, the duties that can reasonably be expected of them. A few have even sought to break down this latter category into the adequacy of current professional auditing standards and the quality of auditors' service delivery (CICA, 1988).

The difficulty in operationalizing these various categorizations of the audit expectations gap is that they rely heavily on the use of the word 'reasonable', and the implicit assumption that there exists one real, absolute way of looking at the audit function. For the purposes of this chapter, the expectations gap will be regarded in more general terms, as a representation of the feeling that *auditors are performing in a manner at variance with the beliefs and desires of those for whose benefit the audit is being carried out.*

The history of the expectations gap
The first use of the phrase 'expectations gap' can be traced to the United States, where the phrase has until recently been given much more public prominence. In early 1974 the Commission on Auditors' Responsibilities (frequently referred to as the Cohen Commission, after its chairman) was set up by the American Institute of Certified Public Accountants (AICPA) with the specific task of making recommendations on the appropriate responsibilities of auditors. In so doing, the Commission's terms of reference stated that

it was to consider 'whether a gap exists between what the public expects or needs and what auditors can and should reasonably expect to accomplish'. The AICPA had been prompted to establish the Cohen Commission by the growing public concern about the criticisms of the quality of auditors' performance. The failure of auditors to detect or disclose failures or wrongdoings by publicly owned corporations (such as Equity Funding) was also officially stated as the reason for the US government establishing a Senate subcommittee (known commonly as the Metcalfe Committee) in the autumn of 1975 to investigate and suggest ways of improving the accountability of publicly owned corporations and their auditors. This was followed in 1976 by the setting up of the House (of Representatives) Subcommittee on Oversight and Investigations of the House Commerce Committee (usually referred to as the Moss Committee, again after its chairman), which was also concerned with standards of corporate accountability. In Canada similar concerns led the Canadian Institute of Chartered Accountants (CICA), in 1977, to establish a group called the Special Committee to Examine the Role of the Auditor, which became known as the Adams Committee and reported in 1978, soon after the Cohen Commission.

Whilst the phrase 'expectations gap' may well have had its roots in North America, similar concerns about the role and accountability of auditors were concurrently being expressed in the UK (again following a number of major corporate scandals and a growing demand for greater corporate accountability – the latter reflected in the issue of the Accounting Standard Committee's (ASC) Corporate Report in 1975). Several Department of Trade investigations in the 1970s were critical of auditing practices and such concern led to the accountancy profession setting up a joint disciplinary scheme to investigate cases of public interest concerning auditors, and the Auditing Practices Committee (APC) which, as noted earlier, developed the first set of auditing standards, published in 1980.

A gap that would not go away

A feature common to many of these studies and investigations was the finding that a gap between performance and expectation did exist, and that this was not due just to ignorance on the part of users of accounting information. According to the Cohen Commission, users generally had reasonable expectations of auditors' abilities and of the assurances they can give. It attributed the expectations gap more to the public accounting profession's failure to react and evolve rapidly enough to keep pace with the changing business and social environment. Similar conclusions were reached by the Metcalfe Commission, which in calling for more visible regulatory procedures noted that 'the public is not willing to accept things on faith today. Government and business leaders must demonstrate that they are worthy of the trust they ask of the public' (Metcalfe Committee, 1978, p. 90).

The congressional findings that an expectations gap existed and that auditors were underperforming were challenged. Benston (1985) undertook a detailed analysis of the congressional recommendations and came to the conclusion that

There is little evidence of collusion and other anticompetitive actions by CPA firms. Audit failures appear to be fewer than the optimal amount as a consequence of enforced minimum standards. Therefore, there would seem to be few valid arguments for additional regulation in the public interest.

In fact, the arguments made in the Moss Report (1976) and in the Metcalfe Committee's Staff Report (1976) are almost completely devoid of empirical or logical support. If enacted, they would increase auditing and regulatory costs and reduce competition. In any event, a principal aspect of the demand for regulation by legislators, journalists, academicians, and public interest activists appears to have been fulfilled. The legislators have had publicity, journalists have gotten copy, academicians received data and the opportunity of writing papers like this, and some public interest activists have had a shot at authority.

(Benston, 1985, p. 74)

However, the notion of an expectations gap would seem to be more than an imaginary problem. With time such problems could be expected to disappear, but the issue of audit expectations has continued to remain at the forefront of debate in the 1980s.

In the USA, in 1985, the accountancy profession was again put under the spotlight of government investigation with the establishment of two congressional committees. The Brooks Committee (officially, the Legislation and National Security Subcommittee of the House Committee on Government Operations) was concerned with the quality of CPA audits of federal expenditure, which had been reported as being substandard (with frequent non-compliance with professional auditing standards). The second committee, the Dingell Committee (officially the Subcommittee on Oversight and Investigations of the House Committee on Energy and Commerce) was established to investigate the 'effectiveness of independent accountants who audit publicly owned corporations and the effectiveness of the SEC who audits those accountants'. Again the setting up of this committee came after a number of notable corporate failures where the role of the auditor had once more been called into doubt (e.g. the cases of ESM Government Securities, Inc. and Beverly Hills Savings and Loan Association).

While the Dingell Committee's hearings were in progress the National Commission on Financial Reporting (a private sector accounting-funded development, chaired by James Treadway, which became known as the Treadway Commission) was established. The Treadway Commission reported in October 1987 with a number of recommendations including restatements of the auditor's responsibility for fraud detection and quarterly reporting. At the same time as the Treadway Commission was conducting its investigations, the profession's Auditing Standards Board (ASB) launched a number of projects with the aim of reducing the expectations gap. These produced ten new statements on auditing standards (becoming known as the 'expectations gap' standards), covering such issues as the detection of fraud and illegal acts; the assessment of internal controls and audit reporting. The standards will all be in force for accounting periods beginning 1 January 1990.

The audit expectations gap has also continued to figure prominently in the 1980s in Canada, the UK and Australasia. In 1986 the CICA established the McDonald Commission (where the majority of members were not chartered accountants) with the specific task of investigating the 'public's expectations of audits'. This found considerable evidence of a gap between the public's expectations of auditors and auditor performance. As with the earlier 1970s studies it concluded that for the most part public expectations of auditors are reasonable and achieveable. In the Commission's view 'expectation gaps will only be narrowed by the profession's acceptance of the need for change and improvement', and its detailed reported contained fifty recommendations as to ways by which the expectations gap could be narrowed. The ICAEW's working party on the 'future of the audit' (ICAEW, 1986) concluded that 'there appears to be a considerable gap between the public's perception of the role of the audit and auditor's perception of that role'. According to Tweedie (1987), the need for the profession to address this issue was the prime reason for the APC establishing its Emerging Issues Task Force in early 1987. Similarly, in Australia in 1987, the president of the Institute of Chartered Accountants called on the profession to respond to public concern about the role of the auditor and to seek ways of narrowing the expectations gap, whilst in New Zealand research has been undertaken to investigate the nature of the expectations gap (Porter, 1988).

THE CONTENT OF THE EXPECTATIONS GAP

Within the confines of this chapter, it is clearly not possible to analyse all the findings and recommendations of the various investigations that have studied the issue of audit expectations in the last twenty years. However, from a review of this literature, it would appear that the debates about audit expectations have tended to focus on three main aspects of the audit function:

1.   audit assurance;
2.   audit reporting;
3.   audit independence.

Many of the relevant issues are covered in much more depth in other chapters of this book. As such, the aim here is not to provide an exhaustive coverage of these issues, but rather to highlight the key elements of concern and in so doing help to illuminate some of the deep-rooted factors underlying the audit expectations gap.

The provision of audit assurance

In reviewing studies of audit expecations and attitude surveys of users of financial statements, what is most striking is the exacting nature of perceptions of the functions performed by the present statutory external corporate audit. Rather than being seen as a probabilistic statement, the audit report has been viewed frequently as a certification, a guarantee of accuracy, even among auditors (Lee, 1970). The audit is also seen as something more than an information credibility assessment. Beck (1973), for example, found considerable support for the view that the audit is designed to give assurance on the efficiency of management and the financial soundness of the company. Such studies have been criticized for methodological weaknesses (see Davidson, 1975) but a similar pattern of findings has continued during the 1970s and 1980s, with users of audited accounts continually perceiving a broader audit function than that performed, or perceived as legitimate by auditors or of that required by legislation (see Turley, 1985 or CICA, 1988 for summaries).

The usual response to such findings among the auditing profession, and unfortunately, often among auditing academics, is to stress the general lack of understanding of the audit function, and to highlight the unreasonable nature of such expectations. Such comments tend, however, to gloss over what is a more fundamentally controversial area. For instance, the view that the audit function is designed to assess management performance does not look that unreasonable when set in the context of public sector auditing. Following the establishment of the Audit Commission and the National Audit Office in the early 1980s, the undertaking of such 'value-for-money', or operational, audits has assumed an enhanced profile in ensuring the accountability of local and central government. Perhaps it is only a matter of time before such investigations become a normal part of the external audit of limited companies? The recent legislation establishing new regulatory frameworks in the financial services sector and for banks and building societies would seem to add support to this view. One aspect of this legislation laid great stress on auditors assuming a responsibility to assess the adequacy of the internal control systems of financial organizations.

The controversial nature of audit expectations is perhaps best illustrated by considering the changing nature of the auditor's responsibility for fraud detection. According to the APC's original Explanatory Foreword to the Auditing Standards and Guidelines, issued in 1980, the primary responsibility for the prevention and detection of irregularities and fraud rests with an enterprise's management. The auditor's principal responsibility is seen as reporting on the truth and fairness of the enterprise's financial statements, and any duty in respect of fraud detection is restricted to planning the audit so as to have a reasonable expectation of detecting any resultant material misstatements in the financial statements (which implies that auditors who executed their audits in a reasonable manner would not be held responsible for any failure to detect material fraud). This all reads very conclusively until it is recognized that until the 1940s the detection of fraud was still seen by auditors as the primary objective of the audit (Brown, 1962). Since that time pronouncements of the professional auditing bodies throughout the world have tended to displace it with the broader objective of reporting on the truth and fairness of a company's financial statements. Lee (1986, p. 23) asserted that such a switch reflected the growing concern of users with the quality of financial information and the tendency of company mangement to assume more responsibility for fraud prevention and detection (through the development of internal control systems). In his view, the increased scale of business transactions was such that the cost of searching out fraud and error by external audit was largely acknowledged as having become uneconomic.

Other writers, however, attribute a much more proactive and self-interested role for the audit profession in bringing about such a change. Brown (1962) suggested that the profession's down-playing of this responsibility was largely a response to the massive undetected fraud revealed in the McKesson and Robbins case of the late 1930s. As Willingham (1975) notes,

perhaps the discussion of the auditor's responsibility for the detection of fraud has not yet diminished because it was a stated audit objective for over 400 years and was removed as an objective by the profession rather than by a change in the demand of clients of accounting firms. A solicitous consuming public could reinstate it.

(Willingham, 1975, p. 19)

Gwilliam (1987) expressed concern at the scarcity of explanation for the changed emphasis with regard to fraud detection, particularly when it was clear that courts or regulatory bodies have continually stressed the importance of the auditor's responsibility in this respect.

The pressure for auditors to assume a broader responsibility for fraud detection has continued in the 1980s. For instance, in the mid-1980s in the UK the government, in response to a serious questioning of the role of the auditor in such scandals as DeLorean and Johnson Matthey Bank (the latter resulting in its auditors paying a reported £25 million to the Bank of England in an out-of-court settlement) and to a growing concern as to levels of corporate fraud, 'invited' the auditing profession to rethink its role regarding fraud detection (*Accountancy Age*, 25 October 1985, p. 4). The deep-rooted and complex nature of the debate over audit expectations is well illustrated by the fact that, some five years elapsed before a finalized auditing guidance on the auditor's responsibilities in relation to fraud and other illegal acts was issued. The difficulty the profession has had in defining such responsibilities is such that the Auditing Practices Committee found itself in the position of issuing a revised Explanatory Foreword to Auditing Standards and Guidelines, which, unlike its predecessor, remained silent on such fundamental responsibilities. It remains to be seen whether the profession will be able to improve on the position noted by the DTI, in 1989, that 'management and shareholders see an important role for auditors generally, and the prevention and detection of fraud in particular and there is a wide gap between these expectations and the view of the auditors' responsibilities offered in the proposed guidelines' (as reported in *Accountancy Age*, 9 March 1989, p. 3).

Audit reporting

Given the misunderstandings and different views of the nature of audit assurance identified in studies of the role of auditing, it is not surprising to find that research on perceptions of the form and content of audit reports has produced similar results. The CICA's (1988) study, for example, found that a significant proportion of the reader/investor public believes that an unqualified audit opinion is only ever issued in circumstances where the company is not presently experiencing financial problems. As Tweedie (1987) noted, in discussing the functioning of the audit report as an early warning/burglar alarm system, it is difficult for lay people to understand how a company can suffer serious financial difficulties, or even collapse, shortly after having received an unqualified opinion. Divergences between the intended message of an audit report and the impression/meanings attributed to it by users have also been revealed in studies of qualified audit reports (see Crasswell, 1985; Holt and Moizer, 1990 for summaries). In certain cases audit qualifications designed to alert readers to material errors in the financial statements have been found not to have influenced subsequent investment decisions by users relying on those financial statements (see Estes and Reimer, 1977; Estes, 1982).

Such findings have served repeatedly to direct discussions on audit expectations to the form and content of the audit report. As such, the expectations gap has been framed very much in terms of a codification problem – that if users better understood the code being used by auditors in reporting their opinions, they would more accurately perceive the messages being given by the various forms of audit reports. Consequently, one of the most frequent solutions that has been put forward as a way of closing the expectations gap has been to change the format of the audit report. In the late 1970s short-form, standardized reporting was typically in favour, in the hope that it would reduce the inconsistency and complexity of audit reports and generate 'at-a-glance' understanding. The continuance of the expectations gap in the 1980s has somewhat discredited this exception-based approach to audit reporting and longer-form reporting has come back into favour (albeit in many cases in a standardized form). Typical of this movement was the ICAEW's (1986) report, entitled *The Future of the Audit*, which called for more consideration of positive reporting and the inclusion in the audit report of explicit statements of assurance regarding each aspect of the auditor's responsibilities. The stylized, short-form reports were seen as employing a rather complex codification system and emphasis was now placed on the 'adoption of a language more understandable to non-expert readers of reports'. This latter form of reporting has recently been adopted in the USA as part of the AICPA's ten expectations gap standards – a change also recommended by the final report of the Treadway Commission (AICPA, 1987). The CICA (1988) also concluded that short-form reports were being misinterpreted and recommended that the Canadian audit report be changed to reflect more closely the new US format. It saw consistency of format across nations as particularly important given the increasingly global nature of capital markets. Given such developments, it is of little surprise to find the APC's study group on audit expectations publicly indicating that it plans to recommend lengthening the present UK audit report.

Interestingly, the new US audit report has itself been the subject of criticism from those who believe it has added to the confusion surrounding the audit process (see *Financial Times*, 17 August 1989). According to Neebes and Roost (1987), the wording of the report will continue to mean different things to different people. Such comments help to get to the heart of the problem facing those seeking to close the expectations gap through such educative initiatives as rewording the audit report. These initiatives would be quite satisfactory if, underneath all the apparent confusion regarding the work of the auditor, there was one all-embracing definition of the audit function. Unfortunately, this is not the case. The previous section illustrated a number of different, and in many cases quite valid, perspectives on the nature of audit assurance. The same is so with audit reporting. For example, whilst the auditor's statutory responsibility to shareholders has remained unchanged for the last forty years, case law in the UK from the 1960s to the early 1980s gradually extented the auditor's responsibilities to third parties such as creditors and investors who bought shares in a company having relied on a previously provided audit opinion. So much so that the ICAEW's (1986) working party on the future of the audit concluded that in the extreme the auditor may well have a liability 'in indeterminate amount for an indeterminate time to an indeterminate class'. More recently, however, the courts have seemed to favour far more restrictive definitions of auditors' responsibilities. Such a shift, though, stands somewhat in contrast to the rulings of the American courts, which have continued to expand the auditor's responsibilities to third parties. They have also come at a time when the UK government has been placing increased emphasis on the public duty responsibilities of auditors, most notably in relation to their reporting of fraud and other illegal acts to supervisory bodies such as the Securities and Investments Board.

Given these divergent views on the role and responsibilities of the auditor, it would seem more appropriate to visualize the audit expectations gap debate as resembling a struggle between respective parties to the audit process, in which each seeks to ensure that a particular view of the audit remains in the ascendancy. In such a context educational initiatives take on a rather less neutral posture and could be seen as a possible mechanism by which certain preferred positions can be protected. As such, it is not surprising to find some commentators noting that the recent changes in the American audit report will not be seen as unselfish, socially orientated concessions on the part of the auditor, but rather as Neebes and Roost (1987, p. 24) suspected it might be seen – as a 'self serving retreat from responsibility' by the audit profession.

The findings of the CICA's (1988) investigation of the audit expectations gap are particularly relevant at this stage. The Macdonald Commission concluded that better communication of the respective roles of auditors and management could have only a limited effect in reducing the expectations gap. In coming to the same conclusion as the earlier Cohen, Metcalfe and Adams investigations (that a gap did exist and that public expectations of the auditor are generally reasonable and achievable), it naturally saw a need for the audit profession to be more adaptive and receptive to change. 'For the most part, expectation gaps will be narrowed only by the profession's acceptance of the need for change and improvement' (CICA, 1988, p. 4). The Commission also had some rather poignant advice for auditors seeking respite in favourable findings of surveys of public attitudes towards their profession:

> it may be of little comfort to the profession to know that a vast majority of the general and reader/investor publics are satisfied with the performance of auditors, if the profession concludes that the views of a substantial portion of both publics are based on a misperception of the role of the auditor.
>
> (CICA, 1988, p. 149)

The basic impression given by the CICA report is that whilst the expectations gap may have little dented the image of the chartered accountant as an independent, responsible professional, there was little ground for complacency on the part of the audit profession. This public trust was seen as a fragile commodity that 'could easily be shattered by a few highly publicized instances of apparent audit failures' (CICA, 1988, p. 4). It was with regard to the independence and professionalism of auditors that the CICA report paid most attention, and it is to this topic that we now turn.

Audit independence

If any topic can be classified as going to the heart of the audit expectations debate, it is the issue of auditor independence. All the above-mentioned investigations of the audit function in the 1970s and 1980s have highlighted the importance of auditors performing, and being seen to perform, in an unbiased, impartial manner. The Metcalfe report, for example, regarded independence as the auditor's single most valuable attribute.

In terms of the expectations gap, the concern has been that auditors have not been operating in a sufficiently independent fashion. Both the Cohen and Metcalfe Commissions were worried that competitive pressures were affecting audit quality. The pressure to acquire or maintain audit clients was seen to be such for Metcalfe to conclude that 'accounting firms have often cut costs to the point where the integrity of the audit is impaired' (Metcalfe Committee, 1978, p. 93). Similar concerns were expressed by the Dingell investigation in the mid-1980s. Its chairman summarized such doubts at the start of the inquiry:

> The system begins with the corporate managers and directors, whose actions are to be audited, going out and choosing the auditor. They hire the independent audit firm, determine the fees to be paid and have the power to fire the auditor for any reason. The independent audit firm often provides tax and management consulting services to the same corporation it audits. Can we really expect an audit firm to remain independent when its audit fees, and perhaps substantial consulting fees, are directly related to pleasing the corporate managers being audited?
>
> (quoted in Miller, 1986, p. 31)

The particular issue of auditors providing non-audit services has been the subject of frequent discussion in the last twenty years, although it should be stressed that all the major investigations have focused on the potential threat to independence, having found little evidence of cases where the provision of such services had compromised independence. This lack of evidence was recently picked up by Hall (1988, p. 26), who commented that 'nothing was broken that required fixing. Critics, regulators, the profession itself had conjured up a problem, based on assumption and repetition, not facts and then busily engaged themselves in finding a cure.' Hall believed that the profession had been too flaccid in fighting off its critics with concessions, and that some members had been unwitting allies of the critics because they had deplored the change from the profession they knew and thought should continue. Hall was confident that in today's litigious environment no firm could afford to stay in practice if it was not committed to high quality audit performance and that those who strayed from these standards would be taken care of by the market. This argument, however, pays little regard to the difficulty of knowing whether an auditor has failed to act independently given the relative unobservability of audit work – a point emhasized by John Dingell, at the Committee's first hearing.

> The accounting firms which audit publicly owned corporations are private organizations which do not file public reports. It may sometimes be hard to understand the operations of their corporate clients from the public reports filed, but it is impossible to understand the operations of the auditors themselves since all we know is the little they choose to tell us. Likewise, when auditors make mistakes, we often do not know the causes of those mistakes because the investigation results are sealed from public view as a condition of an out-of-court settlement.
>
> (quoted in Miller, 1986 p. 30–1)

Given such descriptions of the provision of audit and non-audit services, it is not surprising that the lack of empirical evidence of the latter compromising independence has failed to quell concern. As the Metcalfe Committee stressed, the auditor must be independent in both fact and appearance. Over the last twenty years a whole host of recommendations have been put forward (including peer review systems, the development and strengthening of audit committees, the rotation of auditors, the prohibition of auditors performing non-audit services for a company they also audit, the declaration in the company's financial statements of non-audit fees paid to the auditor, etc.) as ways of bolstering audit independence. And yet the doubts still remain that commercial pressures and the disproportionate power of company management *vis-à-vis* the auditor are hindering in some way the quality of audit work. The CICA (1988) saw much merit in stronger audit committees and less flexible standards of financial reporting, but believed that ultimately the best and only effective strategy to ensure that audit quality was not compromised by commercial pressures was a determination and dedication to professionalism on the part of auditors. There are others, however, who see such a strategy as rather naive, wishful thinking. Apart from the fact that research studies have generally shown that user groups have much stricter views than auditors regarding situations which could jeopardize audit independence, there is a feeling that the days of the disinterested professional are long gone. Stevens (1988), in a survey of the impact of commercialism on the 'Big 8' accounting firms, noted that the way accountants referred to their work as a 'business' (rather than a 'profession') was more than just a matter of semantics:

> The exploding scope of practice is transforming the cultures of the firms themselves. Salesmanship, once a dirty word to accountants, is now critical to the management process and, in many cases, has become the fastest route to promotion and partnership. When Arthur Young or Touche Ross or Price Waterhouse wins a new audit client (more than likely on the basis of a loss leader fee), it uses that opening to bombard the client with sales pitches designed to develop business for the firm's full inventory of services.
>
> (Stevens, 1988, p. 41)

As with nearly all topics discussed in relation to the audit expectations gap, one does not have to look too far for contrary evidence. Just five months after Stevens's article appeared in print, the *Financial Times* ran an article (6 October 1988) illustrating the present attractiveness of the audit market, with the USA-based chairman of Deloitte, Haskins and Sells stating that companies are now more concerned with audit quality than with audit fees. His firm saw a positive marketing advantage in publicizing the fact that they had received fewer writs for substantial negligence claims than had other large audit firms. One could also point to a recent market research survey requiring corporate management to evaluate their auditor (City Research Associates, 1987). This found that audit firms were again rated highly for their independence and objectivity – although it is perhaps difficult to conceive of any corporate management team admitting that their auditors were not independent! In this respect, those of a more conspiratorially minded nature (or at least disbelievers of agency theory) may find it rather disconcerting that such market research shows corporate management (the auditees) as being generally contented with the standard of audit service received.

Even with such contradictory evidence, the debate on audit independence does not appear to be something that can be lightly dismissed in the fashion of Hall (1988, p. 33), who regarded it as a 'controversy in search of an issue'. For instance, the underlying feeling that auditors are too close to company management, and too readily see their loyalties as lying in this direction, can be seen to have been a likely influential factor behind the government's recent legislative changes (permitting auditors to break client confidentiality and report direct to the supervisory bodies in certain matters of public interest). In a similar tone, the Treadway Commission's final report expressed concern at the degree of professional scepticism applied by auditors and felt that the auditor's traditional assumption of management integrity is one of the key areas where guidance is necessary. This produced the response from two leading representatives of the US accountancy profession (Elliott and Jacobson, 1987, p. 20) that 'there can be no audit if the auditor begins with the assumption that management lacks integrity'. In a similar vein, a technical partner in Touche Ross stated, following the Ferranti scandal, that it was virtually impossible for auditors to detect fraud in cases where there was management collusion (*Accountancy Age*, 28 September 1989, p. 17). This portrays a rather intriguing paradox in that the existence of an audit is based on the assumption that company management cannot be trusted sufficiently to act in the shareholders' best interest, yet for the audit to be undertaken it requires management to be trustworthy! Such a paradox produced a response from a reader (*Accountancy Age*, 28 October 1989, p. 17) that auditing was a rather farcical activity if all it could do was to ensure that an honest management did not accidentally mislead shareholders.

In concluding this section, it is perhaps best to leave the final word to the comment by the AICPA secretary:

> We find that the public has believed that the certified public accountant was an infallible superman; that the signature of a CPA invariably meant that everything was perfect; that it was unnecessary to read the accountant's certificate or the financial statements to which it was appended as long as the three major letters were in evidence. . . . Whether through its own fault or not, the accounting profession seems to have been oversold. Its limitations have been overlooked, while its abilities have been emphasized. Now the public has been somewhat shocked to find that even auditors can be fooled by clever criminals.
>
> (quoted in Miller, 1986, p. 35)

The AICPA secretary's comment, though, was not reflecting on the aftermath of the ESM scandal, or that of Equity Funding, but that of McKesson Robbins, the great *cause célèbre* of the 1930s, and were spoken in January 1939! It would appear that in the world of auditing controversy is never that far away.

CONCLUSION

The purpose of this chapter was to cast some light on the role of auditing and the nature of audit expectations. Both from examinations of theoretical perspectives on auditing, and from more practically based studies of the auditing services environment, it is quite clear that the auditing function is not a unitary phenomenon and can be taken as meaning different things to different people. There are a number of competing conceptual perspectives on the role and purpose of auditing and the nature of professionalism which portray some quite radically different scenarios of what can be expected of auditors. When this is coupled with the low visibility of audit work and the resultant uncertainty about what it comprises, it is not surprising to find that auditing has a problem of an expectations gap. Moreover, whilst the term 'expectations gap' has gained prominence recently, the issues it has been seen to incorporate have been in existence for a good deal longer. Fraud detection, public interest reporting, the provision of non-audit services and reliance on management representations have at varying times been the subject of much debate. Indeed, on occasions the similarity of issues giving rise to a questioning of the audit function is of a level where it could almost be said for 1980 read 1970 or 1940 or even 1890.

What is also noticeable is that the major crises to have hit the audit profession, and the major investigations into the nature of the audit services market and its regulation (in both the UK and North America), have been closely related either to the failure of auditors to detect a number of major frauds or to provide an advance warning of an impending corporate collapse. These investigations have then tended to produce a whole host of recommendations as to ways by which the performance of auditors, or perceptions of auditor performance, could be enhanced, followed by a gradual quietening down of debate until the next major scandal. Some have seen this as the natural way of life for the audit profession. Others have argued that corporate crisis (defined broadly to include corporate collapse, undetected major frauds or even social disquiet at any abuse of corporate power) leads to new expectations of and requirements for accountability, which in turn lead to new demands on the audit function and in course produces changes in auditing standards and practice (Tricker, 1982).

Whilst this chapter gives support to such views, it is also argued that this should not be allowed to disguise the fact that the same issues have recurred in many debates over auditing. Thus, whilst it cannot be denied that there have been changes in the extent of an auditor's responsibility, Tricker's thesis, for instance, is not seen as doing sufficient justice to the repetitive nature of the expectations issues confronting the profession. For example, there is a remarkable similarity between many of the recommendations of the Cohen (which is generally regarded as being largely ignored by the profession) and Metcalfe Commissions in the late 1970s and those of the Treadway and Dingell Commissions in the 1980s. Tricker's analysis almost has too cosy an appearance about it, in suggesting that corporate crisis leads to demands for regulation and accountablity, which in turn lead to changes in audit practice. This implies a relatively passive profession, continually responding to the changing expectations of society. From an analysis of the response to the varying historical crises, what appears more appropriate is evidence of a wealth of concern and investigation, followed by reflection and reconsideration on the part of the auditing profession, leading to some change as well but also a watering down of controversial reforms and a settling of the auditing services market until the next crisis or scandal (when more often than not the same issues are addressed and similar recommendations for change put forward).

Such a pattern reflects the existence of conflicts between the interests of society and the interests of the auditing profession. Indeed, the number of conflicting pressures on auditors; the existence of a variety of parties with differing interests in, and demands on the audit function; and the probabilistic nature of audit assurance (which implies that auditors can be routinely expected to miss a number of material errors and irregularities) are all factors that can be viewed as making the existence of an expectations gap somewhat of an inevitablity. Put colloquially, auditors are unlikely to be able to satisfy all the people all the time. Whilst this is also likely to be true of most occupations, what gives the audit function an above average aura of un-met expectations is that good quality audit work remains relatively unobservable, but audit failures have much greater newsworthiness. As Olson (1973, p. 10) noted, 'inherent in serving the public interest is being blamed for what goes wrong and receiving precious little praise when everything goes well'.

A conclusion that an expectations gap may well be an inevitable feature of auditing seems a rather depressing one at a time when the profession is perhaps taking more significant steps than ever before to close the gap. However, the evidence of the past fifty years, with all the ensuing uncertainty and conflict surrounding the audit process, would seem to point more to the former as the likely outcome of the latest initiatives. On a more positive note, it is hoped that the 1990s will see a good deal more consideration being given to the reasons for the existence of an expectations gap. The vast majority of the research documented in this chapter has focused on where a gap exists, rather than seeking to identify the factors underlying people's expectations of auditing. For instance, there is as yet no research study which has provided any meaningful answers to such issues as: Why do people hold auditors in differing levels of regard? Why are different functions expected of an auditor and why are varying levels of responsibility attributed to the auditor for a particular corporate collapse? Why are shareholders and users prepared to leave so much power in the hands of corporate management regarding dealings with the auditor? Answers to such fundamental questions can only help to generate more appropriate audit policy recommendations and thereby assist in a faster closure of any expectations gap.

REFERENCES

AICPA (1987) *Report of the National Commission on Fraudulent Financial Reporting* (Treadway Commission), AICPA, New York.

American Institute of Certified Public Accountants (AICPA) (1978) *Report Conclusions and Recommendations of the Commission on Auditors' Responsibilities* (Cohen Commission), AICPA, New York.

Auditing Practices Committee (APC) (1989) Explanatory foreword to Auditing Standards and Guidelines (revised), in *Auditing and Reporting*, Institute of Chartered Accountants in England and Wales, London.

Beck, G.W. (1973) The role of the auditor in modern society: an empirical appraisal, *Accounting and Business Research*, Spring, pp. 117–22.

Benston, G.J. (1985) The market for public accounting services – demand, supply and regulation, *Journal of Accounting and Public Policy*, Vol. 4, pp. 33–80.

Brown, R.G. (1962) Changing audit objectives and techniques, *Accounting Review*, October, pp. 696–703.

Canadian Institute of Chartered Accountants (CICA) (1988) *Report of the*

Commission to Study the Public's Expectation of Audits (McDonald Commission), CICA, Toronto.

City Research Associates (1987) *Audit and Accountancy*, City Research Associates, London.

Craswell, A. (1985) Studies of the information content of qualified audit reports, *Journal of Business Finance and Accounting*, Spring, pp. 93–116.

Davidson, L. (1975) *The Role and Responsibilities of the Auditor: Perspectives, Expectations and Analysis*, unpublished background paper for the AICPA Commission on Auditors' Responsibilities.

DeAngelo, L.E. (1981) Auditor independence, 'low balling', and disclosure regulation, *Journal of Accounting and Economics*, Vol. 3, December, pp. 113–27.

Elliott, R.K. and Jacobson, P.D. (1987) The Treadway·Report – its potential impact, *The CPA Journal*, November, pp. 20–32.

Estes, R. (1982) *The Auditor's Report and Investor Behaviour*, Heath: Lexington, Mass.

Estes, R. and Reimer, M. (1977) A study of the effects of qualified auditors' opinions on bankers' lending decisions, *Accounting and Business Research*, Autumn, pp. 250–9.

Flint, D. (1988) *Philosophy and Principles of Auditing – An Introduction*, Macmillan, Basingstoke.

Gwilliam, D. (1987) *A Survey of Auditing Research*, Prentice-Hall/ICAEW, London.

Hall, W.D. (1988) An acceptable scope of practice, *The CPA Journal*, February, pp. 24–33.

Haskell, T.L. (1984) Professionalism versus capitalism: R.H. Tawney, Emile Durkheim and C.S. Pierre on the disinterestedness of professional communities, in *The Authority of Experts: Studies in History and Theory*, T.L. Haskell (ed.) Indiana University Press, Bloomington.

Holt, G. and Moizer, P. (1990) The meaning of audit reports, *Accounting and Business Research*, Vol. 20, no. 78, pp. 111–22.

ICAEW (1986) *Report of the Working Party on the Future of the Audit*, ICAEW, London.

Kaplan, R.L. (1987) Accountants' liability and audit failures: when the umpire strikes out, *Journal of Accounting and Public Policy*, Vol. 6, pp. 1–8.

Kent, D., Sherer, M. and Turley, S. (1985) *Current Issues in Auditing*, Harper & Row, London.

Lee, T.A. (1970) The nature of auditing and its objectives, *Accountancy*, April, pp. 292–6.

Lee, T.A. (1986) *Company Auditing*, 3rd edn, Van Nostrand Reinhold, Wokingham.

Mautz, R.K. and Sharaf, H.A. (1961) *The Philosophy of Auditing*, American Accounting Association, New York.

Metcalfe Committee (1978) Improving the accountability of publicly owned corporations and their auditors, *Report of the Subcommittee on Reports, Accounting and Management of the Committee on Governmental Affairs*, United States Senate, Washington. (Reproduced in *The Journal of Accountancy*, January, 1978, pp. 88–96).

Miller, R.D. (1986) Governmental oversight of the role of auditors, *The CPA Journal*, September, pp. 20–36.

Moizer, P. (1985) Independence, in Kent, Sherer and Turley (1985).

Moizer, P. (1988) Towards a theory of the auditor's choice of audit quality in a self-regulated market, unpublished working paper, Department of Accounting and Finance, University of Manchester.

Neebes, D.L. and Roost, W.G. (1987) ASB's ten 'expectation gap' proposals – will they do the job?, *The CPA Journal*, October, pp. 23–5.

Olson, W.E. (1973) Whither the auditors!, speech to the Annual Meeting of the New

York State Society of CPAs, Bermuda, reported in *The Journal of Accountancy*, August, pp. 9–10.

Porter, B.A. (1988) *Towards a Theory of the Role of the External Auditor in Society*, research monograph, Massey University, New Zealand.

Sherer, M. (1985) Auditing today: opportunities and threats, in Kent, Sherer and Turley (1985).

Sherer, M. and Kent, D. (1988) *Auditing and Accountability*, Paul Chapman, London.

Stevens, M. (1988) No more white shoes, *Business Month*, April, pp. 39–42.

Thornton Baker (1983) *Audit Manual*, Nova Communications Ltd, London.

Tricker, R.I. (1982) Corporate accountability and the role of the audit function, in A.G. Hopwood, M. Bromwich and J. Shaw (eds.) *Auditing Research: Issues and Opportunities*, Pitman, London.

Turley, S. (1985) Empirical research in auditing, in Kent, Sherer and Turley (1985).

Turley, S. (1989) Concepts and values in the audit methodologies of large accounting firms, in *Auditing and the Future*, ICAS/ICAEW, Edinburgh.

Tweedie, D. (1987) Challenges facing and auditor: professional fouls and the expectation gap, the Deloitte, Haskins and Sells Lecture, University College, Cardiff, 30 April.

Wallace, W.A. (1980) *The Economic Role of the Audit in Free and Regulated Markets*, University of Rochester, New York.

Willingham, J.J. (1975) Discussant's response to relationship of auditing standards to detection of fraud, *The CPA Journal*, April, pp. 18–21.

DISCUSSION QUESTIONS

1. The expectations gap is due to public ignorance about auditing. Discuss
2. To what extent have developments in audit responsibilities only arisen due to public pressure forcing change on an unwilling profession?
3. The expectations gap is a sympton of the fact that auditing is now a business rather than a profession. Discuss.
4. What strategies would you recommend to reduce or eliminate the expectations gap in auditing?

2
Fraud – Managements' and Auditors' Responsibility for its Prevention and Detection

D.P. Tweedie.

The auditor's responsibility in relation to fraud which may have been committed within an organization being audited has been uncertain and ambiguous for many years. This uncertainty starts from questions about the role of the audit as a control against fraud, and therefore the auditor's responsibility for its detection and prevention, but more recently has also involved issues concerning auditors reporting suspected fraud, particularly to those outside the audited organization.

Although at one time fraud was seen as a major audit objective, as the modern audit function developed objectives in this area became subsidiary to, and interpreted in terms of, a responsibility to report on the quality of the financial statements (Brown, 1962; Lee, 1986). Within the accounting profession, fraud came to be recognized as relevant to the auditor's responsibilities because it is a potential source of error in the financial statements, but not as a major objective of audit investigation in its own right. However, fraud has always remained an area of public concern, and so has never been far from debates about auditors' duties, particularly when evidence of undetected fraud or other irregularity comes to light.

In the last few years responsibility for prevention and detection of fraud by management and auditors in the UK has changed considerably as a result of a number of well-publicized scandals involving the mishandling of private investors' affairs. For example, in the late 1970s building societies' mismanagement hit the headlines, while in the 1980s scandals at Lloyd's and the collapse of Johnson Matthew Bankers led to widespread concern.

In this chapter, the developments and changes which have taken place in the last few years in the auditor's responsibility relating to fraud are outlined and discussed.

THE POSITION OF THE ACCOUNTING PROFESSION

In 1985 it was clear the government was intending to introduce legislation in the area of fraud and the auditor. In response the Institute of Chartered

D.P. Tweedie was technical partner in Peat Marwick McLintock, London and formerly Chairman of the UK's Auditing Practices Committee. He is now Chairman of the Accounting Standards Board. The views and opinions expressed in this chapter are those of the author and do not necessarily reflect those of his present or former colleagues.

Accountants in England and Wales (ICAEW) commissioned two reports on fraud (chaired by I.H. Davison and Lord Benson), the recommendations of which have had a major effect on the profession's thinking.

The reports reached a conclusion similar to that of the Department of Trade and Industry's Consultative Document *The Auditor's Role in the Financial Services Sector*, which recognised (DTI, 1985, para. 3.1) that 'the primary responsibility for safeguarding the assets of any business and for preventing fraud lies with those responsible for its management but the auditor has an important supporting role to play'.

The Davison report

The first ICAEW committee (the Davison Committee) recommended, *inter alia*, that:

1. Legislation should impose more stringent requirements on enterprises as far as accounting records were concerned.

   The government was urged to clarify the statutory requirements that companies should keep proper accounting records. While the auditor is required by the Companies Act to state if in his opinion proper accounting records have not been kept, the legislation is ambiguous, e.g. does the law require a company to be able to construct a picture of its financial position at a single time in the past or does it demand the ability continually to be able to reconstruct that picture at future times? To ensure that directors took more seriously their responsibilities to maintain accounting records, a strong hint was given to the government that failure to keep proper records should be one of the matters warranting the disqualification of a director.

2. Legislation should impose an explicit obligation on certain enterprises to have satisfactory internal controls.

   In particular, the Committee recommended that, as internal controls were often the most cost-effective means of preventing and detecting fraud, legislation should impose an explicit requirement for satisfactory internal controls in:

   (a) enterprises where depositors' and investors' assets were particularly vulnerable where such requirements did not exist already (the Banking Act 1987 is an example of legislation moving in this direction);

   (b) all companies above a certain size or all public companies.

   The report also suggested that a satisfactory internal control system should be a precondition for authorization to engage in investment business.

3. Increased reporting of frauds to the appropriate authorities should be encouraged.

To reduce the number of suspected frauds that go unreported the Davison Committee recommended that employers could be required to report to the appropriate authorities cases of suspected fraud by employees (a secondary reporting responsibility could in this case be imposed upon auditors).

In addition, the Davison Committee recommended that the profession:

1. prepare specialist auditing guidelines for industries that are particularly susceptible to fraud; and
2. revise its existing guidance to members on the reporting of fraud.

This latter guidance, although giving a correct exposition of the existing law, no longer met the expectations of the public so far as concerned the auditor's responsibilities in relation to suspected fraud. The Committee believed the revised guidance should, unlike its predecessor, be designed to have the effect of encouraging an auditor to report to the appropriate authorities any suspected case of serious fraud by a client or client's management.

Finally, the Davison report suggested new responsibilities for auditors in reporting whether satisfactory internal controls and accounting records had been kept.

The Benson report

The second ICAEW report (the report of Lord Benson's Committee to the President) endorsed many of the recommendations of the Davison Committee and similarly suggested a revision of professional guidance.

The Committee asked leading counsel to define fraud and the auditor's responsibilities in relation thereto under the Companies Act. The advice was as follows:

(a) fraud is only established as having taken place when there is a verdict to that effect in the courts.

(b) the suspicion of fraud arises when the transaction or events under enquiry give reasonable grounds to conclude that they are, or may be, dishonestly intended to mislead.

(c) as a result of the auditor's responsibilities under the Companies Act, the auditor would be required to qualify his audit report:

(i) if he is satisfied that the accounting records and/or the accounts upon which he is reporting and/or the directors' report, to the extent that it is inconsistent with the accounts, provide him wih reasonable grounds to conclude that they are, or may be, dishonestly intended to mislead; or

(ii) if he is unable to obtain the information and explanations he requires in relation to such matters.

(ICAEW, 1985, p. 1)

The emphasis in the Benson report was that the normal professional relationship which hitherto existed between the auditor and his or her client should continue in the future without change. If pressures were to be put upon the auditor to act as an informer and to report to outsiders without the client's knowledge, or when there was no *duty* to do so, the profession's integrity would be destroyed. This meant that, whether or not the auditor had any *right* to do so, the Committee believed that the auditor should not disclose any information concerning affairs of the company under audit unless two conditions were fulfilled: the auditor had a duty to qualify the audit report by reason of the statutes or the professional directives set by his or her professional body; and the client was first informed.

As far as fraud or suspected fraud by members of staff was concerned, the auditor would refer to the matter in his audit report only if the true and fair view was affected or if the statutory disclosure requirement had not been met (for example, the disclosure of extraordinary or exceptional items). It would be the auditor's obligation, and the invariable practice, to inform the director or directors responsible for that part of the company's business about the fraud.

The report was, however, more concerned with fraud or suspected fraud by directors. The Benson Committee had no doubts about the auditor's duty if the directors appeared to be involved in fraud which was judged to be material in relation to the affairs of the company: the auditor had to confront the directors and inform them that it was his or her duty and intention to qualify the audit report appropriately. It was considered that the public would be rightly aggrieved if information of suspected fraud undertaken by the directors of a nature which would have a significant influence on a person reading the accounts, and which was within the knowledge of the auditor, was not disclosed by him or her by means of the qualification of the audit report.

It is, of course, more difficult if the auditor has concerns about transactions which are taking place and if he or she cannot obtain satisfactory information. If the auditor were unable to obtain such information he or she would then have to qualify the audit report to the effect that the explanations and information he or she required had not been obtained.

To enable speedy and effective action to be taken if the auditor qualified the audit report on the grounds of suspected fraud by directors (but not otherwise) it was recommended that he or she should forthwith send a copy of the accounts with the audit report to the Companies Division at the Department of Trade and Industry saying that he or she was not satisfied in relation to the matter stated in the report. The client should first be informed. The auditor was advised that as his or her report was a public document it should be straightforward and unequivocal so that the reader would be in no doubt as to the meaning the auditor intended to convey.

In certain cases reporting to the DTI would be inadequate and too late to be effective. For example, the fraud may have been noticed early in the financial year or the auditor's report may be delayed by the client deliberately failing to finalize the accounts. In either event exposure of the matter would have been delayed and this could have been damaging to the public interest. Accordingly, the Benson Committee believed that in such cases the auditor should forthwith inform the DTI that on the basis of information currently available, it was his or her intention to qualify the audit report, and the auditor should include a copy of the qualification he or she intended to make. Once again, however, the client should first have been informed.

THE CURRENT POSITION

Not all of the conclusions of the two ICAEW reports have been accepted by the government or by the accounting profession in general. There has, however, been a major change in the auditor's role in one sector of the economy – a change which has led to the implementation of many of the reports' recommendations and which could well be the benchmark for a general change in the rights and duties of the auditor. Both the law and new professional guidance on the reporting of fraud are extending the auditor's responsibilities.

Statutory requirements

The auditor's role in reporting fraud to the appropriate authorities has been considerably enlarged by recent legislation in the financial sector which does not, however, relate to the generality of companies.

Following Professor Gower's reports on investor protection (1982 and 1984) and the various financial scandals of the past few years, the government introduced three new Acts designed, *inter alia*, to improve investor protection: the Financial Services Act 1986, the Building Societies Act 1986 and the Banking Act 1987.

Broadly, the management of organizations governed by these three Acts will be authorized to conduct business in the appropriate financial sector only if the organizations:

1. keep proper accounting records;
2. have adequate systems of internal controls and have appropriate reporting and inspection systems to enable them to determine whether their control systems are working; and
3. conduct their business in a prudent manner.

The auditor's role is not only to report that a true and fair view is shown in the financial statements but explicitly to report to the regulator whether proper accounting records are kept and, in the case of all bar those organizations covered by the Financial Services Act (many of these organizations are too small to have internal control systems), that the internal control system is adequate. Additionally, under all three Acts the auditor may report to the supervisory authority (the regulator of a particular industry) if the auditor is satisfied that it is expedient to do so in order to protect the interests/ investments of shareholders or depositors or if he or she is requested to do so by the regulator when the latter is so satisfied. This entitlement is notwithstanding any obligation of confidence incumbent upon the auditor. In the financial sector of the economy the auditor is emerging as an adjunct to the regulatory body.

In most cases once the auditor came across a problem he or she would check whether it had been notified by the client to the regulator and, if not, recommend that the client tell the regulator of the problem. If the client refused or delayed unnecessarily then the auditor would report it him- or herself.

Following discussions on the Acts involving the Auditing Practices Committee (APC), the Treasury, the DTI and the regulators it has been agreed that in general the auditor would be expected to exercise his or her right to report to the regulator when it would assist in protecting the interests of depositors/investors because there had been a material loss or there existed a significant risk of material loss. Examples of such situations would be:

1. the extreme situation where there was evidence of imminent financial collapse and where it would be obvious to an auditor that he or she must inform the regulator of the position if the client were unwilling or unable to do so, even if it were only to enable the regulator to organize a rescue or mitigate damage;
2. an occurrence:
   (a) which in the opinion of the auditor gives rise to actual or potential

risk which is or may be material to the security of investments or interests of shareholders and depositors; and

(b)   of which the regulator should be informed but which is not covered by regular monitoring returns (i.e. statistical and financial information regularly supplied by the organization to the regulator); and

(c)   of which the client declines to inform the regulator;

3.   an occurrence which causes the auditor no longer to have confidence in the competence or integrity of directors and senior management to direct and manage the organization in a way which protects the investments and interests of shareholders and depositors or to give a true representation of the position of the organization to the regulator.

In only the exceptional circumstances outlined in item 3 above has it been deemed appropriate for the auditor to report to the regulator without the knowledge of the client. Even then item 3 gives the auditor the *right* not the *duty* to report suspected cases of management fraud. The reason for allowing judgement rather than imposing an obligation is that 'suspected' fraud covers a wide range of uncertainty as to whether an offence has in fact been committed and by whom it has been committed. Where fraud is suspected, there will always be a threshold of certainty below which it would be unreasonable to expect anyone to report his or her suspicions. As the Davison Committee commented, it is impossible to define at what point suspicion of fraud may be regarded as reasonably founded, and there will also be borderline cases where reasonable observers might draw differing conclusions from the same evidence. If the auditor has a right to report his or her suspicions he or she can use his or her judgement as to the occasions on which they are sufficiently well founded to justify making a report. If the auditor has a duty to report there would almost certainly be a tendency for auditors to report their suspicions even when they were not well founded – with the consequences of fractured relationships between auditors and clients and the overloading of the supervisory authorities.

Similarly, it may be appropriate for an auditor to deal with suspected fraud in ways that reporting it would prevent. For example, a company with poor results may try to conceal them in accounts in which profits are materially overstated. It could well not occur to management that it risks committing fraud in doing this and that it might be able to produce arguments to show that it had merely taken the benefit of the doubt in a number of areas in which some judgement was required. The auditor's sensible course of action would be to discuss matters with management and insist on rectification of the accounts. If, however, the auditor had a duty to report fraud he or she could well feel obliged to report to the regulator.

Even with the right to report, however, the auditor could still be at risk where he or she fails to report and consequently, under the present legislation, there is still a problem that over-reporting may take place. Similarly, while the auditor is expected to report only material problems there is always the concern that a small fraud may just be the precursor to a larger one and consequently, when senior management is involved even in a small fraud it is possible that the fact that senior management's integrity is in question will lead the auditor to report to the regulator.

Regulators, however, have realized that auditors cannot be expected to be aware of all circumstances which might have led them to exercise their right to report. Consequently, auditors are not expected to change the scope of their work, or the frequency or the timing of their visits to the client. Similarly, it is accepted by regulators that the auditor does not have the benefit of hindsight when judging whether or not fraud has occurred. Nevertheless, the auditor will have to satisfy him- or herself that his or her decision not to report will stand up to examination at a future date on the basis of what he or she knew at the time, what he or she should have known in the course of his or her work, what he or she should have concluded and what he or she should have done.

The key feature of the relationship between regulator and auditor is that the auditor cannot act as a substitute for or extension of the supervisor – the auditor's role is quite distinct. The auditor's function is to provide additional assurance to the regulator as to the reliability of the information reported to him or her. Only where the auditor believes that the regulator is not being adequately informed or where doubts exist about senior management's integrity will action be taken to ensure that the regulator is aware of the problem.

Professional guidance

While legislation is altering the role of the auditor in the financial sector, views have also been changing in the profession on the auditor's general responsibility for detecting and reporting fraud. Professional guidance on dealing with fraud comes in two forms: in auditing guidelines and in ethical pronouncements.

The UK's Auditing Practices Committee has finalized an auditing guideline, *The Auditor's Responsibility in Relation to Fraud, other Irregularities and Errors* (APC, 1990). The guideline lays out quite clearly the profession's view of the responsibilities of management and auditor. The profession, not surprisingly, agrees with the government that the primary responsibility for the prevention and detection of fraud, other irregularities and errors rests with management: in addition to its business responsibilities, management has the fiduciary roles of safeguarding assets and preparing accounts which give a true and fair view. These duties arise since management is regarded at law as acting in a stewardship capacity concerning the property under its control and is required to keep proper accounting records and to prepare accounts which show a true and fair view. There are other statutory measures relating to management responsibilities. For instance, consenting to and conniving in false accounting is an offence under the Theft Act 1968 and a company's directors have a responsibility to ensure the company does not engage in wrongful trading under the Insolvency Act 1986.

The auditor's responsibility for the detection of fraud

As an officer of a company would be guilty of an offence where he or she knowingly or recklessly made a statement to the company's auditor which was misleading, false or deceptive in a material particular, the auditor would normally accept representations as truthful in the absense of any indication to the contrary and provided these are consistent with other audit evidence obtained. Nevertheless, the UK auditor should evaluate the audit evidence objectively and should adopt an attitude of professional scepticism, i.e. the auditor should neither assume that management is dishonest nor assume unquestioned honesty.

However, it must not be forgotten that because of the characteristics of fraud and other irregularities, particularly those involving forgery and collusion, a properly designed and executed audit may not detect a material fraud or other irregularity. For example, current auditing practice does not normally involve the auditor in establishing the authenticity of original documents. Audit procedures that will usually be effective for detecting a misstatement that is unintentional may be ineffective for a misstatement that is intentional and is concealed through collusion between client personnel and third parties or among management or employees of the client. The auditor's opinion on the financial statements is based on the concept of reasonable assurance: his or her report does not constitute a guarantee that the financial statements are free of misstatement. Therefore, the subsequent discovery that a material misstatement exists in the financial statements is not necessarily evidence of inadequate planning, performance or evaluation on the part of the auditor.

The auditor's responsibility for the detection of fraud would be limited to planning, performing and evaluating his or her work to enable him or her to have a reasonable expectation of detecting material misstatements which could impair the truth and fairness of the view given by the financial statements, whether these mistatements were caused by fraud, other irregularities or errors. The engagement letter should therefore indicate that the auditor would 'endeavour to plan the audit so as to have a reasonable expectation of detecting material misstatements in the financial statements resulting from irregularities or fraud, but that the examination should not be relied upon to disclose irregularities and frauds which may exist'.

If in the course of the audit the auditor's suspicions are aroused, case law and professional guidance demand that he or she does not overlook the problem or leave it alone. The auditor must investigate the matter until his or her anxieties are allayed, or report appropriately.

The auditor's responsibility for reporting fraud to management

The APC guideline agrees with the Benson Committee's view that the auditor should report to the management of an enterprise on employee frauds. The auditor would, however, have no specific responsibility to report fraud or other irregularities in the audit report if the financial statements gave a true and fair view despite the occurrence of a fraud or other irregularity. Nevertheless, the auditor would be expected to qualify the report where he or she concluded that proper accounting records had not been maintained (as required by law) or, for example, where he or she failed to obtain all necessary information and explanations. (In the latter case, it is likely that the scope of the audit would have been restricted and the auditor should also qualify the report appropriately.)

The auditor's responsibility for reporting fraud to shareholders

If the fraud does not warrant qualification of the audit report and the board of directors is neither implicated in the wrongdoing itself nor guilty of improperly condoning or suppressing it, then disclosure of the fraud to the shareholders will ordinarily be unnecessary. The reason is that in such cases it is ordinarily the function of the directors themselves to decide what further disclosure the facts ought to receive.

In particularly serious cases the auditor should compel disclosure by the company to its shareholders by stating his or her intention to resign if disclosure is not made. In the case of a company, the auditor's reasons for resignation would be sent to the shareholders. Under the Companies Act 1989 similar statements are required even if the auditor does not resign but either does not seek reappointment or a resolution to remove him or her is proposed. The cases which call for these extreme measures will generally be those in which the directors themselves are implicated in the wrongdoing or for some other reason are unwilling to deal with the issue in a manner considered appropriate by the auditor.

The auditor's responsibility for reporting fraud to third parties

The most difficult question, of course, is in what circumstances should disclosure be made to a third party, including regulatory bodies or public authorities? In certain situations there is, of course, no option, the auditor is not bound by the duty of confidentiality and has the legal obligation to disclose fraud or other irregularities: for example, if the auditor is obliged to make disclosure by a court or government officer with power to request such information, or has knowledge of terrorist offences connected with Northern Ireland.

The APC has taken legal advice on the present state of the law regarding the auditor's rights and duties. The auditor certainly owes a duty of confidentiality to the company. That duty is not broken by disclosure to its management or shareholders since they are the company for this purpose. The duty would, however, be broken by disclosure to third parties. Counsel has advised that in the present state of the law the furthest that it is possible to go in encouraging disclosure by auditors to third parties is to say that there will be some cases in which an auditor, although not bound in point of law to disclose information to a third party, is entitled to do so. Counsel then suggested that the APC should give guidance as to the circumstances in which the auditor might feel it appropriate to exercise that right.

This view is similar to that given in the ethical statement, *Professional Contact in Relation to Defaults or Unlawful Acts*, revised in 1988. The previous statement, issued in 1980, tended to discourage disclosure. It recommended that members, even if free to do so, should not disclose past crimes or civil wrongs (except treason, which they are legally obliged to disclose) unless they felt that the damage to the public likely to arise from non-disclosure was of a very serious nature. In any such case auditors were advised to take legal advice before making any disclosure. By 1988, however, the Councils of the CCAB bodies believed it would be wrong to encourage members to act in a manner which could leave them vulnerable to legal action by an aggrieved party, and therefore had another draft prepared to reflect the then current state of the law. The revised statement suggested that in certain circumstances information which would otherwise be confidential would cease to be so if the information was such that disclosure was justified in the 'public interest' and should consequently be reported to a third party.

While the public interest is a concept recognized by the courts, no definition of 'public interest' has ever been given. Consequently, the state of the law in the UK leaves the auditor with a difficult decision as to whether matters which he or she may wish to disclose are subject to a duty of confidentiality or whether that duty has ceased because disclosure is justified in the public interest. It is, in any case, clear that exceptions to the duty of confidentiality cover only disclosure to 'one who has a proper interest to receive the information' – presumably the appropriate government departments or regulators. The ethical statement suggested that matters the auditor should take into account when considering whether or not disclosure would be justified in the public interest include:

(a) the relative size of the amounts involved and the extent of the amount of financial damage;
(b) whether members of the public are affected;
(c) the possibility or likelihood or repetition;
(d) the reasons for the client's unwillingness to disclose the matters to the proper authority him- or herself;
(e) the gravity of the matter; and
(f) any legal advice obtained.

The APC guideline offers similar advice. It suggests that matters the auditor may consider before disclosing in the public interest include:

(g) the extent to which fraud or other irregularity is likely to result in a material gain or loss for any person or is likely to affect a large number of persons;
(h) the extent to which the non-disclosure of the fraud is likely to enable it to be repeated with impunity;
(i) the gravity of the matter;
(j) whether there is a general management ethos within the entity of flouting the law and regulations;
(k) the weight of evidence and the auditor's assessment of the likelihood that a fraud or other irregularity has been committed.

The guideline notes that the auditor may need to take legal advice before making a decision on whether the matter should be reported to the proper authority in the public interest.

It can be seen from the above that (g) encompasses (a) and (b) of the ethical statement; (h) is virtually identical to (c); (i) repeats (e) and both the statement and the guideline refer to the seeking of legal advice. The guideline adds new suggestions: (j) concerning management's general attitude towards the law; and (k) recognizing the difficulty in determining whether or not a fraud had occurred. The guideline does not repeat (d) as it was felt that it was less important than the other matters. Nevertheless the guideline does suggest that ideally the client should report to the appropriate authorities. It would be only when there was no evidence to show that the client had reported or when the client refused to inform the appropriate authority that the auditor should report the matter. In certain situations, however, the general guideline on fraud (like the auditing guidelines relating to the financial sector) suggests that where the auditor no longer has confidence in the integrity of senior management, for example where he or she believes that a fraud or other irregularity has been committed or condoned by senior management or there is evidence of the intention of senior management to commit such a fraud or other irregularity, it may be inappropriate to discuss this matter at a more senior level of management. In such cases where the auditor has decided that the matter should be disclosed in the public interest he or she should report direct to the proper authority.

Legal advice to the UK profession indicates that if an auditor forms a view that unlawful acts or defaults have occurred and has communicated the relevant facts to a person who has a legitimate interest in receiving them, he or she will enjoy qualified privilege from liability for breach of duty to the client or defamation. Unless malice is proved against the auditor, that privilege should amount to a valid defence – presumably even if the facts should prove to be wrong. Obviously, however, each case has to be considered on its own merits and any auditor who is in doubt as to the courses properly open to him or her is advised to consult lawyers about his or her rights and duties. Clearly any public announcement or communication direct to shareholders, even if justified by the particular circumstances of the case, could well cause serious damage to the company or to individuals and, consequently, such a step should not normally be undertaken without taking legal advice.

The APC has been advised by counsel that an auditor would not be in breach of any legal duty if although entitled to disclose he failed to do so. His decision whether to do so or not would therefore be a matter of professional judgement and not a matter of law. It should be a decision which reflects the proper expectations which the public has of his profession. Without seeking to define the indefinable, counsel expected the auditor to attach most importance to the following factors now broadly similar to those in the draft guideline:

(i)   The wider interests of the company in a case where the auditor considered that the directors could not be relied upon to apply their minds properly to those interests;

(ii) The gravity of the facts, and in particular the extent to which third parties have suffered or will suffer loss;

(iii) The likelihood of repetition if the public authorities are not informed; and

(iv) The strength of the evidence tending to support the auditor's conclusions.

CONCLUSION

The auditor's role regarding the reporting of fraud in the UK has undergone a major revision since the mid-1980s. Statutory changes were implemented in 1986 and 1987 by three Acts dealing with the financial sector that gave the right to the auditor to report to various regulators in that sector when the auditor had suspicions that fraud perpetrated by senior management had occurred. Changing attitudes towards fraud have lead to a gradual evolution of the auditor's general right to report senior management fraud to third parties. As society's attitudes towards fraud began to harden the auditor's role has changed accordingly – professional guidance now reflects the evolution of public expectation.

REFERENCES AND FURTHER READING

Allan, R. and fforde, W. (1986) *The Auditor and Fraud*, Audit Brief, Auditing Practices Commitee, London.

Auditing Practices Committee (APC) (1990) *The Auditor's Responsibility in Relation to Fraud, Other Irregularities and Errors*, Auditing Guideline, Institute of Chartered Accountants in England and Wales, London.

Brown, R.G. (1962) Changing audit objectives and techniques, *The Accounting Review*, October, pp. 696–703, reproduced in D.R. Carmichael and J.J. Willingham (eds.) (1986) *Perspectives in Auditing*, 4th edn, McGraw-Hill, New York.

Department of Trade and Industry (DTI) (1985) *The Auditor's Role in the Financial Services Sector*, consultative document, DTI, London.

ICAEW (1985) *The Auditor and Fraud – Report of Lord Benson's Committee to the President of the ICAEW*, ICAEW, November, London.

Lee, T.A. (1986) *Company Auditing*, 3rd edn, Van Nostrand Reinhold, Wokingham.

DISCUSSION QUESTIONS

1. Outline the arguments for restricting the auditor's responsibility in relation to fraud to its effects on the financial statements and the arguments for seeing it as an audit objective in its own right.

2. Discuss the conflicts which arise between the auditor's duty of confidentiality to the client and the desirability of auditors reporting suspicions of fraud or other irregularities to regulatory agencies.

3. Should auditors have a right or an obligation to report suspected fraud to regulators?

4. Why should there be limitations on the circumstances in which auditors should be expected to report suspected fraud to company shareholders – will not this information always be of interest to shareholders?

5. What are the arguments for having a different level of auditor responsibility for fraud in the financial sector from that applying to company audits in general?

3
Independence

Peter Moizer

Matilda told such Dreadful Lies,
It made one Gasp and Stretch one's Eyes;
Her Aunt, who, from her Earliest Youth,
Had kept a Strict Regard for Truth,
Attempted to Believe Matilda:
The effort very nearly killed her.
(from 'Matilda' by Hilaire Belloc)

INTRODUCTION

At the heart of the audit process is a belief about human nature. Human beings will speak the truth, unless there is sufficient to be gained by being dishonest. As the managers of an organization are assumed to be able to benefit personally from reporting dishonestly in their organization's published financial statements, there is a presumption that managers will tend to manipulate the financial statements so as to make their performance look better than it actually is. In contrast, auditors are assumed to have no incentive associated with the financial statements to be dishonest. They are presumed to be *independent* of both the organization being audited and its managers and so they can be employed to report on the truthfulness of the managers' financial statements.

If auditors were truly independent of their client this chapter would end here, but they are not. Restricting our attention to company auditing, it can be seen that the directors of a company effectively both appoint the company's auditors and determine the size of the audit fee. The word 'effectively' is used because strictly a company's shareholders appoint the auditors and approve their remuneration, but in practice the shareholders merely rubber-stamp the recommendations of the directors. Hence, the auditors' incentive not to report truthfully is that, if they do, there is the possibility of losing the audit or of having their fee reduced. There is also a sense of loyalty that is built up between an auditor and the managers being audited. An auditor may be reluctant to jeopardize the career of a manager who is a personal friend.

Having allowed that auditors are not truly independent and that they may have some incentive not to report truthfully, there is then a rather interesting paradox. Managers cannot be relied upon to subordinate their own

Peter Moizer, M.A. (Oxon), M.A. (Econ.), F.C.A., is the Professor of Accounting in the School of Business and Economic Studies, University of Leeds.

self-interest to the demands of honesty but auditors can. Why auditors can be assumed to act honestly, even though they are not independent, is the subject of this chapter.

TECHNICAL COMPETENCE

Before addressing the issue of independence, it is helpful to analyse the concept of technical competence, as technical competence can be used to mask dishonest reporting. For the report of the auditor to have any value to the readers of the financial statements, the auditor must be both technically competent and honest. A technically competent auditor will have the necessary expertise to discover all the significant errors and omissions present in a set of financial statements. An honest auditor will ensure either that all significant errors and omissions are corrected or that they are fully disclosed in the auditor's report.

In reality, the concepts of competence and honesty can become interrelated. A dishonest auditor may choose to act in such a way that errors or omissions are not discovered, i.e. to behave in a technically *incompetent* fashion. An illustrious example of the practice was given in 1801 at the Battle of Copenhagen, when Nelson put his telescope to his blind eye to avoid seeing the signal commanding him to withdraw his ships from battle. Auditors can choose to act in a similar fashion, by studiously avoiding those areas where errors or omissions might be found. Since the audit tests have failed to produce any embarrassing revelations, the auditor can produce an unqualified opinion without apparently compromising his or her integrity. In this discussion, such a course of action would be considered to be that of a technically competent person who is not acting honestly.

In cases of alleged audit failure, where subsequent events have shown that the auditor's report was incorrect, it is often difficult to decide whether the auditor made an honest mistake or whether he or she deliberately chose not to examine a particular area or to make some technical error. In this chapter we are concerned with the issue of whether the auditor is acting honestly to the best of his or her abilities.

ANALYSING THE MOTIVATIONS OF AUDITORS

The main issue to be addressed in this chapter is why auditors should behave honestly, even when they are not economically independent of their clients and hence have some economic interest to lose by being honest (either the whole or part of the present value of the net revenues expected to be received from the client in the future). That readers of financial statements do expect auditors to report honestly can be gauged from the fact that many individuals (e.g. investment analysts, bankers and the management of other companies) place considerable reliance on the auditor's report. An honest auditor will behave like someone who is independent, using independence to mean 'an attitude of mind which does not allow the viewpoints and conclusions of its possessor to become reliant on or subordinate to the influence and pressures of conflicting interests' (Lee, 1986, p. 89).

In order to assess what motivates auditors, two principal fields of inquiry will be used: economic analysis and ethical philosophy. These methods of inquiry will be applied to the auditor as an individual and as a member of the auditing profession.

The auditor as a rational economic individual

Rational economic individuals act in such a way as to maximize their own utility (self-interest). This goal is usually considered to have two aspects: the maximization of an individual's economic wealth, i.e. the present value of the stream of future cash flows accruing to the individual; and the minimization of the risk attached to these future cash flows. Antle (1984) has produced a one-period game-theoretical analysis of the situation in which there are three parties: the owner, the manager and the auditor. The language of the paper is difficult to understand, but the result of the analysis is essentially simple. If each party acts purely to maximize his or her self-interest, the implication of the model is that the manager and the auditor should conspire together to the detriment of the owner. This result applies for one period only, the model being too complex to extend to a multi-period situation.

In order to examine the more realistic setting of many periods, so that the auditor is reporting not once only but is producing audit reports on a regular basis, it is necessary to use a less exact form of economic analysis. To understand this analysis, the nature of the product that is auditing needs to be examined. If a set of financial statements is produced without an audit, the reader will expect that the management of the organization will have biased the financial statements in some way, to make the performance of the organization seem better than it actually is. There may also be errors present resulting from genuine mistakes rather than deliberate ones. The effect of having an audit is to reduce the impact of both types of error. By its nature, the audit cannot be expected to uncover all possible errors, since cost considerations prevent the auditor from examining all the transactions that the organization has undertaken in the period. Hence the auditor has to make a decision on how much audit work needs to be undertaken. This process forms the substance of Part II of this book, but for the present we need note only that the auditor makes a judgement on how much audit work he or she considers necessary in order to give an opinion on the financial statements. Different auditors will make different decisions based on their training and their attitudes to risk. As a result it is possible to speak of different qualities of audits. Quality can be measured either by input measures (how much work has been performed) or output measures (the probability that the audited financial statements do not contain a significant error or omission). The difficulty faced by consumers of the audit product (the readers of the financial statements) is that there is no way that they can directly determine the quality of the audit. The unqualified audit report is a document noted for its brevity and consistency. Reading an unqualified audit report gives no indication of the work that has been carried out and so the reader cannot make a direct assessment of the quality of the audit. The only assurance that the reader has is that he or she knows that, if the auditor is found to have behaved in a negligent fashion, the auditor will be liable for a claim for damages (see Chapter 5). Therefore, there is an expectation that the auditor will have performed an audit that will have reduced the chances of a successful negligence suit to a level acceptable to the auditor. In the language of economics, the auditor will perform audit work until the cost of undertaking more work is equal to the benefit the auditor derives in terms of the reduction in the risk of a successful suit being possible. This then represents the minimum amount of work that the reader can expect the auditor to perform. However, all auditors are individuals with different attitudes to risk and return and so one auditor's minimum standard of audit work will not necessarily be that of a colleague.

One further point needs to be considered and that relates to the reputation of the auditor or audit firm. There have been a number of studies which show that different firms have different reputations (see, for example, Moizer, 1989). This result could be explained on the basis of the arguments outlined above, but there is also the possibility of a further effect and this relates to the notion of 'renting a reputation'. If an audit firm has a reputation for performing above average quality work (in the sense that the financial statements the firm has audited have a lower chance of containing significant errors), readers of the financial statements will have more confidence in them. In a world of rational economic individuals who are wealth maximizers and risk minimizers, this increase in confidence should be worth paying for. Such individuals will be prepared to accept a lower return for a lower amount of risk. Hence, auditors with higher reputations can be expected to earn higher fees because their reports are more highly valued. There is thus the possibility that, if an auditor performs work of an above average standard, eventually the reputation of the auditor will rise and he or she will be able to charge more for his or her services. There is, therefore, an incentive mechanism in the market for the auditor to improve the quality of work, although the auditor will have to decide whether the costs of improving quality are justified by the increase in audit fees which arise once the improvement in quality is recognized.

How then does this economic analysis relate to independence or the need to report honestly? Every time that an auditor makes a statement which he or she knows to be false, that individual is risking two things: first, the costs of a successful legal action for negligence (this could be a mixture of money that has to be paid directly to the aggrieved party as a result of a legal settlement and the higher insurance premiums that will inevitably arise if part of the legal settlement is covered by insurance); and, second, the costs of a loss in reputation resulting from the reduction in fee income that the auditor can command. Thus, the auditor has to balance the costs of reporting honestly (the present value of the reduction in net fee income expected to be received from the client) against the long-term benefits of honest reporting (the avoidance of legal costs and the loss of income derived from a good reputation).

The economic value of a self-governing audit profession

Until recently, the members of four professional accountancy bodies were recognized under successive Companies Acts as eligible for appointment as auditors. All UK company auditors were members of one of these bodies, which were self-governing. Following the Companies Act 1989, which implemented the EC Eighth Company Law Directive, the system of regulation of auditing has changed. Rather than specific professional bodies being referred to in the statute, the Secretary of State now has power to designate them as recognized supervisory bodies and individuals, and firms must be registered with, and subject to the rules of, such a body to be eligible for audit appointments. While this change in the law does give the Secretary of State considerable power to ensure the adequacy of the rules of a body on matters such as independence before granting supervisory status, the regulatory structure still relies to a considerable extent on the professional bodies themselves, as self-governing associations, for the development and enforcement of appropriate rules. There are considerable benefits to being a member of such a profession: entry into the profession can be limited by examinations and practising certificate requirements; secrecy can be encouraged (e.g. until recently the rules of the profession prevented professional audit firms from advertising); the regulation of accounting and auditing practice is largely carried out by the profession rather than government; and misconduct can be judged by fellow professionals rather than by some central licensing body such as the Securities and Exchange Commission (SEC) in the USA. All these benefits provide a potentially higher income stream than would be possible under some state scheme and also give the profession's members more flexibility in their work. There is therefore a strong desire on the part of the auditing profession to maintain its self-regulating monopoly and avoid governmental intervention. Government tends to respond to public anxiety, which is usually fuelled by some *cause célèbre*, when the work of the auditing profession is deemed to be of unacceptable quality. Consequently, there is the additional need to report honestly in an independent fashion, because every occasion when dishonesty is discovered increases the possibility of increased governmental intervention and hence the loss of the self-regulatory position that the profession currently enjoys.

Ethical considerations

The considerations above assume that the only motivating forces for individuals are economic considerations. This is only a partial view of human nature. It is hard to believe that real people are completely unaffected by the reach of the Socratic question: 'How should one live?' In this section, we shall examine the view that ethical considerations cannot be totally irrelevant to actual human behaviour.

Two types of ethical reasoning can be distinguished: consequentialism and deontology. In consequentialism actions are judged in terms of the consequences that result, whereas in deontology the view is taken that some acts are morally obligatory regardless of their consequences. The distinction between deontology and consequentialism can be seen by asking:

> Are all the guides to conduct that we want people to follow, and all the constraints on conduct that we want them to accept, of the form – act so as to bring about X as far as is possible (consequentialism); or of the form – do (or do not do) things of kind Y (deontology)?

> (Mackie, 1977, pp. 154–5)

The debate between consequentialists and deontologists has often centred on the doctrine of 'the end justifies the means' (a doctrine which teaches that evil means may be employed to produce a good result). Such a doctrine is an extreme version of consequentialism, however, because it implies that the moral difference between ends and means is such that only the end is important; the means to achieve it having no moral significance at all. The more usual consequentialist view is that there is no morally relevant distinction between means and ends and hence that any badness in the proposed means has to be balanced fairly against the expected goodness of the end. It is therefore possible to justify the use of evil means to achieve a good end, provided that the end is sufficiently good to outweigh the bad created by the means. The deontological view differs, because it assumes that particular aspects of an action determine its moral quality absolutely. Thus a proposed action could be analysed in terms of its moral character and a decision could be made whether it is morally obligatory or morally wrong on the basis of this analysis alone, without considering what else is involved.

In terms of auditor independence and reporting honestly, the ethical position adopted by an auditor will influence his or her decision. Thus an auditor could adopt the deontological stance that it is wrong to be dishonest. Such a person would therefore not write an audit opinion which he or she knows to be wrong, even if the consequences of issuing an honest opinion are expected to be disastrous for a large number of people. Such a person would conform to Aristotle's concept of a sincere or truthful man (*aletheutikos*):

> A man is truthful both in speech and in the way he lives because he is like that in disposition. Such a person would seem to be a good type; for a lover of the truth, who speaks it when nothing depends on it, will speak it all the more when something does depend upon it.
>
> (*Ethics*, translated Thomson, 1976, p. 165)

In contrast, a consequentialist auditor will be concerned about the consequences of issuing a truthful opinion and hence will have to wrestle with his or her conscience when making damaging revelations in the audit report. Perhaps one of the most damaging reports an auditor can issue is the so-called 'going concern' qualification, in which the auditor casts doubt on the organization's ability to continue as a viable entity and, basically, whether it will be able to meet its obligations to its creditors. One inevitable consequence of such a report is that the organization has a greater chance of being put into the hands of a receiver or liquidator. The auditor is therefore aware that his or her report can mean the break-up of an organization, which could spell considerable hardship for a large number of people. In such circumstances, a consequentialist auditor may well conclude that it would be better to say nothing and produce a dishonest report.

The conclusions of the ethical analysis are therefore ambiguous. Auditors who are concerned only with performing the action that is morally obligatory (deontologists) will always report in an honest fashion, but auditors who are concerned about the consequences of their actions may on occasions report in a dishonest way. The profession's ethical guidelines on the subject are unequivocal. For example, the *Guide to Professional Ethics* of the Institute of Chartered Accountants in England and Wales (ICAEW, 1979, p. 3) contains the following statement: 'the overriding requirement [is] that, as a professional man, a member must at all times perform his work objectively and impartially and be free from influence by any consideration which might appear to be in conflict with this requirement'. Such an admonition is entirely deontological; an auditor must be 'free from influence by any consideration', including (one assumes) the consequences of his or her actions. Auditors should report truthfully irrespective of the consequences. To what extent auditors do ignore the consequences of their actions is impossible to answer, because the data to answer the question is unobtainable. However, it has to be allowed that there are ethical reasons that on certain, admittedly rare, occasions an auditor may prefer to report dishonestly from entirely altruistic motives (i.e. taking account of the interests of others rather than the auditor's own self-interest).

The morality of the auditing profession

At this point it is helpful to consider why the morality of the accounting profession exists. Two different explanations can be put forward: egoism and altruism. Egoism is the philosophical theory which propounds the view that self-interest is the basis of morality, and hence would suggest that the morality of the profession can be explained in terms of enlightened self-interest. The apparent conflict between the demands of morality and of personal gain is in reality the conflict between different aspects of self-interest. Personal gain can be represented as direct, short-term self-interest, whereas morality can be represented as indirect, long-term self-interest. The egoistical explanation of the profession's morality can be stated as follows: all the benefits arising from being regarded as a competent, trustworthy auditor stem from the existence of a stable, well-thought-of profession; the observance of certain moral rules is a necessary condition of such a profession; hence auditors have an interest in maintaining the moral order of the profession.

However, the altruistic interpretation of the profession's morality would be that such arguments based on egoism prove only that an auditor has an interest in *other* auditors abiding by the moral rules of the profession. It does not prove that it is in the interest of an individual auditor to abide by the rules. The central argument of altruism is therefore that the explanation of morality cannot be reduced to self-interest. An altruist would argue that it is the interest in people *for their own sake* that is a necessary condition for morality. This notion of the altruistic professional is not confined to auditing; for example, Johnson (1972, p. 13) has noted that professions may be distinguished from other occupations by their altruism, which may be expressed in the service orientation of professional men. To conclude on the subject of the altruistic nature of professionals, however, one can perhaps do no better than quote Haskell (1984):

> The image of the disinterested professional lingers on, but reactions to it range from mild scepticism to curt dismissal. Some modern writers regard it as a harmless myth, possessing like all myths a grain of truth and serviceable as an ideal, perhaps, but certainly not an adequate representation of the actual motives of most professionals, most of the time. Others share Collin's hostile conviction that professionals are wolves in sheep's clothing, monopolists who live by the rule of caveat emptor, but lack the integrity to admit it.
>
> (Haskell, 1984, p. 181)

EXISTING WAYS OF IMPROVING INDEPENDENCE

The foregoing sections analysed the motivational forces acting upon auditors. They reflect what auditors might do given no regulatory restrictions. However, in order to strengthen public confidence in the independence of the auditing profession, a number of rules and guidelines of behaviour have been laid down by Parliament and by the profession itself. To understand the basis behind these rules and regulations, it is necessary to reconsider some of the economic forces which could potentially affect the behaviour of auditors. In terms of professional and legal rules and regulations, four economic factors are relevant:

1. the value of the auditor's economic interest that will be lost if the auditor discloses some error or omission by company management;
2. the probability that the client will dispense with the auditor's services if he or she reports that the financial statements are misstated;
3. the financial loss that will occur as a result of an award of damages if the auditor fails to report a significant error or omission;
4. the loss of future net revenues that will occur as a result of the loss of reputation suffered by the auditor when any misconduct is made public.

The last two factors have not been considered by regulators as ways of improving auditor independence. In the case of the last factor, the reason is presumably because it is too nebulous a concept to legislate for (although the heated discussions that have taken place recently on the subject of 'brand accounting' show that the concept of the value of a firm's reputation is accepted by some accountants). The third factor – the costs of a legal action for damages – has been discussed in the political arena, but not from the point of view of increasing the size of such awards (and hence, one would suppose, increasing independence), but from the viewpoint that damages are too high and that some way should be found of reducing them.

Most of the rules and regulations designed to protect auditor independence can be seen as relating to the first two factors identified above: reducing the size of the auditor's economic interest, and reducing the probability that the auditor will lose the audit by reporting unfavourably on the financial statements. These two factors will now be considered in more detail.

Limiting the size of the auditor's economic interest

In the modern commercial world auditors usually provide numerous other services to complement their audit work. Such services include accountancy and bookkeeping assistance, legal assistance, management consultancy services, personnel recruitment assistance, investigation work, corporate finance advice and tax advice. In some cases the fees from the non-audit services can dwarf the audit fee. Consequently, the costs of losing a client can be considerably more than simply the audit fee. For some audits (e.g. local government audits) auditors are not allowed to be consultants, but for company audits there is no existing legal restriction on the amount of non-audit fee income an audit firm can receive from a client. However, the mood of the EC countries is against auditors also being advisers and so the position in the UK may change.

In the consultative document issued by the Department of Trade and

Industry (DTI) on the implementation of the EC Eighth Directive, comments were invited on the possibility of introducing a prohibition on auditors providing non-audit services to audit clients. No legislation on this point was subsequently introduced in the Companies Act 1989, other than a provision, in itself controversial, allowing the Secretary of State to require disclosure in companies' annual accounts of any fees for non-audit services paid to auditors. It is possible, however, that further EC legislation on the subject of independence may be brought forward in future.

If the EC does set out to prevent audit firms from providing non-audit services, the audit profession could use the interesting defence proposed by Goldman and Barlev (1974). They argue that the more non-audit services are provided to the client, the greater will be the dependence of company management on the audit firm and hence the greater will be the management's desire not to lose the services of that audit firm. Paradoxically therefore, the greater the audit firm's economic interest, the greater will be its independence.

At present, the only restriction on the provision of 'other services' is contained with the ethical guides of the various professional bodies. For example, Statement 1 of the *Guide to Professional Ethics* (ICAEW, 1979) instructs members that a practice 'should endeavour to ensure that the recurring fees paid by one client or group of connected clients do not exceed 15% of the gross fees of the practice'. The logic behind this instruction is that an auditor will be seen to be more independent of a client if revenues from that client form only a small part of the audit firm's total fee income. The recent series of mergers between the large accounting firms should help in this regard.

Likelihood of losing an audit client

This area has attracted the most interest by legislators and the professional bodies as a way of bolstering the independence of auditors. Sections 384 to 394 of the Companies Act 1985 and sections 113 to 117 of the Companies Act 1989 regulate the appointment, removal, resignation and remuneration of the auditor. Auditors have the right to speak against any resolution at a company's general meeting which proposes their replacement and they can also have written representations distributed to shareholders at the company's expense. Hence, company law attempts to place the dismissal of auditors in the hands of the shareholders and not the directors. Unfortunately for auditors, the decisions of the shareholders are likely to be heavily influenced by the view of the directors. In the UK the large majority of shareholders are institutions principally interested in achieving above average portfolio returns and which are therefore unlikely to 'rock the boat' so far as the auditors are concerned.

Further support for auditors is provided by the ethical rules of the institutes. For example, Statement 8 of the ICAEW *Guide to Professional Ethics* contains the following instruction:

> A member who is asked to accept nomination as auditor should . . . (i) request the prospective client's permission to communicate with the auditor last appointed. If such permission is refused he should decline nomination. (ii) on receipt of permission, request in writing of the auditor last appointed, all information which

ought to be made available to him to decide whether he is prepared to accept nomination.

(ICAEW, 1979)

This recommendation appears to be effective for public companies listed on the UK Stock Exchange, principally because of the publicity that surrounds the replacement of auditors. Lack of communication with the old auditor would diminish the reputation enjoyed by the new auditor.

The Companies Acts ensure that the remuneration of auditors is determined at the annual general meeting, but apart from this there is little to protect them from a reduction in either audit fees or fees from non-audit work should they upset client company management. There has been a increasing tendency to put audits 'out to tender', with the ostensible aim of reducing audit fees. Such reasons may be a way of making the removal of an audit firm more acceptable to the public at large, as well as lowering fees. In such cases company management must decide whether the set-up costs of a new audit firm are worth paying (e.g. the new audit firm will have to waste company employees' time learning about the company).

Another feature of the modern audit environment which might be expected to give some support to the independence of auditors is the existence of accounting and auditing standards and guidelines. If these were comprehensive and enforced in a vigorous and visible manner, the power of the auditor would be increased. Both auditors and company management would know that all audit firms would reach a similar conclusion as to what ought to appear in the company's financial statements and, hence, that the advantages of changing audit firms would be non-existent. That this is not the case can be seen from the practice of 'opinion shopping', where client management will telephone various audit firms asking their opinion on a particular aspect of its company's financial statements. The effect of such practices is to weaken the position of existing auditors, once company management can say that another audit firm would act differently.

One further form of support for auditors that is employed is the use of audit committees. These committees are manned by several members of the board of directors, including usually one or more non-executive directors. These committees can provide a buffer between the audit firm and company management, although their exact effectiveness will depend on the independence of the non-executive directors. As most non-executive directors are people with a reputation to lose, the presumption is that they will act in an honourable fashion and hence support the auditors when their cause is a fair one.

ADDITIONAL WAYS OF IMPROVING INDEPENDENCE

The previous section outlined what presently exists to support the independence of auditors. In this section we shall examine further ways that have been suggested.

Legal prohibition of financial interests in client companies

At present there are no legal requirements to prevent an auditor from having a financial interest (such as holding shares) in a client company. There are not even any legal requirements that an auditor should disclose such financial interests. The ethical guidelines of the professional bodies make clear that financial interests in clients should be avoided and the large accounting firms regularly produce lists of the companies in which members of the firm cannot invest. The effect of a legal requirement not to hold shares will probably therefore have little effect in most cases, although it should improve the outside world's perception of the independence of auditors. The reasoning behind this last statement is subtle and runs like this: beneficial shareholdings in audit clients create an incentive for the auditor to act in such a way as to maintain the market value of the client; maintaining a false market value of a company is against the interests of future shareholders at whose expense an existing shareholder (such as the auditor) could profit by selling shares at an inflated value; hence an auditor shareholder has an incentive to mislead potential shareholders and therefore not to act in an independent manner. Furthermore, an auditor has access to insider information (information not yet in the public domain) and could potentially profit by this information. It might be argued that the laws prohibiting insider dealing should prevent such trading by the auditor, but it should be realized that the law operates only when someone makes a loss as a result of another person acting on the basis of insider information. There is nothing to prevent an auditor from gaining from the use of insider information provided no one else apparently loses. For example, an auditor can choose when *not* to sell his or her shares or when *not* to buy.

Rotation of audit appointments
One suggestion to reduce the dependence of the auditor is that audit appointments should be rotated on a regular basis, say every five years. This system should mean that the loss of economic interest will be minimized, since the audit fee income would last for only a short period. If auditors know that they will be replaced soon, they are less likely to be concerned about the attitudes of a company's management. The obvious drawback of the suggestion is that there will inevitably be set-up costs every time the audit changes.

Rotation of audit appointments was something the DTI invited comments on when planning implementation of the EC Eighth Directive, but nothing on the subject was included in legislation.

Peer review
Another suggestion designed to improve performance is that one audit firm's audit working papers should be reviewed by another firm. This 'peer' review would check that the original audit firm had performed all the audit work necessary and that all discovered significant errors and omissions had been either corrected or disclosed in the audit report. The principal drawback of this system is who should bear the costs of the review: the client or the profession. Neither appears particularly willing.

Independent audit-appointing and fee-setting body
The intention behind this proposal is to reduce the power of directors over the appointment of auditors. A governmental body would be set up under the auspices of the Department of Trade and Industry or some specially constituted State Auditing Board. This body would be responsible for the

appointment of auditors and determining the size of their remuneration. The audit fee could also be paid by the governmental body out of a system of levies on companies. The main disadvantage of such a system is that it would be difficult and costly to implement.

SUMMARY

Individuals who use company financial statements when making decisions need to be reassured that the information contained in the financial statements is reliable. The audit is the main mechanism for providing this reassurance, but the modern auditor is effectively hired and paid by the directors of a company. Accordingly, there is an economic incentive for the auditor not to offend the directors and hence for the auditor not to be independent. However, there are also economic reasons that auditors should act in an independent manner. If an auditor fails to report some error or omission in the financial statements, there are two directly associated economic costs: the costs of an award of damages for negligence, and those associated with a drop in the levels of fee income the auditor can command as the auditor's reputation among users falls. There is also an indirect cost to the firm in that every case of auditor negligence reduces the esteem in which the audit profession is held by the general public and therefore increases the likelihood that the self-regulatory monopoly which the profession currently enjoys will be withdrawn by government.

An analysis of the ethical position of auditors shows that in the vast majority of cases the ethical decision is to tell the truth. However, it is possible to envisage situations in which an auditor who was concerned about the consequences of reporting honestly might ethically justify dishonest reporting on the grounds that the harm caused by the act of dishonesty is outweighed by the expected overall increase in good. The notion that 'independence is an attitude of mind' is tenable only for individuals who hold the deontological view of life (i.e. certain actions are morally obligatory regardless of the consequences that result).

In order to increase the independence of auditors it is necesssary to reduce the expected gains from not telling the truth. Therefore, it is necessary either to reduce the size of the auditor's interest in the client or to reduce the powers of the directors of the client company to sack the audit firm or reduce its income from the company. A number of methods for supporting and improving auditor independence are in use and have been suggested. A common thread linking all of them is that someone (be it directors, auditors or shareholders) must make some sacrifice. Consequently, proposals to improve independence can succeed only if backed by an effective means of producing this sacrifice. The most obvious way is via specific legislation, although there may be a role for self-regulation by the profession, provided the enforcement procedures are tough enough.

REFERENCES

Antle, R. (1984) Auditor independence, *Journal of Accounting Research*, Spring, pp. 1–20.
Aristotle, *Ethics*, translated by J.A.K. Thomson (1976), Penguin, Harmondsworth.

Goldman, A. and Barlev, B. (1974) The auditor–firm conflict of interests: its implications for independence, *The Accounting Review*, October, pp. 707–18.

Haskell, T.L. (ed.) (1984) Professionalism versus capitalism: R.H. Tawney, Emile Durkheim and C.S. Pierre on the disinterestedness of professional communities, in *The Authority of Experts: Studies in History and Theory*, Indiana University Press, Bloomington.

Institute of Chartered Accountants in England and Wales (1979) *Guide to Professional Ethics*, ICAEW, London.

Johnson, T.J. (1972) *Professions and Power*, Macmillan, London.

Lee, T.A. (1986) *Company Auditing*, 3rd edn, Van Nostrand Reinhold, Wokingham.

Mackie, J.L. (1977) *Ethics – Inventing Right and Wrong*, Penguin, Harmondsworth.

Moizer, P. (1989) The image of auditors, chapter 8 of *Auditing and the Future*, Institutes of Chartered Accountants in Scotland and England and Wales, Edinburgh/London.

FURTHER READING

Further discussion of the issues raised in this chapter can be found in the following:

Carey, J.L. and Doherty, W.O. (1970) The concept of independence – review and restatement, in W.S. Boutell (ed.) *Contemporary Auditing*, Dickenson Publishing, Belmont, California.

Flint, D. (1988) *Philosophy and Principles of Auditing – An Introduction*, Macmillan, Basingstoke, pp. 54–86.

Lee, T.A. (1986) *Company Auditing*, 3rd edn, Van Nostrand Reinhold, Wokingham, pp. 88–102.

Mautz, R.K. and Sharaf, H.A. (1961) *The Philosophy of Auditing*, American Accounting Association, New York, pp. 204–31.

Sherer, M. and Kent, D. (1983) *Auditing and Accountability*, Pitman, London, pp. 24–35. (Reprinted 1988, Paul Chapman, London)

DISCUSSION QUESTIONS

1. Explain what is meant by the concept of auditor independence.
2. Given that the directors of a company effectively hire the company's auditors and determine the size of their audit fee, explain to a non-accountant why he or she should rely on the audit report contained in a company's financial statements.
3. Suggest ways in which an audit firm can acquire a reputation for performing audit work of a particular quality.
4. Discuss the ethical arguments on whether an auditor should always tell the truth.
5. Compare and contrast the role of the external auditor with that of a chartered surveyor advising a client on a house purchase.
6. Discuss why company shareholders allow their directors so much power in the appointment of a company's auditors.

4
Regulating the Auditing Profession

Stuart Turley and Michael Sherer

Most aspects of business activity are subject, at least to some extent, to regulation in one form or another. In support of regulation it is argued that it can promote efficiency, improve allocation of resources and prevent abuse of position or power; in short, that it helps deal with market failure.

Market failure can take a number of forms. Two of these are relevant to the auditing profession. On the supply side market failure is seen to exist when a monopolist is able to charge above the competitive price for its products or services. In the context of auditing this may arise because the profession is able to control membership through a closed system of examinations and training and to prevent other groups from establishing themselves as alternative professional bodies. Market failure can also be observed when the demand for services is not satisfied by the supplier. An example of this in relation to auditing might be the demand by investors that auditing provide some kind of certificate that there has been no major fraud in the company. The latter may in fact be seen as an example of the supposed expectations gap, which was discussed in Chapter 1.

The regulation of the auditing profession may be considered necessary in order to promote and sustain certain desirable characteristics, for example cost effectiveness, independence and appropriate education and training. Regulation may also help to strengthen the position of those who have an interest in the financial performance of the company but who may not have a contractual relationship with the auditor. In addition to potential investors, creditors, employees and taxpayers, this will probably include most existing shareholders of companies since in practice the auditor is appointed and remunerated by the managers. On the other hand, it may be argued that, more negatively, regulation is associated with intervention, unnecessary or ineffective constraints on freedom and the imposition of costs on those having to comply with stipulated requirements.

Regulation affects both the demand for and the supply of auditing services. The volume of auditing demanded by companies and other organizations is influenced by the existence of statutory requirements for audit; and the type of auditing supplied, and who the suppliers are, reflect both the need to meet such requirements and also additional controls applied by the professional accountancy bodies and the courts. Although it can be argued that sufficient incentives exist which could ensure that an economically efficient level of audit services will be demanded and supplied even in the absence of legal requirements (Jensen and Meckling, 1976; Wallace 1980), in practice auditing exists as a regulated activity. At least to some extent, audits are carried out in reponse to, defined by and subject to monitoring and control through various forms of regulation. Changes in the content of regulatory requirements and the boundaries between different sources of regulation can therefore have important implications for the nature of auditing activity.

Following implementation in the Companies Act 1989 of the EC Eighth Company Law Directive the structure of the regulatory framework relating to auditors has been changed significantly. These changes, which are the subject of this chapter, have affected mainly the supply side of the auditing services market, concerning who should be eligible to audit companies and how their activities should be supervised and controlled. In order to provide a background against which the significance of the recent changes can be judged, the regulatory structure that has historically applied to auditing in the UK is outlined first. The significant issues arising out of the way in which the Directive has been implemented and its impact on those structures are then discussed.

Before going on to consider the regulatory changes from the 1989 Act, it should be noted that in recent years other legislative changes have also affected the position of auditors. The two areas where this is most noticeable are the public sector and the financial services sector. In the public sector, legislation in the early 1980s changed the type of audits organization are subject to by introducing more emphasis on value-for-money considerations. Similarly, in the financial services sector requirements relating to internal control are now part of the auditor's responsibilities, and the auditor's role in reporting to regulatory authorities has come under scrutiny. These issues are discussed elsewhere in this book. This chapter concentrates on the regulation of auditors themselves under the new companies legislation.

THE TRADITIONAL FRAMEWORK OF REGULATION OF AUDITING IN THE UNITED KINGDOM

The manner in which the supply of audit services has been organized and controlled in the UK has involved three main sources of regulation: Parliament, through statute law and the operations of governmental agencies; the accounting profession, which includes four professional bodies whose members commonly undertake audits of private sector enterprises; and the courts, which provide interpretation of statutory and other responsibilities in the context of specific cases.

Parliament, statute law and governmental agencies

The primary sources of regulation of auditing are Parliament, which enacts statutory legislation, and the governmental agencies charged with implementing, applying and ensuring adherence to these statutes. In one sense the statutory requirements can be seen as the means by which government attempts to represent and, at least to some extent, define the role of auditing in society. Under this view, legal provisions should reflect societal perceptions of the need for and desired contribution of, an audit. National legislation is also the means by which regulatory policies determined and agreed at the level of the European Community affect the control of activities, such as auditing, within individual states.

Evidence of the relationship between changing societal values with respect to auditing and the content of relevant UK statutory requirements can be found in the successive revisions to company law in the course of this century.

For example, a shift in the balance of emphasis in the objectives of the audit – away from the detection of fraud and protection of investment towards the reliability of information as a basis for financial decisions – was recognized in the Companies Act 1948, which changed the criterion for the auditor's opinion from 'truth and correctness' to 'truth and fairness' and extended the audit to include the profit and loss account as well as the balance sheet. The same statute also introduced a requirement for the auditor to be a suitably qualified professional accountant, reflecting a feeling that a certain level of technical expertise was necessary to carry out the audit of increasingly complex financial statements, which were being used in connection with significant economic decisions.

Until the recent changes resulting from implementation of the Eighth Directive, the main pattern of statutory regulation of audits established in the 1948 Act has been sustained in subsequent statutes. Although intervening legislation did alter significantly the financial statements subject to audit, major changes in the audit requirements occurred only in certain restricted sectors.

For most private sector companies, the main statutory provisions relating to an individual audit are contained in the Companies Act 1985, which consolidated previous legislation, together with some provisions introduced in the Companies Act 1989. Requirements are specified governing the appointment, removal and resignation of an auditor, the manner in which the auditor's remuneration is to be set, the qualifications necessary to be allowed to act as a statutory auditor and the auditor's rights, for example to have access to information and explanations, and to communicate with shareholders. In addition, the legislation specifies the auditor's duties and reporting responsibilities. On all audits, the auditor must report an opinion on the truth and fairness of the financial statements and their compliance with the accounting requirements in legislation. The auditor must also report when the following conditions do not hold: proper accounting records have been maintained; the accounts agree with those records; all information and explanations required have been received; and consistency between the financial statements and the directors' report. All active companies, irrespective of their size, are required to have an annual audit of their financial statements. For further details of the provisions relating to auditing in the Companies Acts 1985 and 1989, see Woolf (1990) and Swinson (1990).

The principal government agency responsible for the enforcement of business and audit regulations is the Department of Trade and Industry (DTI). For example, the DTI has the power to appoint inspectors to investigate a company's affairs where there is a suggestion of some irregularity in the running of the company. Although investigation tends to be used only in extreme circumstances, in a number of cases inspectors have commented on the work of auditors, often critically. A fuller discussion of the criticisms of auditors made in DTI investigations can be found in Chapter 6.

The accountancy profession
Within the statutory framework, the professional accountancy bodies whose members undertake audits have had a significant role in the regulation of auditing. This role has included control of educational standards, through the process of qualification for membership of the bodies, influence over the

content of audits, through recommendations on standards of practice, and the policing of auditing, through the possibility of disciplinary action against members. Hence the UK system has often been described as one of 'self-regulation', where the profession is responsible for both developing and monitoring the standards of behaviour which are to apply to its own members. In this situation it can be argued that incentives exist to set professional standards at the minimum level likely to be acceptable to the courts or to avoid more direct governmental control and the removal of self-regulatory powers (Moizer, 1988).

Before implementation of the Eighth Directive, the members of four accountancy bodies were recognized specifically in company law as qualified for appointment as auditor. These were the Chartered Association of Certified Accountants, the Institute of Chartered Acountants in England and Wales, the Institute of Chartered Accountants in Ireland and the Institute of Chartered Accountants of Scotland. The recognition of professional bodies and of individuals for eligibility to carry out audits is one of the main areas of change resulting from the Directive.   .

The professional bodies have sought to regulate the performance of audits by issuing guidance about audit procedures and the conduct of an audit, and also recommendations on the application of ethical considerations to audit situations and relationships. Since 1980 the practice recommendations have been in the form of auditing standards and guidelines, prepared by the Auditing Practices Committee and issued by the individual bodies. Standards and guidelines have different status. Auditing standards are mandatory and are expected to be applied whenever an audit is carried out. Disciplinary action could be taken by the professional bodies for non-compliance with standards. In contrast, guidelines are intended to be persuasive but are non-mandatory. This distinction is important when it is recognized that, at 1 April 1990, only two standards but thirty-three guidelines were in force.

An additional aspect of professional regulation has been the operation of a joint disciplinary scheme (JDS) by the English and Welsh, Scottish and certified bodies. The introduction of the JDS can be linked to government disquiet about regulation of auditors following a number of critical reports from DTI investigations in the mid-1970s. The scheme has tended to deal only with instances of direct complaint about auditors or where allegations of inadequate performance have been made. There has been no active monitoring of auditor behaviour or adherence to standards and the operation of the JDS has not been very visible publicly. Again, this is an area where change is likely as a result of the Directive.

The courts and professional liability
Regulation of auditing is also affected by the way in which the courts interpret and apply the nature and extent of the auditor's statutory and other responsibilities. The UK legal system comprises two main strands, statute law and common law. In the context of auditing, statute law creates liability for both civil and criminal offences, for example knowingly making false or misleading statements in order to induce investment, while common law is concerned mainly with the circumstances under which a liability for negligent behaviour might be held.

Most court cases relating to claims of inadequate auditing concern the auditor's common law responsibility for the quality of the audit work and the reported opinion. The judgements in such cases have a significant role to play in the regulation of auditing, in that deciding the existence or otherwise of liability for negligence involves both specifying the standards of behaviour which are regarded as desirable and also determining the type of relationship between auditors and other parties where liability can arise. These judgements will therefore have an influence on the approach and standards followed by auditors generally.

Many of the issues raised in this very brief review of the regulatory framework surrounding auditing are discussed in more detail in other chapters in this book. Court decisions on the auditor's liability are reviewed in Chapter 5 and the role of DTI investigation in Chapter 6. Professional regulation on ethical matters is covered in Chapter 3, on auditor independence, while practice standards and guidelines are discussed in Chapter 7. What remains to be examined in this chapter are the changes in the broad regulatory structure which have resulted from the Eighth Directive.

IMPLEMENTATION OF THE EIGHTH DIRECTIVE

The previous section has outlined the main elements in the system of regulation and control of auditing in the UK prior to the implementation of the Eighth Directive – in summary, that statute law provided a general framework concerning audit responsibilities, that the major emphasis for standards of practice and ethical behaviour for the fulfilment of statutory requirements was placed on self-regulation by the accounting profession, but that this self-regulatory action operated within constraints which could result from potential intervention by governmental agencies and from what the courts were willing to impose on auditors. It is against this background that the impact and significance of the Eighth Directive for UK auditing can be assessed.

The Eighth Directive was implemented by statute in the Companies Act 1989. As well as the auditing provisions, the Act dealt with a variety of issues in companies regulation, including the Seventh Directive on group accounts, aspects of mergers and financial markets, and administrative arrangements in small companies.

Many of the details of the new regulatory system are not yet known and in a number of areas the precise manner of the implementation will be determined by statutory instrument, following discussion with the relevant parties. It is, however, possible to outline the main areas of structural change resulting from the Companies Act 1989 and their significance in the UK context. In the consultative document issued by the DTI to elicit views on implementation of the Directive (DTI, 1986), three main issues were identified: whether regulation should remain with the professional bodies or be transferred to a new quasi-governmental body; the need for rules to guarantee the independence of auditors; and whether audit firms should be allowed to incorporate.

The regulatory position of the professional bodies

As has already been described, the position before the 1989 Act was that four professional accountancy bodies were recognized specifically in law and only members of those bodies could be appointed as auditors. In the consultative document, three possible regulatory regimes were suggested:

1. to give statutory powers to the professional bodies;
2. to allow the Secretary of State to recognize professional bodies for the purpose of both qualification and supervision, such recognition being revocable; and
3. to create a new tier of regulatory control involving representatives of the profession and the state in some form of supervisory council.

A number of points are worth noting about these possible changes in the profession's regulatory position. Whichever alternative was adopted, the status of any self-regulatory roles would inevitably change. The intention of the Directive was that the regulation of auditors should be legally enforceable in the sense that the rules governing auditors should be matters of public law and not simply private rules within self-regulating bodies. Although option 2 was perhaps closest to the existing position on regulation of the auditing profession, there were precedents in other areas for both options 1 and 3. The role of the Law Society with respect to the legal profession is an example of option 1. This would be difficult to achieve in auditing because of the number of professional bodies. An example of option 3 is offered by the legislative changes that were made in the mid-1980s in the area of investment business and related financial services. In that case, the government delegated supervisory authority to a new Securities and Investments Board, which in turn recognizes professional bodies. The response of the accounting profession to the three possible regimes was not unanimous. The Scottish Institute favoured course 1, the English and Welsh course 2 and the certified accountants, perhaps sensing an opportunity to remove some of the differences from the chartered accountants' bodies, course 3 (Cooper *et al.*, 1989). In the 1989 Act the choice adopted was course 2, i.e. the power of approval of professional bodies has been given to the Secretary of State.

Individual professional bodies may now be recognized for two purposes: supervision (as recognized supervisory bodies – RSBs) and qualification (as recognized qualifying bodies – RQBs). Bodies can apply to the Secretary of State for an order granting recognized status. Once granted, recognition can be revoked at any time if the Secretary of State believes the conditions for recognition are no longer being complied with.

In order to be recognized for supervisory functions, a professional body must be operating rules governing both eligibility for appointment as auditor and the content of audit work, which are binding on members and others subject to the body's rules. A supervisory body will be recognized only on satisfying a number of conditions dealing with the following issues:

1. that those eligible for appointment as auditor hold an appropriate qualification;
2. that those eligible for appointment are fit and proper persons;
3. professional integrity and independence;
4. technical standards applying to audit work;
5. procedures for maintaining competence;
6. arrangements for monitoring and enforcement of rules;
7. rules governing membership, eligibility and discipline;

8.   investigation of complaints;
9.   auditors' ability to meet claims arising from audit work;
10. a register of auditors;
11. the cost of compliance with rules;
12. the promotion and maintenance of high standards of integrity.

In line with the Directive, conditions are also imposed for recognition for qualifying purposes, in the areas of:

1.   entry requirements;
2.   theoretical instruction;
3.   professional experience;
4.   examination;
5.   practical training;
6.   monitoring compliance with the Act.

In addition to the conditions in these specific areas, the Secretary of State must also receive a report from the Director General of Fair Trading concerning whether a body's rules are likely significantly to restrict, distort or prevent competition, before a decision is taken on recognition as a supervisory or qualifying body.

Taken together, the various conditions for approval and the power of the Secretary of State to determine whether the conditions have been met represent a major departure from the position that applied previously in the UK. Some aspects of the conditions, for auditors to have the appropriate technical expertise and to be independent and subject to adequate practice rules, may have been implicit in the reliance on the professional bodies under the old regime. The changes in the 1989 Act, however, make such objectives and criteria a great deal more explicit and potentially more onerous.

The requirement to establish a register of auditors is a good example of the more regulated environment facing the auditing profession in the 1990s. The Companies Act 1989 requires RSBs to maintain an up-to-date list of approved auditors, both individuals and firms. This list or register must be made available to the public, although how this is to be achieved and many other details concerning the register will be determined only after consultation between the professional bodies and the DTI. Notwithstanding this, some of the details have already been clearly signalled by the DTI. For example, the register will have to identify those qualified individuals who are responsible for company audit work on behalf of firms, and it will include the names and addresses and the RSB to which individuals and firms belong. It may seem surprising that there has not been, until now, a requirement for a publicly available register of authorized auditors, although it may be argued that the list of members published by the Institute of Chartered Accountants in England and Wales performs such a function. Perhaps there has been some reluctance to establish a formal, official register because of the existence of several professional bodies with different criteria for qualification as auditors. Or, perhaps, the reluctance stems from the belief that the establishment of an official register of members is often a response by a self-regulating body to public disquiet about the 'unprofessional' activities of some of its members.

It is generally expected that all the bodies referred to in the 1985 Act will apply for recognition as both RSBs and RQBs. However, this is not the only possible outcome. Given that it is now possible for a firm or an individual to be registered as eligible to undertake audits, it is possible that firms whose staff are qualified with more than one body may choose to register with the supervisory body where the associated costs are lowest. This behaviour would cause the per capita costs in other bodies to rise and potentially could threaten the viability of some bodies accepting supervisory status. In addition, even where a body meets the necessary conditions, the Secretary of State may decline to grant a recognition order if it is felt unnecessary, for example because of the existence of other bodies. Suggestions have even been made by members of Parliament that, as a matter of policy, the government should recognize only one supervisory body (Smith, 1990). The issue of which bodies become recognized as RSBs and RQBs and what rules will be required to achieve this has yet to be resolved. It is expected that the order recognizing RSBs will not be issued until the spring of 1991.

These changes in the regulatory position of the professional accountancy bodies are significant in a number of ways. As already noted, they make much more explicit than before the areas in which standards must be applied in order to ensure the adequacy of auditing activity, while leaving open the question of exactly what those standards should be. As a result of the new requirements, the Secretary of State is able to exercise great control over the way in which the supervisory bodies regulate the auditing profession, by deciding whether the bodies' rules are acceptable. Perhaps the greatest threat to the profession's existing approach is likely to be in the areas of monitoring and disciplining auditors' performance. In the past the UK profession has had little active monitoring of compliance with rules and it is clear that new procedures will be required in this area. In addition, the mechanisms for investigating and taking effective action in respect of complaints are likely to come under close scrutiny. The powers of the Secretary of State could further be used to influence not only the profession's regulatory activities, but also the structure of the profession itself. Decisions on the kind of rules required and on the recognition of individual bodies could be used to promote greater unification in the currently fragmented UK auditing profession.

Maintaining auditor independence

In the area of auditor independence, the DTI consultative document included a number of possibilities which went considerably further than anything in the Eighth Directive itself. Comments were invited on the suggestions that there should be a statutory requirement for periodic rotation of audit appointments and for prohibition of the provision of non-audit services to audit clients. Both of these possibilities, which are concerned with the auditor's dependence on the audited company, would mean radical changes in the UK market for audit services.

The suggestions, which caused considerable disquiet in the profession, were raised only tentatively in the consultative document, however, and it is possible that the DTI intended simply to give a warning to the profession as to the type of solutions which could be imposed if adequate professional rules were not introduced. Inclusion of these possibilities in the document does suggest at least that the DTI regards independence as an important issue.

In the 1989 Act, apart from some changes involving possible disclosure of information on non-audit fees and on changes in auditor, no statutory measures on auditor independence were introduced. Rather, 'professional integrity and independence' are left as an area in which the professional bodies must convince the Secretary of State of the adequacy of their rules before being recognized for supervision. Specifically, the bodies must have rules to ensure that:

1. company audit work is conducted properly and with integrity;
2. persons are not appointed as auditors in circumstances where a conflict of interest could arise;
3. audit firms have arrangements to prevent unqualified members of the firm or outsiders exerting influence on the conduct of an audit in a way which could jeopardize its independence and integrity.

The UK government has therefore opted largely for a continuation of the status quo regarding regulation and independence. Little in the way of new statutory control has been introduced, and reliance continues to be placed on professional rules. Whether the Secretary of State will use the powers in relation to recognition to secure any changes in existing professional rules on independence is as yet uncertain.

Incorporation of audit firms

Historically, in the UK it has not been possible for a corporate body to be appointed as the auditor of a company, in contrast to the situation in a number of EC countries. This prohibition has been lifted by the 1989 Act, although the practical significance of this move will depend in part on the subsequent response of the professional bodies on this issue. The change in law to allow appointment of a firm as auditor, whether a corporate body or a partnership, does remove one anomaly in UK company law, where previously the Companies Act referred to individuals but in practice partnerships were often appointed.

The possibility of audit firms incorporating raises additional issues of independence concerning the ownership and control of the firms. The Act includes provisions to ensure that decision-making is controlled by individuals holding recognized qualifications. Similarly, as noted above, RSBs are required to have rules to ensure that non-qualified persons cannot exercise influence over audit practice in a way that could threaten independence. The professional bodies have produced their own report on this issue, suggesting that a minimum of 75 per cent of the voting rights in an incorporated firm should be held by qualified auditors and, further, that non-auditor and outsider shareholders and directors should agree to be subject to the rules and discipline of the RSBs. These proposals have been questioned by the DTI, however, on the grounds that more stringent requirements than those in law could be regarded as anti-competitive.

This example provides an interesting illustration of the kind of debate that is likely to take place between the professional bodies and the government over the detail of the bodies' rules in a variety of areas before recognized status is granted. The Act gives sufficient discretionary power to the Secretary of State in determining the acceptability of such rules to force the profession to adopt particular standards regarded as desirable or essential by the government.

One particular effect of the possibility for audit firms to incorporate and be registered as firms is that it is forcing the professional bodies increasingly to recognize within their structures, and to regulate, firms as well as individual members. This development reflects the realities of the audit services market, but also represents a significant departure from the traditional UK idea of a profession, which places emphasis on the individual as a 'professional', not on his or her employing entity.

IMPLICATIONS OF THE COMPANIES ACT CHANGES

The environment within which auditing services are provided to companies continually changes in response to economic factors affecting companies and auditors, societal expectations and regulatory demands. In this chapter we have seen how recent regulatory developments will affect the future auditing environment in the UK. As well as their formal effects, these changes also indicate possible wider implications for the auditing profession.

The Eighth Directive has been implemented in a way which is to a considerable extent similar to the pre-existing position in the UK and without the radical suggestions for either the regulatory structure in general or specific areas such as auditor independence which were raised in the DTI consultative document on implementation. Nonetheless, it is clear that the regulatory changes which have been introduced are of major significance for UK auditors in a number of ways.

1. It is likely that there will be an increase in the volume of regulations affecting auditing.
2. Particular areas of regulation may become more important and more visible than previously, notably in the monitoring and enforcement of standards, discipline and independence.
3. The change in status of many matters from private self-regulatory rules to public law is an important structural change in the regulatory system.
4. Similarly, the power of the Secretary of State to influence directly the volume, content and effect of the rules of the professional bodies represents a major change in the balance of power in auditing regulation.
5. The separate recognition of professional bodies for qualifying and supervisory status introduces greater flexibility in the government's control of the auditing profession.
6. The power of the Secretary of State on rules and recognition could be used, if desired, to encourage change in the structure of the profession, for example to force greater unity between the accountancy bodies for certain functions.
7. The recognition of firms as auditors represents a change from the traditional UK understanding of a professional person as an individual to reflect the economic reality that it is normally the firms that are the relevant entities for regulation.

Many of the applications of the new system have yet to be worked out and it will be some time before the full impact of these developments in the general structure of auditors can be assessed. What is already clear, however, is that the Companies Act 1989 marks the beginning of a new phase in the relationship between auditing and the state. There is now statutory backing for the intervention of the state, in the form of the DTI and its Secretary of State, in the affairs of the auditing profession.

AUDITING AND THE STATE

It is appropriate, therefore, to conclude this chapter on regulation by reviewing the relationship between the auditing profession and the state, and in particular why it is generally in the interest of the state to support an independent, self-regulating profession. Throughout the history of auditing in the UK there has always been a close relationship between auditing and the state. This is most apparent in the statutory basis for an audit, as prescribed in the Companies Acts. What is perhaps not so apparent is that the legal requirement that companies be subject to an audit has generated benefits not only for the auditing profession, by creating barriers to entry and a guaranteed source of income, but also for the state, by providing an effective, low-cost means of maintaining the confidence of investors in the securities market (Merino and Neimark, 1982).

As an inevitable consequence of the regulatory role played by auditing on behalf of the state, however, this relationship has also been characterized by a significant amount of tension. The primary cause of this tension has been the extent to which the profession should be allowed to govern itself and determine its own rules and procedures. The nature of the problem can be seen more clearly be adopting an agency relationship framework. The state, as the principal in the relationship, wants to ensure that the auditing profession, the agent, is contributing to the objectives of the state, which specifically means maintaining confidence in the capital markets by enhancing the credibility of company financial statements. A problem arises if the credibility of the auditing profession, in terms of its expertise or its independence, is put in doubt. This becomes apparent when adverse comments about the auditors are made in Department of Trade investigations. The reaction of the state, as we have seen above, was to consider direct regulation of the auditing profession in order to restore the credibility of auditing. Direct state control of auditing could take a number of forms, for example passing legislation to specify how an audit should be conducted and restricting the type of non-audit work which can be performed by the auditor; or even making auditors employees of the state, as in France where the *commissaires aux comptes* are responsible to the Ministry of Justice.

However, any of these forms of direct state control would be an unpalatable solution to both parties in the UK. The advantages to the profession of self-regulation are no doubt self-evident, but self-regulation is also very convenient to the state; partly because it avoids the high administrative costs associated with direct control, but mostly because it ensures that the audit function in society is seen as independent of the state. In particular, the auditing function performs a valuable role for the state by helping to maintain stability in the financial markets, but it can only do this because it has the *de jure* responsibility of protecting the interests of investors.

The state has also seen that an independent auditing function can serve other valuable roles in addition to its traditional role of maintaining confidence in the securities market. Auditors, and particularly those from the large international firms of accountants, are engaged in an increasing amount of public sector work. Approximately one-third of all local authority audits are in the hands of private sector auditors. There had been for some time a statutory provision which allowed local authorities to appoint approved private sector auditors, but only a small number of authorities ever took advantage of this. Under the Local Government Finance Act 1982, however, auditors are required to report on the economy, efficiency and effectiveness, or value for money, of local authorities, in addition to conducting a normal regularity audit. The Audit Commission, which now has the responsibility for appointing auditors, considers that private sector auditors have the necessary expertise to do this type of work.

In direct response to glaring weaknesses in internal control and the need to reduce central government expenditure, there has also been a resurgence of interest in auditing within central government, again with an emphasis on evaluating the value for money of departments and services. Clearly, not all this public sector audit work is undertaken by private sector accounting firms. However, the greater use made of auditing in the public sector, and the legitimation of its role there, has been facilitated by the strength of the aura associated with auditors. If, within a basically self-regulating framework, the auditing profession is seen to be responsible, independent and accountable, and to have control over its members, the state, as well as the profession, will benefit.

CONCLUSION

The Companies Act 1989 has given the Secretary of State the power to regulate the auditing profession and, as a consequence, the DTI will be concerned that there is a vigorous and credible mechanism for setting auditing standards. This may well lead to a review of the role and future objectives of the Auditing Practices Committee as suggested by Patient (1990). However, it is doubtful whether the new regulatory framework for auditing will fundamentally change the essentially symbiotic relationship between the auditing profession and the state. Self-regulation is dead, long live self-regulation!

REFERENCES

Cooper, D., Puxty, A., Lowe, A., Robson, K. and Wilmott, H. (1989) (In)stalling European standards in the UK: the case of the Eighth Directive on the regulation of auditors, paper presented at the EIASM Workshop on the Regulation of Auditors, Brussels.

Department of Trade and Industry (DTI) (1986) *Regulation of Auditors: Implementation of the EC Eighth Company Law Directive – a Consultative Document*, DTI, London.

Jensen, M.C. and Meckling, W.H. (1976) Theory of the firm: managerial behaviour, agency costs and ownership structure, *Journal of Financial Economics*, Vol. 3, October, pp. 305–60.

Merino, B.D. and Neimark, M.D. (1982) Disclosure regulation and public policy: a sociohistorical reappraisal, *Journal of Accounting and Public Policy*, Vol. 1, no. 1, pp. 33–58.

Regulating the Auditing Profession

59

Moizer, P. (1988) Towards a theory of the auditor's choice of audit quality in a self-regulated market, unpublished working paper, University of Manchester.

Patient, M. (1990) Auditing Practices Committee: time to review? *Accountancy*, August, p. 27.

Smith, T. (1990) One supervisory body to serve the public interest, *Accountancy Age*, 3 May, p. 16.

Swinson, C. (1990) *A Guide to the Companies Act 1989*, Butterworths, London.

Wallace, W. (1980) *The Economic Role of the Audit in Free and Regulated Markets*, University of Rochester, N.Y.

Woolf, E. (1990) *Auditing Today*, 4th edn., Prentice-Hall, London.

DISCUSSION QUESTIONS

1. Critically evaluate the arguments for and against the regulation of the auditing profession.
2. What are the implications of the new regulatory framework for the role of the Auditing Practices Committee in setting auditing standards?
3. 'The implementation of the Eighth Directive will hasten the integration of the professional accountancy bodies in the UK.' Discuss.
4. What do you understand by the 'aura' of auditing? To what extent does this explain the increased use of auditing in the public sector?
5. Discuss the relationship between the state, the auditing profession and a company's investors, creditors and employees. Are the state and the auditing profession impartial between these interests?

5
The Auditor's Liability to Third Parties

David Gwilliam

In a company audit the underlying contractual relationship is between the auditor and the company in its capacity as an artificial person. To fulfil this contract the auditor must comply with the specific Companies Act requirements for audit together with any duties accepted as implicit in the term 'audit' but not spelt out as such in the Companies Act, for example the duty to report detected or suspected fraud and error to management at the earliest possible opportunity. Satisfactory performance of this contract requires the exercise of reasonable skill and care on the part of the auditor. The parties may agree additional duties but section 310 of the Companies Act 1985 prevents the parties contracting for a lower standard of audit.

Other parties which choose to rely on the information contained in audited financial statements will not normally have a contractual relationship with the auditor. These may include shareholders of the company, prospective shareholders, actual and prospective creditors of the company, etc. For such parties to recover losses which they sustain consequent to their reliance upon an auditor's work they normally have to establish:[1]

1. that the auditors owed them a duty of care (the duty of care issue);
2. that the auditors were negligent in the auditing of the accounts (the negligence issue);
3. that they (the third party) suffered loss in consequence of the negligence of the auditors (the causation issue);
4. the amount of loss they suffered (the quantum issue).

The question arises whether these separate issues are independent. In a certain sense they are interdependent, an interdependence which one judge referred to in the following terms:[2]

> Duty of care is a thing written on the wind unless damage is caused by that breach of duty; there is no actionable negligence unless duty, breach and consequential damage coincide . . . for the purpose of defining liability in a given case, each element can be defined only in terms of the others.

In practice, however, the courts have treated these criteria as essentially separate and in the interests of judicial efficiency have on more than one

David Gwilliam M.A., F.C.A., is a lecturer at the Judge Institute of Management Studies, University of Cambridge. He is a member of the ICAEW Auditing Research Foundation.

occasion taken the duty of care issue as a preliminary point in its own right. Nevertheless, one interrelationship which has been suggested by an eminent UK judge is that the extension of the duty of care in recent years has had 'the almost indefinable and subconscious consequence of lowering the standard of proof which the courts require before inferring negligence' (Oliver, 1988, p. 174).

A related question with important practical implications for auditors is whether the exercise of the skill and care necessary to defeat a negligence claim in contract, i.e. one made by the company client, is sufficient to defeat a claim made by a third party. Here there has been no suggestion in the courts that a higher standard of care would ever be owed to third parties, but the question whether there is any interaction between the extent of negligence and the scope of a duty of care has not, in an auditing context, been directly considered by the courts.

This chapter addresses the specific question of the circumstances in which an auditor may be held to owe a duty of care to a third party. If there is no duty of care, questions of negligence, causation and damage will not normally arise. This is not to say that they are not important. On a number of occasions where a duty of care has been held to exist the plaintiff has been unable to recover losses because the auditor has been held not to be negligent (as in *Lloyd Cheyham*) or because losses were not caused by reliance upon the audited financial statements (as in *JEB Fasteners*)[3] or because the quantum of damage, if any, could not be determined (as in *Scott* v. *McFarlane*).[4]

DEVELOPMENT OF THIRD-PARTY LIABILITY

In the nineteenth-century case *Cann* v. *Willson*[5] the House of Lords held that a valuer instructed by a mortgagor was liable to a mortgagee for failure to carry out the valuation with reasonable skill and care. However, five years later the 'wrong turning'[6] taken in *Le Lievre* v. *Gould*[7] effectively overruled this judgment and reaffirmed the doctrine of privity of contract other than in cases of deliberate misrepresentation. Although in the twentieth century *Donoghue* v. *Stevenson*[8] opened the door to duties outside contract where physical injury was suffered as a consequence of a negligent act or omission, it was not until *Hedley Byrne* v. *Heller*[9] that the House of Lords was again prepared to find that a duty of care was owed to a party which had suffered economic loss as a consequence of reliance upon a negligently made statement. Following *Hedley Byrne* came the influential decision in *Anns* v. *Merton London Borough*.[10] In this case Lord Wilberforce put forward a two-tailed test for establishing whether a duty of care was owed, which was subsequently interpreted and applied in a number of cases so as to extend significantly the scope of liability for negligence. Lord Wilberforce stated that in order to establish whether a duty of care arose in a particular situation it was necessary to answer in the affirmative two questions:[11]

> First one has to ask whether, as between the alleged wrongdoer and the person who has suffered damage there is a sufficient relationship of proximity or neighbourhood such that, in the reasonable contemplation of the former, carelessness on his part may be likely to cause damage to the latter – in which case a prima facie duty of care arises. Secondly . . . it is necessary to consider whether

there are any considerations which ought to negate or to reduce or limit the scope of the duty or the class of person to whom it is owed or the damages to which a breach of it might give rise.

For a time, the policy of the courts in their interpretation of the *Hedley Byrne* and *Anns* decisions seemed to be toward expanding the duty of care within limits set by reasonable foresight and an increasingly wide definition of proximity.[12] More recently, there has been evidence of a judicial reaction against this extension of care outside contract[13] and both the *Anns* test and its subsequent interpretation have been criticized in higher courts. For example, in *Yuen Kun-yeu* Lord Keith said:[14] 'Their Lordships venture to think that the two-stage test formulated by Lord Wilberforce for determining the existence of a duty of care in negligence has been elevated to a degree of importance greater than it merits, and greater perhaps than its author intended.' In their retreat from the highwater mark of the expansion of the duty of care for economic loss which, it is generally agreed, was reached in *Junior Books*[15] the courts have been particularly concerned to ensure that foreseeability or the reasonable contemplation of likely harm did not in itself become a sufficient test for proximity. In *Hill* v. *Chief Constable of West Yorkshire*[16] Lord Keith stated: 'It has been said almost too frequently to require repetition that foreseeability of likely harm is not in itself a sufficient test of liability in negligence. Some further ingredient is invariably needed to establish the requisite proximity of relationship.'

Instead, there has been an emphasis on the need to approach questions of whether a duty of care is owed to a third party by reference both to the specific circumstances of each particular case and by analogy with previous similar categories of case. This approach has checked the perceived widening of the scope of a duty of care but it has still permitted third parties to recover losses in certain circumstances. For example, in two cases heard together – *Smith* v. *Eric S. Bush* and *Harris* v. *Wyre Forest District Council*[17] – the House of Lords held that a surveyor making an inspection on behalf of a mortgagee owed a duty of care to a plaintiff house-buyer. Here Lord Griffiths set out the basis on which he considered decisions as to whether a duty of care was owed should be decided. He stated:[18]

> in what circumstances should a duty of care be owed by the adviser to those who act on his advice? I would answer: only if it is foreseeable that if the advice is negligent the recipient is likely to suffer damage, that there is a sufficiently proximate relationship between the parties and that it is just and reasonable to impose the liability.

THIRD-PARTY LIABILITY IN AUDITING

Judgements in UK cases where third parties have sought to bring actions against auditors have mirrored the developments in negligence law as a whole. In *Candler* v. *Crane Christmas*,[19] heard over a decade before *Hedley Byrne*, the majority of the Court of Appeal followed *Le Lievre* v. *Gould* in holding that a third party, on whose behalf accounts had been drawn up and audited, was not owed a duty of care by the auditors even though the auditors knew the purpose for which the accounts were being prepared and audited.[20]

However, it was Lord Denning's dissenting judgement which was approved by the House of Lords in *Hedley Byrne*. Lord Denning asked himself to whom accountants owed a duty, and answered:[21]

> They owe the duty, of course, to their employer or client, and also, I think, to any third person to whom they themselves show the accounts, or to whom they know their employer is going to show the accounts so as to induce him to invest money or take some further action on them. I do not think, however, the duty can be extended still further so as to include strangers of whom they have heard nothing and to whom their employer without their knowledge may choose to show their accounts. Once the accountants have handed their accounts to their employer, they are not, as a rule, responsible for what he does with them without their knowledge or consent.

More recently, lower court decisions in *JEB Fasteners* and *Twomax*[22] relied heavily upon the *Anns* test in finding that in certain circumstances third-party investors, of whose existence the auditor had no direct knowledge at the time of the audit, were owed a duty of care by the auditors of the company in which they subsequently invested. These decisions, and those in a number of other Commonwealth cases, have been well documented (in, for example, Savage, 1983; Kent, 1985; Baxt, 1987; Gwilliam, 1987).

Both the *JEB Fasteners* and *Twomax* decisions were, in respect of the duty of care issue, those of single judges (both were appealed but in neither case was the duty of care issue heard before the higher court). However, in *Caparo*[23] the question whether auditors owed a duty of care to either actual or prospective shareholders was considered in both the Court of Appeal and in the House of Lords.

This important case arose following the takeover by Caparo of a company called Fidelity. On 21 May 1984 the auditors of Fidelity signed an unqualified audit report on the accounts of the company for the year ended 31 March 1984. On the following day Fidelity released a preliminary statement of the results. In early June Caparo purchased its first block of shares and by 12 June, the day the annual report was published to the shareholders, held approximately 1.3 per cent of the equity in Fidelity. Caparo continued to purchase shares after the publication of the annual report and by the end of the first week of July had increased its stake to 29.9 per cent. On 4 September Caparo made a full takeover bid. Initially contested, a subsequent, slightly higher, bid was recommended by the directors of Fidelity. By 25 October Caparo held or had received acceptances for 91.8 per cent of the issued share capital and was able to proceed to acquire the entire equity of Fidelity.

The takeover was not a success and in 1985 a writ was issued against the auditors of Fidelity alleging loss resulting from the negligence in the performance of their auditing duties, in particular failure to detect alleged overvaluation of stock and other irregularities which, according to Caparo, resulted in a reported profit of £1.3 million as compared to a true deficit of at least £400,000.

In the lower court[24] the judge directed that the question whether Caparo was owed a duty of care by the auditors should be taken as a preliminary issue in abstraction from the questions of negligence, causation and quantum. In the outcome he found that the auditors did not owe Caparo a duty of care in its capacity either as an existing shareholder at the time the audit report was made or as a potential shareholder at that date. Although a duty of care might be owed by the auditors to shareholders as a body this could be enforced only by shareholders suing as a class. Even if there was such a duty it would not in all the circumstances of the case have been just, fair and reasonable to impose a duty either to shareholders individually or as a class.

Caparo appealed and the Court of Appeal[25] decided by a majority of two to one that Caparo was owed a duty of care in its capacity as a shareholder at the time of the audit report (but that had it not been a shareholder it would not have been owed a duty of care as a potential investor).

All three Court of Appeal judges considered the issues within the framework of reasonable foresight, proximity and whether it was just, fair and reasonable to impose a liability.

The foreseeability of economic loss to Caparo as a shareholder at the time the auditors' report was published was effectively common ground. The auditors knew that their report would be sent to the members and they must have known that some shareholders would rely upon the report in making investment decisions. They also knew that an unqualified report, negligently made, might cause individual shareholders to suffer loss by selling (if the accounts undervalued the company's worth) or buying (if the accounts overvalued it).

It was on the question of proximity that opinion was divided. Bingham LJ interpreted proximity within the context of the neighbourhood principle defined by Lord Atkin in *Donoghue* v. *Stevenson* as 'such close and direct relations that the act complained of directly affects a person whom the person alleged to be bound to take care would know would be directly affected by his careless act'.[26] In this context he saw the relationship between the shareholders as a class and the auditor to be very close to a contractual relationship. He noted that although the auditor's contract is made with the company it is a contract made on the company's behalf by the shareholders; the auditor's fee is paid out of company funds which would otherwise be available for distribution to the shareholders; and the object of the contract is to obtain a report to shareholders made independently of the company itself. Although the analogy with contract was less compelling when applied to the shareholders as individuals rather than as a class, he was nevertheless satisfied that this relationship was sufficiently close to satisfy the requirements of proximity.

Taylor LJ agreed that the appointment of the auditor by the shareholders created a nexus close to contract and that the relationship between the parties was sufficiently close and direct for the requirement of proximity to be satisfied. However, O'Connor LJ, dissenting, held that any statutory duty owed by auditors to shareholders was owed to them as a body.

He considered that the wide-ranging requirement that it should be fair, reasonable and just to impose a liability covered the same ground as the second stage of the *Anns* test (the factors that ought to negate responsibility) and also what had been described in earlier cases as policy. He suggested that if the imposition of a duty on a defendant would be for any reason oppressive, or would expose him, in Cardozo CJ's famous phrase, to 'liability in an indeterminate amount for an indeterminate time to an indeterminate class',[27] this would weigh heavily, probably conclusively, against the imposition of a duty. A duty would be more readily found, however, where a defendant is voluntarily exercising a professional skill for reward, where the victim of his carelessness has no other means of redress, where the duty contended for arises naturally from a duty which already exists or where the imposition of a duty is thought to promote some socially desirable objective.

He was satisfied that it was in all the circumstances just and reasonable to impose a duty of care toward individual shareholders. The imposition of such a duty would not require the auditor to change the nature of audit work significantly nor was it likely that auditors would be subjected to hundreds or thousands of claims because the difficulty and cost confronting parties seeking to make such claims would deter all but large shareholders. Here he emphasized that in the ordinary way such a claim would be very hard to establish as not every oversight or blunder, even if negligent, would significantly affect the share price.

Having decided that Caparo was owed a duty of care as a shareholder the question whether it was owed such a duty in its capacity as a potential investor alone did not strictly arise. Nevertheless, he expressed his opinion that the absence of sufficient proximity prevented such an extension of potential liability. Nor was he persuaded that at this present time it would be just and reasonable, or politic, that the law should be extended so as to impose a duty on the basis of the facts in the case.

Taylor LJ agreed that there was a sufficiently close and direct relationship between the auditors and individual shareholders to meet the requirements for proximity and that it would be fair, just and reasonable for an individual shareholder to have a remedy against a negligent auditor. However, a lack of proximity prevented the investor at large being owed such a duty of care even where that investor was a potential suitor in situations where it was arguable that a company was vulnerable to takeover. (In a number of previous cases, for example *Scott* v. *McFarlane*, *JEB Fasteners* and *Twomax*, the argument that the nature of the client company's financial status should have alerted the auditors to the existence of a class of potential investors, who were likely to choose to rely on the audited accounts in making their investment decisions, had an important bearing on the decision as to whether a duty of care was owed.)

The dissenting judge, O'Connor LJ, considered that the statutory duty imposed upon auditors was one which was owed to shareholders as a body. Furthermore, even if under statute a duty was owed to shareholders as individuals, that duty would have to be confined to transactions in which a shareholder can participate only because he is a shareholder. Whereas selling shares may be such an activity, buying shares is not. (This argument was considered by both Bingham and Taylor LJ but rejected partly on the grounds that it would not be just and reasonable to deny a duty on this basis. However, it subsequently received some support in the House of Lords where Lord Bridge referred to the 'specious equation of "investment decisions" to sell or to buy as giving rise to parallel claims'.)[28] Consequently, he did not consider that the auditors owed a duty to Caparo; something more, which was not present, was required to create the necessary linkage.

In the interval between this Court of Appeal decision and the further appeal to the House of Lords, this decision was applied and interpreted in *Al Saudi Banque* v. *Clarke Pixley*.[29] Here an action was brought against the auditors of a company whose main business had been the provision of credit to overseas customers. The plaintiffs, a group of banks which had lent money to this company (some of which were creditors at the time of the audit report and some of which subsequently became creditors), alleged that the business was essentially fraudulent – the transactions amounting to little more than the provision of credit to connected companies which were hopelessly insolvent. (As in *Caparo* the case came to court on the preliminary issue whether a duty of care was owed by the auditors to the plaintiffs.)

In this judgement Millett J noted that it was common ground between the parties that for a duty of care to be owed to a third party on the basis of a negligent misstatement:

1. it must be reasonably foreseeable that the statement would be relied on;
2. the relevant degee of proximity between the parties must exist;
3. it must be just and reasonable in all the circumstances to impose a duty of care.

He saw the Court of Appeal decision in *Caparo* as binding authority for the following propositions.

1. Foreseeability was a necessary but not sufficient criterion for liability. In addition, it was necessary to establish a nexus or relationship between the parties sufficient to create a duty of care.
2. Whether a relationship was sufficiently close to satisfy the requirements of proximity was something that necessitated close analysis in each individual case. In some cases it might be useful to consider whether there had been a voluntary assumption of responsibility.
3. Company members had that relationship as a consequence of the statutory requirements for auditors to report to the members of the company.
4. That relationship might exist if there had been an implied representation of the accuracy of accounts to the plaintiff or perhaps where they provided accounts with the intention or in the knowledge that it was the company's intention that they were to be supplied to the plaintiff or to persons in a class of which the plaintiff was one.
5. The relationship was not necessarily restricted to one type of transaction.
6. The necessary relationship did not exist between a company's auditors and potential investors.

In this context the plaintiffs asserted that because of the nature of the business the auditors must have reasonably foreseen that the company would show its accounts to the lending institutions and that the banks would rely on them accordingly.

In the outcome Millett J took the view that on the facts of the case the position of the lending bankers who were not creditors at the time of the audit report was similar to that of potential investors and in consequence no duty of care was owed to them. Nor was a duty of care owed to those bankers who were creditors at the time of the audit report as even the limited nature of the class to which they belonged did not create a relationship which satisfied the test of proximity as there was no statutory obligation to report to them nor were copies of the audit report supplied to them.

In the House of Lords the Court of Appeal decision that Fidelity's auditors did owe a duty of care to Caparo in its capacity as a shareholder at the time of the publication of the annual report was reversed. In reaching their unanimous decision the Law Lords again cautioned against an approach based on the application of underlying principles common to the whole field of negligence and in favour of a more traditional approach based on the categorization of 'distinct and recognizable situations as guides to the existence, the scope and the limits of the varied duties of care which the law imposes'.[30] Three of the Law Lords referred with approval to the view expressed by Brennan J in the Australian High Court:[31]

> It is preferable in my view, that the law should develop novel categories of negligence incrementally and by analogy with established categories, rather than by a massive extension of a prima facie duty of care restrained only by indefinable 'considerations which ought to negate, or to reduce or limit the scope of duty or the class of person to whom it is owed.'

Such an approach reduced the emphasis placed on the tripartite test (foreseeability; proximity; just and reasonable) adopted in the lower courts as the basis for deciding whether a duty of care was owed. Lord Oliver, noting both the difficulties of applying such a test and the overlap between its constituent parts, stated:[32]

> one looks in vain for some common denominator by which the existence of the essential relationship can be tested. Indeed it is difficult to resist a conclusion that what have been treated as three separate requirements are, at least in most cases, in fact merely facets of the same thing, for in some cases the degree of foreseeability is such that it is from that alone that the requisite proximity can be deduced, whilst in others the absence of that essential relationship can most rationally be attributed to the court's view that it would not be fair and reasonable to hold the defendant responsible. 'Proximity' is, no doubt, a convenient expression so long as it is realized that it is no more than a label which embraces not a definable concept but merely a description of circumstances from which, pragmatically, the courts conclude that a duty of care exists.

Lord Roskill was just as emphatic:[33]

> Phrases such as 'foreseeability', 'proximity', 'neighbourhood', 'just and reason-able', 'fairness', 'voluntary acceptance of risk' or 'voluntary assumption of responsibility' will be found used from time to time in the different cases. But, as your Lordships have said, such phrases are not precise definitions. At best they are but labels or phrases descriptive of the very different factual situations which can exist in particular cases and which must be carefully examined in each case before it can be pragmatically determined whether a duty of care exists.

For each of the four Law Lords who gave separate judgements a key aspect was the purpose for which the relevant information was given. This in turn led to consideration of the purpose of the statutory provisions making compulsory for companies both an annual audit and the filing of audited accounts. This their Lordships interpreted in the restricted sense of giving shareholders the information necessary to enable them to exercise their powers in a general meeting. They emphasized that these statutory provisions were not for the purpose of enabling investors to make investment decisions *per se*. This position was clearly put by Lord Jauncey, who stated:[34]

There is nothing in . . . [Part VII of the Companies Act 1985] . . . which suggests that the accounts are prepared and sent to members for any purpose other than to enable them to exercise class rights in general meeting. I therefore conclude that the purpose of annual accounts, so far as members are concerned, is to enable them to question the past management of the company, to exercise their voting rights, if so advised, and to influence future policy and management. Advice to individual shareholders in relation to present or future investment in the company is no part of the statutory purpose of the preparation and distribution of the accounts.

In that Caparo's claim was based upon a use of the statutory accounts other than one which, even if it could be foreseen, was not intended by statute, the necessary degree of proximity did not exist. Lord Oliver stated the general principle as follows:[35]

> Thus *Smith v. Eric S. Bush*, although establishing beyond doubt that the law may attribute an assumption of responsibility quite regardless of the expressed intentions of the adviser, provides no support for the proposition that the relationship of proximity is to be extended beyond circumstances in which advice is tendered for the purpose of the particular transaction or type of transaction and the adviser knows or ought to know that it will be relied upon by a particular person or class of persons in connection with that transaction.

On this basis Evans (1990) suggests that in its decision in this case the House of Lords has rejected both the three-part test of foreseeability, proximity and whether it is just and reasonable to impose a liability, and the test of the voluntary assumption of responsibility. Instead it has proposed a new test: liability for negligent misstatement is to be confined to cases where the statement has been given to a known recipient for a specific purpose of which the maker was aware, and upon which the recipient had relied and acted to his detriment.

FUTURE DEVELOPMENTS

How significant a restriction the House of Lords decision in *Caparo* places on the actual liability of auditors is open to debate. Very few third-party actions which came through the courts were in fact completely successful although the growing acceptance of the existence of a wider duty of care may have resulted in settlements being made which would otherwise not have been. Following *Caparo* what categories of third-party claims may still succeed in establishing that a duty of care was owed?

Claims made by or on behalf of the company are normally made within the contractual relationship between the company and the auditor. The direct and indirect beneficiaries of such claims may include existing shareholders or shareholders who have purchased shares subsequent to the breach of contract or creditors of the company. For example, in the Australian case *Cambridge Credit*[36] although the case was brought in contract the actual beneficiaries were creditors of the collapsed company, a situation referred to by one of the judges in the following terms:

> This leads to the paradox that, although the trustee relied on the certificates, it is not making any claim for damages; while Cambridge, which did not rely either on

the certificates or the events constituting the breach of contract, is the party claiming the damages. What is more, if damages are recovered by Cambridge, they will go to pay the creditors as at September 1974, most or all of whom probably did not rely on the 1971 accounts or certificates in making their investments.

Although third parties may be the ultimate beneficiaries of many such actions, however, the decision to bring them is in the hands either of the company itself or of a liquidator (who may of course be appointed by the creditors). In *Caparo* Lord Bridge considered that in practice the interest of the shareholders in the proper management of their company's affairs is indistinguishable from the interest of the company itself, and any loss suffered by the shareholders will be recouped by a claim against the auditors in the name of the company, not by individual shareholders. Lord Bridge found it difficult to visualize a situation in which an individual shareholder could claim to have suffered a loss in respect of an existing shareholding, referable to the negligence of the auditor, which could not be recouped by the company. Such an analysis needs to consider the situation in which shares are undervalued; it also needs to consider the incentives for management not to bring an action against an auditor if they are likely to be shown in an unfavourable light and, perhaps most important, the incentives for existing shareholders to bale out by selling to unsuspecting third parties who will then have no right of recourse against the auditor.

Outside contract, application of the test proposed in *Caparo* would clearly suggest that in circumstances similar to those in *Candler*, where an auditor shows a set of audited accounts to a prospective investor, a duty of care to that investor will exist. In *Lloyd Cheyham*, where the potential investor refused to go through with the investment until audited accounts were available and where these accounts had been handed to him by the auditor, Woolf J had little doubt that a duty of care was owed:[37]

> It is clear beyond peradventure in this case that the defendants knew that their audited accounts were required by the plaintiffs in relation to their proposed agreement in respect of Trec. In these circumstances, subject to reserving his position if the case should go to appeal, counsel for the defendants . . . accepts that the defendants owed to the plaintiffs a duty of care in auditing the accounts of Trec. On my view of the law this is undoubtedly the position.

Whether an auditor who knows that a client intends to show audited accounts to a prospective investor or creditor similarly owes that third party a duty of care is less clear. It may be that the courts will follow the example of the New York courts in drawing a distinction between situations in which an auditor has positively evidenced his awareness (and implied acquiescence in) of the accounts being shown to third parties and those where there is no such evidence. In *Caparo* at least one judgement appeared to allow the possibility that a duty of care might exist where there was constructive or inferential knowledge that the accounts would be communicated to a third party, and it has been suggested (Evans, 1990) that this might be an area in which liability could be extended in the future.

Another type of claim, which may arise in either contract or tort, is where a special report is commissioned from the auditor. In *Caparo* Lord Roskill referred to this situation accordingly:[38]

If a would-be investor or predator commissions a report which he will use, and which the maker of the report knows he will use, as a basis for his decision whether or not to invest or whether or not to make a bid, it may not be difficult to conclude that if the report is negligently prepared and as a result a decision is taken in reliance upon it and financial losses then follow, a liability will be imposed on the maker of that report.

In such circumstances, however, it may be open to the auditor to avoid liability by means of an appropriate exclusion caluse. As Lord Roskill noted:[39] 'there may be cases in which the circumstances in which the report was commissioned justify the inclusion of the reliance on a disclaimer such as succeeded in the *Hedley Byrne* case but by reason of subsequent statutory provisions failed in *Smith* v. *Eric S. Bush*'.

In many instances reports requested by third parties are commissioned and paid for by the company itself. For example, a bank deciding whether to lend money to a company may require that company to provide it with a special report from the auditor. In that the auditor knew the purpose of such a report it may be conjectured that a duty of care would be owed by the auditor to the bank. This conjecture is strengthened by the outcome of a recent case[40] in which a company, at the specific request of its bankers, instructed professional advisers to undertake an investigation into its financial affairs and report to its directors, with copies to its bankers. It was held that the resulting contract was between such advisers and the bankers alone; so that such advisers owed no contractual duty of care to the company or to its directors or shareholders or guarantors.

Another group of third parties which may be able to establish that they were owed a duty of care might include those regulatory authorities to whom the auditor is required to report directly on a regular or *ad hoc* basis. The most comprehensive of these reporting requirements are those found under the Financial Services Act 1986 (for a discussion of which, see Sweeney-Baird, 1990). There are also circumstances, e.g. those in connection with the issue of prospectuses, where further statutory provision may enable a successful action to be brought. This was noted by Lord Denning in *Candler* v. *Crane Christmas*: 'It is perhaps worth mentioning that Parliament has intervened to make the professional man liable for negligent reports given for the purposes of a prospectus: see sections 40 and 43 of the Companies Act 1948'. (These provisions are now contained in sections 67 and 68 of the Companies Act 1985). In *Anns* Salmon LJ seemed to envisage a wider duty of care based in common law:[41]

> There are a wide variety of instances in which a statement is negligently made by a professional man which he knows will be relied on by many people besides his client, e.g. a well-known firm of accountants certifies in a prospectus the annual profits of the company issuing it and unfortunately, due to negligence on the part of the accountants, the profits are seriously overstated. Those persons who invested in the company in reliance on the accuracy of the accountants' certificate would have a claim for damages against the accountants for any money they might have lost as a result of the accountants' negligence.

It has been argued (see Evans, 1990) that the incorporation of the greater part of the Stock Exchange *Yellow Book* rules as subordinate legislation made under the Financial Services Act 1986 may have an impact upon the scope of the duty of care owed by auditors. The *Yellow Book* rules require audited accounts expressly for the purpose of informing the investing public of the financial standing of a public company both on admission to listing and as a continuing requirement. This contrasts with the more limited view of the role of published accounts as a means for enabling shareholders to review the performance of management with a view to exercising their collective rights to replace management or to take other appropriate action. The *Yellow Book* rules had not been incorporated into statute at the time of Caparo's takeover of Fidelity and were not referred to in any of the judgements, however, as Evans (1990, p. 80) notes: 'it would be a brave advocate who argued that the decision in *Caparo* is no longer binding because the Stock Exchange rules were not then on a statutory footing, and consequently auditors do now owe a duty to all shareholders'.

PUBLIC INTEREST AND POLICY

If the *Caparo* decision does significantly restrict the scope and extent of third-party actions against auditors, it is necessary to ask whether this is in the interests either of the audit profession or of the economy as a whole. Has the House of Lords been over-protective to auditors? And in so doing has it failed to take into account the realities of the present-day role of the auditor in making possible the efficient functioning of the capital markets?

The classic floodgates argument, as expressed in Cardozo CJ's oft-quoted assertion that auditors should not be exposed 'to a liability in an indeterminate amount for an indeterminate time to an indeterminate class' is couched in terms of protecting auditors as suppliers of audit services and has been criticized in these terms. For example, in *Scott* v. *McFarlane* Woodhouse J stated:[42]

> the attraction and force of the language ought not to lead to uncritical acceptance. . . . It is, of course, substantially a plea in mitigation on behalf of [auditors] that they should be altogether excused from liability for their negligent conduct because the consequences are too serious to justify responsibility. It may be regarded as a rather one-sided argument, particularly when it is set up in favour of those who are in business to give advice.

It is at least arguable, however, that the long-term interests of the audit profession are better served by a wider scope of liability. To take an analogy from auditing history, there is little doubt that over the years the prestige and fee-earning capacity of the profession have risen hand in hand with the rise in requisite standards of auditor care and expertise. If, as was argued in *Leeds Estate Building and Investment Company* v. *Shepherd*,[43] the work of the auditor was restricted merely to verifying the transcription of the entries in the underlying books of account to the financial statements, it is difficult to see how the profession could have reached its present status and eminence. Even if there is no direct gain to the audit profession from an extended duty of care it would be surprising if, operating as audit firms do, in a market in which there is effectively a minimum guaranteed demand for audit that any additional costs could not be passed on to clients and, indirectly, to the economy as a whole.

This brings us to the wider, and more important, question whether such a restriction of liability is in the public interest. Here two separate lines of argument may be distinguished. The first is that if existing levels of investor protection are in fact higher than would hold in a free market then any reduction in the level of protection is likely to increase welfare. Although investors who have suffered loss will *ex post* seek to recover this loss from other parties it may well be that *ex ante* they would not support the blanket imposition of protection. Some evidence to support this argument may be seen in the fact that when privity of contract was enforced to prevent recovery by third parties, prior to *Hedley Byrne*, there was little evidence of separate contracting practices between third parties and auditors (see Goldberg, 1988).

The second line of argument develops out of the general proposition that negligence rules should be developed so as to impose penalties upon those parties which can at the least cost take the action necessary to avoid the perceived harm. (The design of negligence rules to maximize economic welfare has been pioneered by writers such as Coase, 1960, Calabresi, 1970 and Posner, 1977.) Extending the scope of an auditor's duty of care will not necessarily require additional audit work as the exercise of reasonable skill and care sufficient to fulfil the contractual audit requirements is also sufficient to defeat a third-party claim. In *Caparo* Bingham LJ noted that the plaintiffs' contention that the imposition of a duty of care to individual shareholders would oblige an auditor to do nothing that he was not already obliged to do under his contract with the company, and was satisfied that recognition of such a duty would not lead to any significant change in audit practice. In contrast, the hiring by every potential investor of an auditor to undertake a separate audit would clearly be inefficient (as was the practice of all prospective purchasers of a house commissioning their own structural survey).

CONCLUSIONS

Recent developments in the law relating to negligent misstatements have shown a reaction against the development of the scope of a duty of care based upon reasonable foresight alone and have emphasized that the proximity necessary for a duty of care to be owed requires some further linkage between the parties. More generally, the courts have rejected overall tests of proximity based upon reasonable foresight, voluntary assumption of responsibility or other grounds, and have instead emphasized the need for gradual development of the law based upon analogy to previous cases and categorizations of negligence. This incremental approach focuses upon the existence of a close and direct relationship between the parties and actual knowledge of the purpose for which the negligently made statement is to be used.

In *Caparo* a key aspect of this approach was consideration of the nature and purpose of statutory accounts. Here the House of Lords finding that statutory accounts are prepared, audited and publicly filed primarily for the purpose of providing information useful to shareholders in the exericse of their class rights, and not to assist either shareholders or others in the making of investment decisions, almost certainly flies in the face of general expectations in the investment community and the public at large. However, although the House of Lords decision has been criticized as a retrograde step, the question whether such a restriction of liability is in the long-term interests of either the audit profession or the investing public is, for the reasons discussed above, an open one.

NOTES

1. As set out by Woolf J in *Lloyd Cheyham & Co.* v. *Littlejohn & Co.* [1987] BCLC 303, 305.
2. Per Brennan J in *John Pfeiffer Pty Ltd* v. *Cannay* [1981] 148 CLR 218, 241–2.
3. *JEB Fasteners Ltd* v. *Marks Bloom & Co. (a firm)* [1981] 3 All ER 289; affd [1983] 1 All ER 583, CA.
4. *Scott Group Ltd.* v. *McFarlane* [1978] 1 NZLR 553, NZ CA; affg [1975] 1 NZLR 582, NZ SC.
5. (1888) 39 Ch D 39.
6. As it was referred to by Bridge LJ in *Caparo Industries plc* v. *Dickman* [1990] 1 All ER 568, 575, HL.
7. [1893] 1 QB 491, CA.
8. *Donoghue (or M'Alister)* v. *Stevenson* [1932] AC 562, [1932] All ER Rep 1, HL.
9. [1963] 2 All ER 575, [1964] AC 465, [1963] 3 WLR 101, HL.
10. [1977] 2 All ER 492, [1978] AC 728, [1977] 2 WLR 1024, HL.
11. [1978] AC 728, 751.
12. For example, as in *Ross* v. *Caunters (a firm)* [1979] 3 All ER 580, [1980] CH 297, [1979] 3 WLR 605; *Yianni* v. *Edwin Evans* [1981] 3 All ER 592.
13. As evidenced by the decisions of the House of Lords in *Peabody Donation Fund (Governors)* v. *Sir Lindsay Parkinson & Co. Ltd* [1984] 3 All ER 529, [1985] AC 210, [1984] 3 WLR 953, HL, and *Yuen Kun-yeu* v. *A.-G. of Hong Kong* [1987] 2 All ER 705, [1988] AC 175, [1987] 3 WLR 776, PC.
14. *Yuen Kun-yeu* [1988] AC 175, 191.
15. *Junior Books Ltd* v. *Veitchi Co. Ltd* [1982] 3 All ER 201, [1983] 1 AC 520, [1982] 3 WLR 477, HL..
16. [1988] 2 All ER 238, 241.
17. [1989] 2 All ER 514.
18. Ibid., 536.
19. [1951] 1 All ER 426, [1951] 2 KB 164, CA.
20. At the time the accounts, which were prepared by the auditors, were shown to the third party an audit report was not attached. However, the third party was assured that they had been audited and an audit report was provided a few days later.
21. [1951] 1 All ER 426, 434.
22. 1982 SC 113, Outer House, rvsd by consent 1984 SLT 424, Inner House.
23. 25 *Caparo Industries plc* v. *Dickman* [1990] 1 All ER 568, HL.
24. [1988] BCLC 387.
25. [1989] 1 All ER 769.
26. [1932] AC 562, 581.
27. *Ultramares Corp.* v. *Touche* (1931) 255 NY 170, 179.
28. [1990] 1 All ER 568, 580–1, HL.
29. *Al Saudi Banque and Others* v. *Clarke Pixley and Another* [1989] 3 All ER 361.
30. [1990] 1 All ER 568, 574, HL.
31. *Sutherland Shire Council* v. *Heyman* (1985) 60 ALR 1, 43–4.
32. [1990] 1 All ER 568, 585, HL.
33. Ibid., 581–2.
34. Ibid., 607.

35. Ibid., 592.
36. *Cambridge Credit Corp.* v. *Hutchinson & Ors* (1983) 8 ACLR 513, (1985) 9 ACLR 545, [1987] ACLC 587.
37. [1987] BCLC 303, 310.
38. [1990] 1 All ER 568, 582, HL.
39. Ibid.
40. *Huxford & Ors* v. *Stoy Hayward*, *The Times*, 11 January 1989.
41. [1978] AC 728, 769.
42. [1978] 1 NZLR 553, 571–2.
43. (1887) 36 ChD 787. Here counsel for the auditor argued (at 795) that it was his duty 'to see that the balance sheet represented, and was a true result of, what appeared in the books of the company, and his certificate goes no further than that. The auditor is a machine for this purpose only.'

REFERENCES AND FURTHER READING

Baxt, R. (1987) *Auditors and Accountants: Their Role, Liabilities and Duties*, North Ryde, N.S.W. 3rd edn, CCH Australia.
Calabresi, G. (1970) *The Costs of Accidents*, Yale University Press, New Haven.
Coase, R.H. (1960) The problem of social cost, *Journal of Law and Economics*, October, pp. 1–44.
Evans, H. (1989) Auditors' duty of care to third parties: *Caparo* v. *Dickman* in the Court of Appeal, *Professional Negligence*, January/February, pp. 16–18.
Evans, H. (1990) The application of *Caparo* v. *Dickman*, *Professional Negligence*, June, pp. 76–80.
Goldberg, V.P. (1988) Accountable accountants: is third party liability necessary?, *Journal of Legal Studies*, June, pp. 295–312.
Gwilliam, D.R. (1987) The auditor, third parties and contributory negligence, *Accounting and Business Research*, Winter, pp. 25–35.
Jones, M.J. (1990) Negligence and the auditor's duty of care after Caparo, *Professional Negligence*, June, pp. 69–75.
Kent, D. (1985) The auditor's liability to third parties, in D. Kent, M. Sherer and S. Turley (eds.) *Current Issues in Auditing*, Harper & Row, London.
Oliver of Aylmerton, Lord (1988) Nought for your comfort, *Professional Negligence*, November/December, pp. 173–9.
Posner, R.A. (1977) *Economic Analysis of Law*, 2nd edn, Little, Brown & Co., Boston.
Savage, N. (1983) Auditors: a critical review of their role, *The Company Lawyer*, Vol. 4, no. 5, pp. 187–98.
Sweeney-Baird, M. (1990) The implications of the financial Services Act 1986 for accountants, *Professional Negligence*, March, pp. 30–5.

DISCUSSION QUESTIONS

1. What criteria must be satisfied if an action for negligence is to be successful?
2. Discuss the extent to which reasonable foresight of loss consequent upon a negligent misstatement will impose a duty of care upon the party making that statement.
3. References by the courts to criteria such as 'proximity' and 'just and reasonable' have been described as no more than 'sublimely meaningless ritual incantations' which serve to conceal rather than guide judicial reasoning. Discuss.

4. The oft-repeated assertion that auditors should not be exposed to a liability in an indeterminate amount for an indeterminate period to an indeterminate class represents no more than special pleading that they should be relieved of liability for negligence because the consequences are too serious to warrant the imposition of such a responsibility. Discuss.

5. In *Hedley Byrne* the House of Lords developed a coherent test for determining the duty of care in negligent misstatement cases on the basis of voluntary assumption of responsibility only for the issue to be subsequently clouded by notions of foreseeability and proximity which by their nature are incapable of precise definition. Discuss.

6
Department of Trade and Industry Investigations

Peter Russell

INTRODUCTION

In this chapter we look at Department of Trade and Industry (DTI) investigations into the affairs of companies. This is an important yet somewhat unexplored area, as noted by Hatherly (1980, pp. 2–4), who stated that the criticisms by inspectors of the accountancy and auditing profession contained in the published reports of investigations contributed much to the 'crisis to confidence' within the profession during the 1970s.

We consider first the legal background and then the extent and procedures, conduct and results of investigations. Next, we look at the 'statutory fact-finding capacity' of inspectors and seek to identify the most important issues arising from reports published during the 1970s and 1980s. Finally, we examine the implications of the reports for the accountancy and auditing profession.

LEGAL BACKGROUND

Under Part XIV of the Companies Act 1985 and section 177 of the Financial Services Act 1986 the DTI has powers to appoint inspectors to investigate the affairs of a company, its membership and dealings in its securities. This chapter will concentrate on investigations into the affairs of a company, rather than those into membership and dealings in shares, since this type of investigation is of more direct relevance to the accountancy and auditing profession.

Leigh, Joffe and Goldberg (1987, p. 258) suggest that the principal purpose of an investigation is to establish the facts where, *prima facie*, some irregularity has been shown in the way a company has been run, and to report those facts to the DTI. Gower *et al.* (1979, p. 679) point out that DTI investigations supplement the basic philosophy of disclosure on which successive Companies Acts have been based, since investigations may help members to obtain further information or to establish that their rights have been infringed. Investigations also supplement the other remedies a member has against oppression, as the DTI itself may institute proceedings as a result of the investigation. Leigh, Joffe and Goldberg (1987, p. 258) noted that over and above this the reports of investigations often provide a basis for public discussion and action by government and professional bodies on aspects of the law,

Peter Russell is Lecturer in Accountancy and Finance at the University of East Anglia.

administration and professional practice which are shown to be in need of reform.

Farrar (1988, p. 461) states that the power to appoint inspectors to investigate the affairs of a company was first granted to the Board of Trade under the Joint Stock Companies Act 1856 and was based on equivalent legislation in the New York Business Corporations Act. The powers of the Board of Trade (now the DTI) and the rights and duties of inspectors have been expanded and refined in succeeding Companies Acts and by decisions in the courts. A detailed discussion of the legal provisions may be found in most up-to-date texts in company law (see 'Further reading' at the end of the chapter). All that is attempted here is a brief summary of the main points.

Under Part XIV of the Companies Act 1985 the provisions for the appointment of inspectors to investigate the affairs of a company fall into two categories: where the DTI *may* appoint inspectors and where it *must* appoint them.

By far the more common case is where the DTI appoints inspectors on its own initiative. Section 432 of the 1985 Act is the one most frequently used as a basis for an investigation since it permits the DTI to appoint inspectors if there are circumstances suggesting any of the following:

(a) that the company's affairs are being or have been conducted with intent to defraud its creditors or the creditors of any other person or otherwise for a fraudulent or unlawful purpose, or in a manner which is unfairly prejudicial to some part of its members, or

(b) that any actual or proposed act or omission of the company (including an act or omission on its behalf) is or would be so prejudicial, or that the company was formed for any fraudulent or unlawful purpose, or

(c) that persons concerned with the company's formation or the management of its affairs have in connection therewith been guilty of fraud, misfeasance or other misconduct towards it or towards its members, or

(d) that the company's members have not been given all the information with respect to its affairs which they might reasonably expect.

Under this section the DTI may appoint inspectors even though the company is in the course of being voluntarily wound up.

The DTI may also appoint inspectors to investigate a company's affairs following an initiative by the company or its members. Section 431 of the 1985 Act permits an application to the DTI, either by the company or by a specified minimum number of members, requesting it to appoint inspectors. The application must be supported by evidence showing good reason for requesting the investigation, and, in addition, security to cover costs may be required by the DTI. The DTI may also appoint inspectors following an initiative by the Director of Public Prosecutions where, in the course of a voluntary winding up, it has appeared to the liquidator that a past or present officer or member has been guilty of a criminal offence against the company (Insolvency Act 1986, s. 218(4) and (5)).

Under section 447 of the 1985 Act the DTI has powers of preliminary inquiry and may demand the production of books and documents and require explanations to be provided. A preliminary inquiry enables the DTI either to resolve matters at an early stage or to proceed to a full investigation.

The only occasion where the DTI *must* appoint inspectors is under section

432(1) of the 1985 Act, if a court orders that the affairs of the company ought to be investigated.

There are occasions other than an investigation of a company's affairs when the DTI may appoint inspectors. Under section 442 of the 1985 Act inspectors may be appointed to investigate share ownership for the purpose of determining the true persons who are or have been financially interested in the company or in the position of being able to control or materially influence the company's policy. Inspectors may also be appointed under section 446 of the Act to investigate contraventions of section 323 thereof, involving directors dealing in options in the securities of their company, or contraventions of section 324 and Schedule 13 of the Act, involving directors disclosing their interests in the securities of their company. In this connection it is worth mentioning that under section 177 of the Financial Services Act 1986 the DTI has taken new powers to appoint inspectors to investigate the possibility of insider dealing in contravention of sections 1, 2, 4 or 5 of the Company Securities (Insider Dealing) Act 1985.

EXTENT OF INVESTIGATIONS

It is interesting to examine how extensively the DTI uses its power to investigate the affairs of a company. The DTI publishes such figures on an annual basis, and Table 6.1 shows the number of cases considered for investigation for the period from 1971 to 1987–8 and the way the DTI dealt with them.

From Table 6.1 it can be seen that over those seventeen years an average 523 cases for possible investigation were considered by the DTI each year. In only 22 per cent of cases was an investigation approved. Of the remaining cases considered, 55 per cent either did not go to investigation or the application was refused, while 23 per cent were held over to the following year. From the published figures it is not possible to establish exactly what happened to the carried forward cases, but if the same percentage that applies to the cases decided upon during the year applies to all cases then in only about 28 per cent of the cases brought to its attention does the DTI approve an investigation.

For an investigation to be carried out inspectors must be appointed under particular section(s) of the Companies Act 1985. An analysis of the approved investigations is given in Table 6.2. The table shows that 88 per cent of investigations represent the use of the DTI's powers of preliminary inquiry. Unfortunately, it is not possible from the published figures of preliminary inquiries to establish the proportion that go on to full investigation; but an examination of the figures in Table 6.2 indicates that the proportion is very low. A full investigation is proceeded with in only 12 per cent of the cases approved for investigation by the DTI. In fact, if all the cases actually decided upon in a year are considered then only 3 per cent go on to full investigation.

An important point which has not so far been mentioned is the number of public companies that become subject to investigation. The consequences of an investigation for a public company, with potentially a much larger number of shareholders than a private company, can be very serious. An indication of the number of public companies receiving a full investigation can be obtained from the number of reports published by the DTI. Under section 437 of the

Table 6.1 Number of DTI investigations

	B/f	Received during year	Total	Approved	Not proceeded with	Refused	C/f	Total
1971	65	432	497	117	159	149	72	497
1972	72	403	475	115	173	117	70	475
1973	70	408	478	93	186	76	123	478
1974	123	438	561	158	192	110	101	561
1975	101	456	557	177	209	97	74	557
1976	74	447	521	152	150	98	121	521
1977	121	374	495	115	191	100	89	495
1978	89	343	432	101	111	110	110	432
1979	110	261	371	79	91	37	164	371
1980	164	395	559	81	188	102	188	559
1981	188	412	600	103	239	93	165	600
1982	165	408	573	91		365	117	573
1983	117	374	491	112		290	89	491
1984	89	449	538	101		331	106	538
1985	106	528	634	116		444	74	634
1986–7	79	495	574	134		350	90	574
1987–8	90	441	531	135		341	55	531
TOTAL	1,823	7,064	8,887	1,980		5,099	1,808	8,887
Average	107	416	523	116		300	107	523
%				22%		57%	21%	100%

Note: Calendar years to 1985, then 1 April 1986 to 31 March 1987, thereafter 1 April to 31 March. Break in series cannot be reconstructed from published data.

Source: DTI, *Companies in 1987–88* and previous editions.

Table 6.2 Analysis of approved investigations

	s.431	s.432	Companies Act 1985			Other	Total
			s.442	s.632	s.447 (preliminary inquiry)		
1971	24	—	—	—	93	—	117
1972	6	—	—	—	109	—	115
1973	1	9	1	—	82	—	93
1974	1	25	2	—	130	—	158
1975	3	16	2	6	150	—	177
1976	—	10	—	12	130	—	152
1977	1	14	2	9	89	—	115
1978	2	8	1	20	69	1	101
1979	—	4	—	1	74	—	79
1980	—	1	2	4	74	—	81
1981	—	2	—	2	98	1	103
1982	—	9	—	3	79	—	91
1983	—	6	3	—	103	—	112
1984	—	1	1	—	99	—	101
1985	—	1	3	1	111	—	116
1986–7	—	1	3	—	130	—	134
1987–8	—	2	—	—	133	—	135
TOTAL		147	20	58	1,753	2	1,980
Average		9	1	3	103	—	116
%		8%	1%	3%	88%		100%

Notes:
1. Calendar years to 1985, then 1 April 1986 to 31 March 1987, thereafter 1 April to 31 March. Break in series cannot be reconstructed from published data.
2. Sections 431, 432, 442 and 442 were formerly sections 164, 165 and 172, respectively, of the Companies Act 1948; section 632 was formerly section 324 of the 1948 Act, now section 218 of the Insolvency Act 1986; section 447 was formerly section 109 of the Companies Act 1967.

Source: DTI, *Companies in 1987–88* and previous editions.

1985 Act the DTI has the power to publish the inspectors' reports of their investigations, and it is the DTI's general practice to publish in the case of a public company; if legal proceedings are under consideration or are in progress, however, publication may be delayed. Reports on private companies are published only in those cases where they raise issues of general interest (DTI, 1986, para. 74). The number of reports published each year is set out in Table 6.3. A list of all reports published by the DTI during the period from 1971 to 1988 is given in the Appendix to this chapter.

Finally, it is worth pointing out that the cost to the DTI of company investigations is quite substantial although such cost may be recovered under certain circumstances. These costs are given in Table 6.4. The amounts in columns 1 and 2 represent the fixed costs the DTI has to bear. In addition, there are the variable costs of the outside inspectors appointed to conduct the investigations. Thus, this part of the DTI's 'wacthdog' role is expensive.

PROCEDURES, CONDUCT AND RESULTS OF INVESTIGATIONS

The discussion of this topic is particularly reliant on the helpful *Handbook of the Companies Inspection System* (DTI, 1986) and also DTI (1988).

Initially, cases are considered by the Companies Investigation Branch, which is part of the Investigations Division of the DTI. The sources for requests for investigations into the affairs of companies during 1987–8 are shown in Figure 6.1.

It should be noted that the DTI does not simply wait passively for complaints but is also on the alert for comments in the press and specialized journals on company activities, statements and accounts. From within the DTI requests for investigations during 1987–8 came from the divisions shown in Figure 6.2.

A flowchart, showing in very general terms the way the DTI follows up a complaint, is shown in Figure 6.3.

Where it is decided that a full investigation is warranted, the normal practice in the case of a large public company is for the DTI to appoint two inspectors, one of whom is usually a senior partner in a firm of chartered accountants and the other a Queen's Counsel or a leading solicitor. The firm of accountants is able to provide the large number of professionally skilled staff who may be needed to assist the task of investigation. The DTI makes a public announcement when inspectors have been appointed to investigate a public limited company. The courts have decided that as long as the DTI acts in good faith it is not obliged to disclose to a company the material in its possession, to give reasons for the investigation, to inform the company in advance or to allow the company an opportunity to comment before the appointment is made (*Nortwest Holst Limited* v. *Secretary of State for Trade* [1978] 3 WLR 73).

Sections 433 and 434 of the 1985 Act give the inspectors the power to investigate the affairs of a related corporate body, e.g. a subsidiary or holding company. Past and present officers and agents of the company or related corporate body or any other person considered by the inspectors to be in possession of relevant information are required to produce all books and documents to the inspectors, to attend before the inspectors when required to do so, and to give to the inspectors all assistance which they are reasonably

Table 6.3   Numbers of published reports of DTI investigations

1971	2	1982	2
1972	2	1983	2
1973	2	1984	1
1974	2	1985	1
1975	5		
1976	8	1986–7	1
1977	3	1987–8	1
1978	6		
1979	7		
1980	7	TOTAL	61
1981	9	Average	4

Note: Calendar years to 1985, then 1 April 1986 to 31 March 1987, thereafter 1 April to 31 March.

Source: DTI, *Companies in 1987–88* and previous editions; HMSO, *Annual Catalogue 1988* and previous editions.

Table 6.4   Administrative costs of investigations (£000)

	Basic staff costs and costs of common services (1)	Accommodation (2)	Cost to Department (1) + (2)	Payments to outside inspectors	Total
1971	n.a.	n.a.	n.a.	n.a.	n.a.
1972	83	16	119	n.a.	n.a.
1973	128	51	179	n.a.	n.a.
1974	181	70	251	634	885
1975	282	85	367	759	1,126
1976	316	91	407	763	1,170
1977	392	90	482	999	1,481
1978	411	103	514	919	1,433
1979	478	117	595	781	1,376
1980	582	117	699	773	1,472
1981	628	174	802	538	1,340
1982	658	166	824	266	1,090
1983	719	168	887	924	1,811
1984	732	185	917	1,062	1,979
1985	774	191	965	773	1,738
1986–7	918	166	1,084	1,531	2,615
1987–8	1,000	200	1,200	2,500	3,700

Note: Calendar years to 1985, then 1 April 1986 to 31 March 1987, thereafter 1 April to 31 March. Break in series cannot be reconstructed from published data.

Source: DTI, *Companies in 1987–88* and previous editions.

Requests

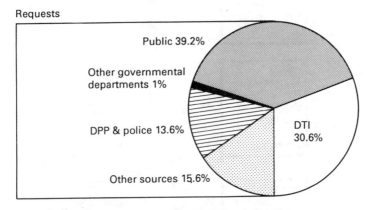

Figure 6.1   Sources of external requests for DTI investigations
Source: DTI (1988)

Departmental

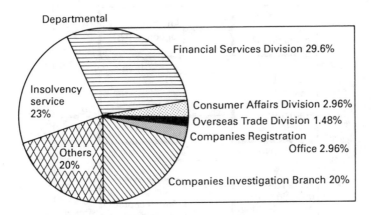

Figure 6.2   Source of internal requests for DTI investigations
Source: DTI (1988)

able to give. The inspectors may examine on oath any person required to give evidence and such persons may have to give evidence even though it may be used against them. Under section 435 the inspectors may require directors to produce all documents relating to bank accounts maintained by them.

Under section 436 failure to produce any book or document to the inspectors, refusal to attend before the inspectors and refusal to answer questions put by the inspectors, may be referred to the court and offenders may be punished as if they had been guilty of contempt of court.

Section 437 states that when the inspectors have completed their investigation they must report their findings to the DTI. In addition, the inspectors may inform, or be directed to inform the DTI of any matters coming to their knowledge and they may submit, or be directed to submit

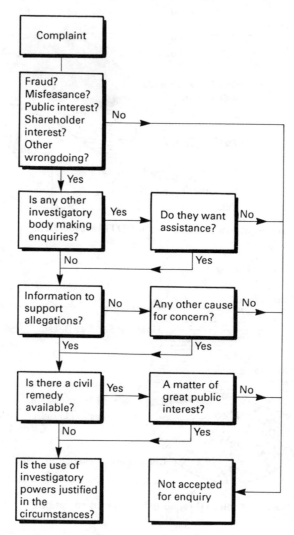

Figure 6.3 Follow-up of complaint to DTI
Source: DTI (1988)

interim reports. On receiving the inspectors' report the DTI must forward a copy to the court if the inspectors were appointed by direction of the court and the DTI may forward a copy to the company, to various parties with legitimate interests in the report and have the report printed and published (see preceding section and Appendix).

Legal proceedings may be instituted as a result of the report. Members may take action on their own behalf or the DTI may initiate actions. This may occur in a variety of ways: first, section 438 permits the DTI to bring a civil action in the company's name if it appears that such proceedings are in the public interest; second, section 440 permits the DTI to petition the court for the company to be wound up in the public interest; and, third, section 460 enables the DTI to petition the court for an order to give members relief against oppression either in addition to or instead of a winding-up petition. Under section 441 the inspectors' report may be used in any legal proceedings as evidence of the inspectors' opinion in relation to any matter contained in the report. Under section 439 the DTI may seek repayment of the expenses of investigation and consequent proceedings as a result of a successful action in the courts.

FINDING OUT THE FACTS

In evidence to the Jenkins Committee (1962, Minutes of evidence, Vol. 20, p. 1572) on the reform of company law, the DTI took the view that the basic function of inspectors in an investigation was to ascertain and report on the facts. Thus, inspectors should be limited to what has been termed a 'statutory fact finding capacity' (Hadden, 1977, p. 356).

Two Court of Appeal decisions, referred to at length in DTI (1986), involved consideration of the role of inspectors in carrying out their investigation. In delivering judgement in the first case, *Re Pergamon Press Ltd* [1970] 3 All ER 535–46, Lord Denning, Master of the Rolls, made some pertinent observations, and it is worth quoting from his judgement:

> It is true, of course, that the inspectors are not a court of law. Their proceedings are not judicial proceedings. They are not even quasi-judicial, for they decide nothing; they determine nothing. They only investigate and report. They sit in private and are not entitled to admit the public to their meetings. They do not even decide if there is a *prima facie* case.

This statement might, at first sight, imply that the inspectors' role is relatively simple and uncontroversial. Yet their task should not be underestimated. Lord Denning continued: 'They [the inspectors] may, if they think fit, make findings of fact which are very damaging to those whom they name. They may accuse some; they may condemn others; they may ruin reputations or careers'.

In getting at the facts there are no set procedures for the inspectors to follow. Lord Denning referred to this in detail in his judgement in the second case, *Maxwell v. Department of Trade and Industry and Others* [1974] 2 All ER 122–34:

> He [an inspector] has himself to seek out the relevant documents and to gather the witnesses. He has himself to study the documents, to examine the witnesses and to have their evidence recorded. He has himself to direct the witnesses to the relevant matters. He has himself to cross-examine them to test their accuracy or their veracity.

In both cases it was held that, whatever procedures the inspectors adopt, their overriding duty is to be fair and then to make their report accordingly. Lord Denning, again in *Re Pergamon Press*, said: 'They [the inspectors] should be subject to no rules save this: they must be fair. This being done they should make their report with courage and frankness, keeping nothing back.

The public interest demands it.' In practice, inspectors go to considerable lengths to ensure fairness, and this requirement may prevent them from submitting a quick and timely report. However, the DTI has laid down a general time scale of twelve months to which investigations should conform and, if an inspection cannot be finally completed within the time limit, an interim report must be produced (DTI, 1986, App. F, para. 8). It is likely that this requirement will conflict with the requirement for fairness. In fact, the inspectors of both Fourth City and Commercial Investment Trust Limited (1982, para. 1.6) and Scotia Investments Limited (1981, paras. 1.4 and 1.5) made the point that submission of their reports was considerably delayed by the overriding obligation of fairness (the two reports are listed in the Appendix).

The DTI (1986, App. B, paras. 33 and 34) notes that inspectors may need to point the 'finger of criticism'. However, as there is no appeal against the validity of any criticisms made by the inspectors – except, of course, in the event of unfairness – the DTI has asked inspectors writing their reports to exercise great restraint when making critical comment, and to avoid super-fluous epithets and the eye-catching phrase likely to lead to unbalanced comment, so as not to jeopardize the value of the reports. In addition, inspectors are asked to give careful thought to the question whether or not to include a summary of the findings and, if so, how the summary should be drafted. This is because when a summary has been included, attention has frequently been focused on the summary alone, with the rest of the report being ignored.

DTI INVESTIGATIONS

(Note that in this section details of the investigation reports cited will be found in the Appendix at the end of the chapter, not in the 'References' section.)

The published reports of DTI investigations often arouse considerable public and professional interest. Inspectors take their fact-finding role very seriously and their reports contain a wealth of information about the day-to-day affairs of a company, and about the decisions and actions of company officers and agents. Such detailed information about the internal workings of a company otherwise rarely comes to light.

In a number of these reports the inspectors have been openly critical of the accountancy and auditing profession. The inspectors' findings on these matters have been taken seriously by the profession, practices have changed and disciplinary action has been taken.

It is impossible to cover all the reports and to do justice to the richness and variety of the inspectors' findings within the confines of a single chapter. Therefore, the aim is to consider a selection of those reports that have something important to say to the accountancy and auditing profession, and to encourage readers to go back to the original reports and read them for themselves.

The 1970s

The first set of investigations to make headline news were those into Pergamon Press Limited ('Pergamon') and related companies (1971, 1972 and 1973).

Pergamon's chairman was Robert Maxwell, then a Labour MP, and Pergamon had also been involved in two controversial stock market transactions – the first was a bid to take over a major national newspaper, the *News of the World*, and the second a proposed merger with an American company, Leasco. It was the events leading to the collapse of the merger with Leasco that gave rise to the DTI investigation into the affairs of Pergamon and related companies. The inspectors were expressly instructed by the DTI to report whether the members of Pergamon had been given all the information they might reasonably have expected with regard to, first, Pergamon's interest in and relations with International Learning Systems Corporation Limited (ILSC), and, second, Pergamon's transactions with Maxwell Scientific International Incorporated (MSI Inc.).

The inspectors made three reports amounting to a total of 664 pages excluding appendices. O'Neil (1973) points out that the summary of conclusions contains fifty-six heads, each of which is critical of Maxwell in some degree. The inspector's answers to the questions they were expressly instructed to consider were that, in their opinion, the members of Pergamon had not been given all the information they might reasonably have expected with regard to both ILSC and MSI Inc., and that, in the case of ILSC, the information the members were given was untrue and that any person receiving the information would have been misled by it; and, further, that there was a lack of disclosure regarding the general nature of transactions with the Maxwell family companies and their bearing on the accounts of Pergamon (Pergamon, 1971, para. 320; 1973, para. 1223). The inspectors were highly critical of Maxwell (see, for example, Pergamon, 1971, paras. 338–43).

The inspectors were also critical of Pergamon's published accounts for the accounting periods between 1 November 1964 and 31 December 1968. The inspectors said that, with hindsight, they were not satisfied that any of these accounts showed a true and fair view of the affairs of Pergamon at the material time or of the profits reported for the relevant period (Pergamon, 1973, paras. 1147–8). For the period ended 31 December 1968 the published accounts showed a *profit* of £1,503,000 and an *increase* in net assets of £1,285,000. On reassessment, with the benefit of hindsight, by another firm of accountants, the corresponding figures became a *loss* of £60,000 and *decrease* in net assets of £1,288,000 (Pergamon, 1973, para. 1219).

The inspectors said that the auditors should not have been satisfied with Maxwell's explanations and that they failed to 'rumble' him, although the inspectors also listed a series of extenuating circumstances (Pergamon, 1973, paras. 1245–53). The inspectors reported that throughout the investigation Maxwell had tried to shift responsibility on to others, not least the auditors and other professional men, but concluded that responsibility lay on Maxwell's shoulders (Pergamon, 1973, para. 1254). However, it is clearly a matter of the utmost concern that the auditors, who were there to protect the interests of the members of Pergamon, could have been misled in such a manner.

The next published report of a DTI investigation which aroused widespread public and professional interest was that on Rolls-Royce Limited (1973). One of Britain's most famous companies had gone into receivership in February 1971, and under section 165(a)(i) (now repealed) of the Companies Act 1948 the members of Rolls-Royce declared, by special resolution, that the affairs of the company ought to be investigated and requested the DTI to appoint inspectors.

The inspectors' report provided a fascinating insight into the RB-211 aero-engine project (Russell, 1981). The inspectors were not directly critical of the accountancy and auditing profession but pointed out that in 1961 Rolls-Royce changed its accounting policy of writing off research and development expenditures as they were incurred, to a policy of capitalizing such expenditures (Rolls-Royce, 1973, paras. 81–91). This change of accounting policies and its effects were shown in the 1961 accounts but the inspectors demonstrated that if the original policy of ·writing off research and development expenditures as they were incurred had been adopted in the nine years from 1961 to 1969, in 1961 a loss instead of a profit would have been reported and in 1962, and in each of the three years from 1967 to 1969, profits would not have been sufficient to cover the dividends paid. At the time, however, such a treatment of research and development expenditures in the accounts was considered acceptable by the accounting profession.

The failure of a number of banks during the secondary banking crisis of 1973–5 (for an account of this, see Reid, 1982) led the DTI to appoint inspectors to investigate the causes of failure, e.g. London and Counties Securities Group Limited (1976) and London Capital Group Limited (formerly British Bangladesh Trust Limited) (1977).

In the London and Counties report (1976, paras. 13.09–28) the inspectors concluded that the group accounts, and the accounts of the principal subsidiary, for the period ended 31 March 1973 were unsatisfactory and misleading. In neither case should the auditors have signed an unqualified audit report. The auditors were in possession of information about a material inflation of cash balances, and could have discovered at least some of the ways in which profits were materially overstated, had their audit work been more penetrating and effective. As in Pergamon, however, there were mitigating circumstances since in several transactions the directors deliberately intended to mislead the auditors, whilst in other transactions the directors negligently failed to inform the auditors of matters which had a significant impact on the accounts. Eventually the auditors ceased to trust their client. The inspectors were highly critical of the chairman and managing director of London and Counties, Mr Caplan, and of his co-director, Mr Pepperell, both of whom defrauded the principal subsidiary of substantial sums (London and Counties, 1976, paras. 3.01–23 and 3.76–85).

In the case of London Capital Group, the inspectors concluded that the accounts and directors' report for the period ended 30 June 1973 were grossly deficient and misleading, and that the auditors had improperly issued an unqualified report (London Capital Group, 1977, section IX, para. 9). The two principal items of concern were a deliberate breach of an undertaking given in the prospectus, and the failure to disclose substantial advances made to directors and associated companies. The inspectors went on to list eleven separate facts that were concealed from the shareholders and the public, which meant the accounts did not show a true and fair view (op. cit., para. 52). The inspectors were in no doubt that, had all the facts been disclosed, the subsequent history of the company would have been very different, since the accounts were used to support an application for a banking certificate for the company and later a rights issue (op. cit., paras. 53–4).

Other reports of DTI investigations published during 1976 and 1977 contained such serious criticisms of the accountancy and auditing profession that the DTI asked the profession what it intended to do in reponse. As Sherer and Kent (1983, pp. 44–5) relate, the outcome was the Cross report (1977), which in turn led to the Grenside report (1979) whose main proposal was that the three professional bodies – the ICAEW, the Institute of Chartered Accountants in Scotland and the Association of Certified Accountants – should set up a joint disciplinary scheme to inyestigate cases of public interest involving members and their firms, and that the findings should be binding on the disciplinary committees of the individual bodies.

Further reports, highly critical of auditors, continued to appear. These reports added to the debate already set in motion by the Cross and Grenside reports. The Grenside proposal for a joint disciplinary scheme was accepted by the three accountancy bodies (*Accountancy*, July 1979, p. 4). In addition, in 1980 the major accountancy bodies introduced a series of auditing standards and guidelines, laying down principles and practices to be observed by the auditor.

The 1980s

The published reports of DTI investigations in the early 1980s were as critical of the accountancy and auditing profession as were those in the 1970s. A sample of headlines in *Accountancy* illustrates this: 'Scotia auditors slated' (March 1981, p. 21); 'Inspectors slate 3 chartered firms' (May 1981, p. 22); 'Gilgate inspectors' report throws up concealment, breaches and false accounting' (October 1981, p. 11). Most of these investigations were, however, reporting on activities that had taken place during the 1970s, and after 1981, when a record nine reports were published, only one or two reports were published each year during the rest of the 1980s until 1988–9, when the figure crept up to four (see Table 6.3). This is probably due to a combination of three things: first, in the 1980s there had not been a crisis, such as the secondary banking crisis in the 1970s, causing a large number of companies to fail in suspicious circumstances; second, the accountancy and auditing profession had responded to the crisis of confidence in the profession by tightening up its working practices and disciplinary procedures; and, third, the DTI may have been less inclined to exercise its full investigatory powers.

From 1982 to March 1989 only twelve reports of DTI investigations were published. The reports of particular interest to the accountancy and auditing profession are those on Ramor Investments Limited (formerly Bryanston Finance Limited) and Derritron Limited ('Bryanston') (1983) and Milbury plc and Westminster Property Group Limited ('Milbury') (1989).

In the case of Bryanston the inspectors were appointed by the DTI in response to an application from shareholders. The inspectors discovered that the books and papers of the various companies were voluminous and extremely disordered, and, on examination and together with the gathering of oral evidence from witnesses, led to a picture emerging of serious wrongdoing over a wide field (Bryanston, 1983, paras. 1.04 and 1.05). After a lengthy investigation the inspectors concluded (op. cit., paras. 20.01–07) that the story of Bryanston was the story of abuse of position by two men, both directors of the company. The inspectors observed that the majority shareholder, Mr Smith, was unwilling and perhaps at times unable to make the distinction between the assets of the public group and his own pocket. They described the other, Mr Hegard, as cold, calculating, ruthless, devious and unscrupulous in his activities. The inspectors believed that the first line of defence for the shareholders against these directors abusing their position should have been the non-executive directors. But the non-executive directors assumed that all was continuing in order notwithstanding that the warning signs were there to be seen. The second line of defence should have been the auditors, but the auditors failed on three counts. First, they did not follow up certain points revealed during an audit which, had they done so, would have shown that all was not well with the conduct of the two directors; second, in the following year's audit certain activities were undertaken by the two directors, of which the auditors were or should have been aware, that should have led to a qualified audit report; and, third, the auditors, on becoming unhappy about the dubious activities of the two directors, resigned without revealing to the shareholders or the incoming auditors the reasons for their resignation. A committee of inquiry under the joint disciplinary scheme reprimanded the auditors and ordered them to pay £270,000 towards the cost of the inquiry (*Accountancy*, April 1987, p. 8).

The Milbury inspectors were appointed by the DTI as a result of an application to the court by a minority shareholder. Two earlier DTI investigations, Saint Piran Limited (1980, 1981) and Westminster Property Group Limited ('Westminster) (1985), formed background material to the Milbury investigation since a leading personality in the St Piran report, Mr Raper, played the leading role in the Milbury story, and the ownership of Westminster had been investigated prior to its acquisition to Milbury. The original reason for the Milbury appointment was to investigate the sale of the shares in Westminster, which on acquisition by Milbury had cost £9.8 million, for £1 million. In addition, the inspectors discovered that two further issues needed investigation: the decisions to allow Milbury shares to be relisted in the Stock Exchange and its simultaneous acquisition of Westminster, and the audited accounts of the Milbury group for 1984.

As with Bryanston a lengthy investigation ensued, requiring the examination of numerous books and records and the taking of oral evidence. Again as with Bryanston, the inspectors concluded (Milbury, 1988, paras. 16.01–16) that the Milbury affair was the story of a dominating and unscrupulous man, Raper, whose activities were inadequately controlled. Earlier, in 1980, the Takeover Panel had declared Raper 'unfit to be a director of a public company'. Raper had also come under criticism in the St Piran report mentioned above. The inspectors were highly critical of the way in which the Stock Exchange agreed to the relisting of Milbury – in which Raper not only was a director but had effective control through his investment vehicle, St Piran. The inspectors also found that the 1984 Milbury group accounts should have been qualified by the auditors as, in the inspectors' opinion, the accounts did not show a true and fair view of the group's financial position. This was because the Milbury board was keen to present the group's trading position in the best possible light. In the inspectors' opinion the results for 1984 were materially overstated, probably by £1 million and possibly by as much as £2 million, which, taken together with the misleading presentation of other items in the accounts, obscured the true financial position of the group. Not only this, the preceding and following interim reports also gave a distorted impression. The result was that the world at large was being given a picture of prosperity but, by late 1984, the financial problems were already serious. As in the case of Bryanston, a committee of inquiry under the joint disciplinary scheme has been set up to scrutinize the actions of Milbury's auditors (*Accountancy*, September 1989, p. 8).

Thus, whilst the Bryanston and Milbury reports contained familiar criticisms of the accountancy and auditing profession, the brickbats were thrown neither as fast nor as frequently as had been the case during the 1970s. It could be argued that the DTI reports of the 1970s had been so critical that the reports of the 1980s could hardly be anything other than an improvement. It would, perhaps, be fairer to the profession to say that the improvement in the 1980s was probably due to a consolidation and implementation of the harsh lessons learnt during the 1970s.

IMPLICATIONS FOR AUDITING

Lee (1982), after examining the underlying objectives and postulates of company auditing, concluded that the main concepts of company auditing may be taken to be as follows. First, *auditor independence* – that is, auditors should be in a position of complete independence so that their audit may be objective, and the credibility of the financial statements they are attesting to, enhanced; second, *auditor responsibility* – that is, auditors can be held responsible, legally and professionally, for the conduct and quality of their work and opinions; third, *truth and fairness* – that is, the financial statements are based on generally accepted accounting principles which, taken together with statutory requirements, result in the financial position of the company being truly and fairly described; fourth, *audit evidence* – that is, the auditor has collected sufficient competent evidence to support his or her audit opinion.

DTI investigations have never seriously questioned the independence of auditors, although inspectors have been critical of auditors who failed to stand up to company chairmen with strong personalities. Auditor responsibility has considerably improved as a result of DTI investigations, notably through the setting up of the joint disciplinary scheme. They have also contributed to the debates on truth and fairness and audit evidence, which were already going on within the accountancy and auditing profession. The reports have given additional stimulus to the accounting standards programme and were instrumental in leading to the auditing standards and guidelines programme.

In conclusion, it is clear that DTI investigations have had a significant impact on the accounting and auditing profession, and there is no doubt that the reports contributed to the 'crisis of confidence' within the profession during the 1970s. The main advantage of DTI investigations to the accountancy profession is that they may highlight, in a very dramatic way, the shortcomings of the profession. In the short run this was a painful and embarrassing experience. In the long run the profession responded by taking positive steps to overcome the criticisms voiced by inspectors, and this led to an improvement in professional standards and practice. DTI investigations should be welcomed by the accountancy and auditing profession, as the reports may demonstrate where the profession is at fault and the profession is put in the position of having to remedy the situation. Thus, DTI investigations represent an important mechanism by which the accountancy and auditing profession *learns*.

ACKNOWLEDGEMENT

The figures and tables in this chapter are reproduced with the permission of the Controller of Her Majesty's Stationery Office.

REFERENCES

Cross report (1977) Report of a Committee under the Chairmanship of the Rt Hon. Lord Cross of Chelsea, *Accountancy*, December, pp. 80–6.

DTI (1986) *Handbook of the Companies Inspection System*, 2nd edn, HMSO, London.

DTI (1988) *Companies in 1987–88*, HMSO, London.

Farrar, J.H. assisted by Furey, N. and Hannigan, B. (1988) *Farrar's Company Law*, 2nd edn, Butterworths, London.

Gower, L.C.B., Cronin, J.B., Eason, A.J. and Lord Wedderburn of Charlton (1979) *Gower's Principles of Modern Company Law*, 4th edn, with Second Cumulative Supplement (1988), Stevens, London.

Grenside report (1979) Report of the Joint Committee appointed to consider the Cross Report and related matters, *Accountancy*, June, pp. 124–32.

Hadden, T. (1977) *Company Law and Capitalism*, 2nd edn, Weidenfeld & Nicolson, London.

Hatherly, D.J. (1980) *The Audit Evidence Process*, Anderson Keenan.

Jenkins Committee (1962) Report of the Company Law Committee, Chairman the Rt Hon. Lord Jenkins, Cmnd 1749, HMSO, London.

Lee, T. (1982) *Company Auditing*, 2nd edn, Gee, London.

Leigh, L.H., Joffe, V.H. and Goldberg, D. (1987) *Northey and Leigh's Introduction to Company Law*, 4th edn, Butterworths, London.

O'Neil, G. (1973) Third report blames Maxwell, *Accountancy* December, pp. 19–20.

Reid, M. (1982) *The Secondary Banking Crisis 1973–75: Its Causes and Course*, Macmillan, London.

Russell, P.O. (1981) Accounting implications of Department of Trade Investigations: a case study of Rolls-Royce, unpublished M.A. (Econ.) dissertation, University of Manchester.

Sherer, M.J. and Kent, D. (1983) *Auditing and Accountability*, Pitman, London. (Reprinted 1988, Paul Chapman, London)

FUTHER READING

There is no substitute for reading the original reports, although they are not particularly easy to get hold of and are quite expensive to buy. Fortunately, the professional accountancy magazines, for example *Accountancy*, give good coverage to the reports and this is perhaps the best place for the interested reader to start.

DTI investigations do not appear much in accountancy and auditing textbooks. The exceptions – although each contains only a few pages on the subject – are Hatherly (1980), pp. 2–3, Lee (1982), pp. 124–7, Sherer and Kent (1983), pp. 42–5, and J.R.H.H. Pockson, *Accountants' Professional Negligence: Developments in Legal Liability* (Macmillan, 1982), p. 190.

The legal background may be found from any good company law textbook, for example Farrer *et al.* (1988), Gower *et al.* (1979), A.J. Boyle *et al.*, *Boyle and Birds' Company Law* (2nd edn, Jordan and Sons, 1987) and L.H. Leigh, V.H. Joffe and D. Goldberg, *Northey and Leigh's Introduction to Company Law* (3rd edn, Butterworths, 1983).

DISCUSSION QUESTIONS

1. Describe the main statutory provisions by which the Department of Trade may appoint inspectors to investigate the affairs of a company.
2. What is the role of inspectors appointed to investigate the affairs of a company and to what extent has case law contributed to an understanding of this role?
3. Explain how Department of Trade investigations contributed to the crisis of confidence within the accountancy and auditing profession.
4. How has the accountancy and auditing profession responded to the criticisms contained within the reports of Department of Trade investigations?
5. In a report of a Department of Trade investigation that you are familiar with, describe the inspectors' main criticisms of the company's auditors. How would you change audit work to avoid these criticisms?
6. Assess the usefulness of Department of Trade investigations as part of the overall provisions for the control and regulation of the corporate sector.

APPENDIX: DEPARTMENT OF TRADE INVESTIGATIONS – REPORTS PUBLISHED 1971–1988/9

Note: Section numbers refer to the Companies Act 1948 except where otherwise stated.

1971

1. International Learning Systems Corporation Limited
   Pergamon Press Limited
   Report and interim report by R.O.C. Stable QC and Sir Ronald G. Leach CBE, FCA, under section 165(1)(b).
2. Pinnock Finance Company (Great Britain) Limited and associated companies
   Report by B. Wigoder QC and P. Godfrey FCA, under section 165(1)(b).

1972

1. E.J. Austin International Limited
   Interim report by J.L. Eley QC and D. Garrett FCA, under section 165(1)(b).
2. Pergamon Press Limited
   Further interim report by R.O.C. Stable QC and Sir Ronald G. Leach CBE, FCA, under section 165(1)(b).

1973
1. Maxwell Scientific International (Distribution Services) Limited
   Robert Maxwell & Co. Limited
   Pergamon Press Limited
   Report and final report by R.O.C. Stable QC and Sir Ronald G. Leach
   CBE, FCA, under section 165(b).
2. Rolls-Royce Limited
   Report by R.A. MacCrindle QC and P. Godfrey FCA, under section
   165(1)(a)(i).

1974
1. First Re-Investment Trust Limited
   Nelson Financial Trust Limited
   English and Scottish Unit Trust Holdings Limited
   Interim report by D.C.H. Hirst QC and R.N.D. Langdon, under section
   165(1)(b).
2. Kwik Save Discount Group Limited
   Report by D.S. Mangat and J.H. Dickman, under section 32 of the
   Companies Act 1967.

1975
1. Court Line Limited
   Interim report by J.P. Comyn QC, D.S. Morpeth TD, BCom, FCA and
   J. Hamilton MA, under section 165(1)(b).
2. John Willment Automobiles Limited
   Report by P.J. Millett QC and M.R. Harris FCA, under section
   165(1)(b).
3. Bernard Russell Limited
   Report by D.A.C. Smout MA, LLM and B.E. Basden MA, FCA, under
   section 165(1)(b).
4. Blanes Limited (now named Black Arrow Group Limited)
   Report by D.A.L. Smout MA, LLM and B.E. Basden MA, FCA, under
   section 165(1)(b).
5. Australian Estates Limited
   First Re-Investment Trust Limited
   Nelson Financial Trust Limited
   English and Scottish Unit Trust Holdings Limited
   Second and final report by D.C.H. Hirst QC and R.N.D. Langdon FCA,
   under section 165(1)(b).

1976
1. London and Counties Securities Group
   Capebourne Limited
   Standfield Properties Limited
   Hilbernian Property Co. Limited
   Bremian Properties Limited
   Avon Land Securities Limited
   Report by A.P. Leggatt QC and D.C. Hobson FCA, under sections
   165(1)(b) and 172.
2. Hartley Baird Limited

Report by J.B.R. Hazan QC, T.G. Harding FCA and A.M. Troup, under section 172.
3. Hartley Baird Limited
   Report by J.B.R. Hazan QC, T.G. Harding FCA and A.M. Troup, under section 164.
4. The Vehicle and General Insurance Company Limited
   Report by T.M. Eastham QC and R.T.M. McPhail MBE, CA, under section 165(1)(b).
5. E.J. Austin International Limited
   Final report by J.L. Eley QC and D. Garrett FCA, under section 165(1)(b).
6. Lonrho Limited
   Report by A. Heyman QC and Sir William Slimmings CBE, CA, under section 165(1)(b).
7. Dwell Constructions Limited
   Yorks and Lancs Construction Company Limited
   Southern and Provincial Estates Limited
   Southern and Provincial Investments Limited
   Boulters Court Development Limited
   Report by R.G. Waterhouse QC and J.J.C. Steare FCA, under section 165(1)(b).
8. Roadships Limited (formerly known as Ralph Hilton Transport Services Limited)
   Report by B.A. Hynter QC and I. Irvine FCA, under section 165(1)(b).

1977
1. Edward Wood and Company Limited
   Report by D.J. Clarkson QC and K.A. McKinlay CA, under section 165(1)(b).
2. New Brighton Association Football and Athletic Club Company Limited
   Report by A. Ranbin QC and T. White FCA, under section 165(1)(b).
3. London Capital Group Limited (formerly British Bangladesh Trust Limited)
   Report by M. Sherrard QC and I.H. Davison FCA, under section 165(1)(b).

1978
1. Court Line Limited
   Final report by J.P. Comyn QC, D.S. Morpeth TD, BCom, FCA and J. Hamilton MA, under section 165(1)(b).
2. Electerminations Limited (formerly known as A.P.T. Electronic Industries Limited)
   Report by A.J.D. McCowan QC and A.P. Humphries FCA, under section 165(1)(b).
3. Kuehne and Nagel Limited
   Report by Dame Rose Heilbron QC and S.D. Samwell FCA, under section 165(1)(b).
4. The Birmingham and Midland Canal Carrying Company Limited
   Report by A.M. Belchambers and J. Nunn, under section 165(1)(b).
5. Land and General Developments Limited
   Napet Securities Limited

Report by M.C. Nourse QC and P.W.G. DuBuisson FCA, under sections 164 and 172.
6. Rajawella Produce Holdings Limited
Report by R.A.T. Stanley and J.M. Buttimer, under section 165(1)(b).

1979
1. Peachey Property Corporation Limited
Report by R.I. Kidwell QC and S.D. Samwell FCA, under section 165(1)(b).
2. North Devon Railway Company Limited
Words in Action Limited
Report by B.M. Hooper and J.M. Buttimer, under section 165(1)(b).
3. Ferguson and General Investments Limited (formerly known as Dowgate and General Investments Limited)
CST Investments Limited
Report by J. Jackson QC, MA, LLB and K.L. Young TD, FCA, under section 165(1)(b).
4. Larkfold Holdings Limited
Report by D.J. Nicholls QC and E.K. Wright MA, FCA, under section 165(1)(b).
5. Burnholme and Forder Limited (in liquidation)
Brayhead Limited (in liquidation)
Report by T.M. Dillon QC and D. Garrett FCA, under section 165(1)(b).
6. Ashbourne Investments Limited
Report by R.E. Auld QC, H.H. de C. Moore FCA and I. Glick, under sections 164 and 172.
7. AEG Telefunken (UK) Limited
Chasgift Limited (formerly known as Credit Collections Limited)
Report by D.J. Freeman and P.J. Oliver FCA, under section 165(1)(b).

1980
1. Ozalid Group Holdings Limited
Report by N.M. Butter QC and B.A. Kemp FCA, under sections 165(1)(b) and 172.
2. Darjeeling Holdings Limited
Interim and final reports by P.J. Millett QC and I.M. Bowie CA, under sections 164 and 172.
3. Bandara Investments Limited
Bandarapola Ceylon Company Limited
Report by P.J. Millett QC and I.M. Bowie CA, under section 165(1)(b).
4. The Central Provinces Manganese Ore Company Limited
Data Investment Limited
Report by P.J. Millett QC and I.M. Bowie CA, under section 165(1)(b).
5. Consolidated Gold Fields Limited
Report by B.J. Welch and M.C.A. Osborne, under section 172.
6. Saint Piran Limited
Interim report by G.M. Godfrey QC and A.J. Hardcastle FCA, under section 172.

7. Cornhill Consolidated Group Limited (in liquidation)
   Report by D.C. Calcutt QC and J.A.P. Whinney FCA, under section 165(1)(b).

1981
1. Kina Holdings Limited
   Report by W.E. Denny QC and K.W.G. Webb FCA, under section 165(1)(b).
2. Scotia Investments Limited
   Report by L.J. Bromley QC and J.S. Hillyer OBE, FCA, under section 165(1)(b).
3. Gilgate Holdings Limited
   Raybourne Group Limited
   Calomefern Limited
   Desadean Properties Limited
   Report by R.A. Morritt QC and P.L. Ainger FCA, under section 165(1)(b).
4. Aveley Laboratories Limited
   Report by A.J.D. McCowan QC and A.P. Humphries FCA, under section 165(1)(b).
5. Peek Foods Limited
   Report by A.W. Hamilton QC and P.W. Foss FCA, under section 165(1)(b).
6. Orbit Holdings Limited
   Report by A.H.M. Evans QC and R.H. Morcom FCA, under section 165(1)(b).
7. The United Industrial Company Limited
   Report by G.J.K. Coles QC and P.H. Dobson JP, FCA, under sections 164 and 172.
8. Saint Piran Limited
   Final report by G.M. Godfrey QC and A.J. Hardcastle FCA, under section 172.
9. Dunlop Holdings Limited
   Interim report by C.W.M. Ingram and F.H. Puling, under section 172 (a very short final report will not be published).

1982
1. Fourth City and Commercial Investment Trust Limited
   Excelads Limited
   Systematic Tooling Limited
   Cambramain Limited
   Report by J. Blofled QC and B. Currie FCA, under sections 164 and 165(1)(b).
2. Norwest Holst Limited
   Report by J. Davies QC and T.G. Harding FCA, under section 165(1)(b).

1983
1. Ramor Investments Limited (formerly Bryanston Finance Limited)

Report by H.B.H. Carlisle QC and J. Darby FCA, under section 164, *and*
2. Derritron Limited
Report by H.B.H. Carlislie QC and J. Darby FCA, under section 172.

Note: These two reports published as one volume.

1984
1. House of Fraser plc
Interim report by J. Griffiths QC, under section 172.

1985
1. Westminster Property Group Limited
Interim and final reports by B.J. Welch and F.H. Pulling, under section 172.

1986–7
1. Minet Holdings plc and W.M.D. Underwriting Agencies Limited
Interim report by S.C. Boyd QC and P.W.G. DuBuisson FCA, under section 165(1)(b).

1987–8
1. Aldershot Football Club Limited
Report by N.D.F. Bohen and A.S. Ridler, under section 442 of the Companies Act 1985.

1988–9
1. Equity & General plc (formerly Emray plc)
Report by P.H. Bovey and I.G. Salter, under section 172.
2. The Greenbank Trust plc
Report by G.M. Abercrombie and A.H.S. Robertshaw, under section 165(1)(b).
3. Milbury plc, Westminster Property Group Limited
Report by H.B.H. Carlisle QC and M.G. Lickiss FCA, under sections 432(1) and 442 of the Companies Act 1985.
4. Summer International plc (formerly Sumrie Clothers plc)
Report by Sir Michael Kerry and K.S. Carmichael, under sections 442 and 446 of the Companies Act 1985.

Source: DTI, *Companies in 1987–88* and previous editions; HMSO, *Annual Catalogue 1988* and previous editions.

7
Auditing Standards and Guidelines

Rod Ferrier

INTRODUCTION

In the time since the UK accountancy profession introduced auditing standards, those standards have come increasingly to dominate auditors' actions. It might even be suggested that the need for auditor judgement is steadily being eroded, ultimately to result in audits becoming a purely technical exercise. The purpose of this chapter is to examine the nature, purpose and future of auditing standards in the UK, in order to provide some indication of the seriousness of the 'threat' which is now faced by the auditor.

Professional regulation of auditing has its roots in the purpose of the audit function. Many explanations could be given for appointing an auditor. Apart from the obvious reason that companies legislation requires the appointment of auditors, the audit function has been explained in terms of the need to ensure that managers adequately discharge their duty of accountability to the owners of the business, in terms of the need to ensure that financial information provided by business managers is reliable, and in terms of the need to discourage managers from committing frauds.[1]

Each of these explanations is based on the auditor acting as an intermediary between managers and people who might be disadvantaged if those managers act unscrupulously. It seems that the appointment of auditors is to be explained primarily on the grounds that there is a potential conflict of interest between the owners and managers of a business, and that the auditor is necessary to ensure that managers do not abuse their power to the disadvantage of owners. In short, the auditor is a referee.

However, this generalized explanation does not always stand up; in some organizations there is little, if any, distinction between owners and managers. Small, family-owned and managed companies are an example. Yet the law still requires the appointment of an auditor. To explain the appointment of auditors under these circumstances, it is necessary to interpret the phrase 'people who might be disadvantaged if managers act unscrupulously' as including more than the owners of a business.

It may be suggested that the benefits of limited liability could be exploited to the detriment of creditors, the government and society at large. Under these circumstances, auditors can be considered to be acting on behalf of society at large (despite what the Companies Act says), under conditions in

Rod Ferrier, Ph.D., A.A.S.A., is Partner, Corporate Services, at Ernst and Whinney, chartered accountants, Sydney, New South Wales, Australia. The views and opinions expressed in this chapter are those of the author and do not necessarily reflect those of Ernst and Whinney.

which there could arise a conflict of interest between owner/managers and members of society. And again the auditor acts as a referee.

All would be well in this scenario were it not for the fact that managers (or owner/managers) are able to wield considerable influence over auditors, not least because power over the auditor's remuneration and working conditions rests, *de facto*, with management. In the case of companies, for example, the audit fee is usually determined as a result of negotiations between management and the auditor, with the shareholders merely 'rubber stamping' that agreement. If we accept that there could be a conflict of interest between management and those to whom the auditor reports, we must accept the possibility that management could attempt to influence the decisions and actions of the auditor.

How, then, can we be assured that the actions adopted and decisions taken by auditors are acceptable? How can we be assured that the auditor is not unduly influenced by management and that the audit report is reliable? The answer (or part of it, at least) lies with the provision of auditing standards.

THE BACKGROUND TO AUDITING STANDARDS

The accountancy profession in the UK began to issue statements on auditing in 1961, with the publication by the ICAEW of Statement U1 'General Principles of Auditing'. Before this time, there was no formal guidance of auditors by the professional associations.

As the U Series developed, it became increasingly clear to the major professional bodies in the UK that a joint approach to the regulation of auditing (and accounting) was desirable. Accordingly, the Consultative Committee of Accountancy Bodies (CCAB) was set up in 1974, with the inaugural meeting of that committee held on 24 May that year. Under its terms of reference, this body was to 'consult on matters of common concern, make joint representations to Government Departments and the EEC, and monitor progress in areas where collaboration is already operational'.[2]

The wheels of professional regulation move slowly, however, and it took some rather strident criticism of auditors to force the CCAB to act in the area of auditing standards. In particular, the publication of the report of the inspectors into London and Counties Securities 'stirred up a fury of criticism in the press' (Davison, 1976, p. 26) and it was this that ultimately led to the establishment of the Auditing Practices Committee (APC – a committee of the CCAB) in March 1976.

This committee was set up specifically to consider the generation of auditing standards: at its first meeting it adopted a programme of work which included the establishment of personal, operational and reporting standards for the auditor. At the time, it was said that the APC 'has had as its principal intention "disseminating information about auditing practices with the objective of improving audit quality". The main medium for doing this was, and is, to be the publication . . . of auditing standards' (Davison, 1976, p. 26).

Four years after the APC was set up, pressure was mounting for the profession to issue a statement of auditing standards and to take firm steps to ensure that auditors who succumbed to the pressure placed upon them by management were suitably punished. In 1978, for example, pressure for the publication of a statement of the basic principles of auditing and of a code of operating practice was thought to be due to a 'number of well-publicized lapses' (Gough, 1978, p. 118). These pressures for auditing standards were reinforced by the development of accounting standards in the UK, auditing standards in the USA and criticism of audit procedures expressed by Department of Trade inspectors (de Paula and Attwood, 1982).

In response to these pressures, a joint disciplinary scheme was introduced from 1 January 1980, and in April of that year the APC issued its definitive statement on auditing standards and guidelines (APC, 1980). This document not only provided auditors with an authoritative indication of what constituted 'best practice', it also demonstrated that the UK profession was able to respond to criticism through a process of self-regulation.

It is apparent that there were a number of factors operating at the time which resulted in the issue of auditing standards and guidelines. Later in this chapter these factors and the role(s) that they imply standards should fulfil will be discussed in further detail. For the moment, however, it is important to stress that the issue of the 1980 standards and guidelines was only the start of professional regulation of the audit process, and that the APC has not been idle since that time.

THE APC'S PROGRAMME

The APC has not confined itself to the issue of standards and guidelines. Two further sources of information which indicate the APC's thinking on the regulation of audit procedures are 'Audit Briefs' and the Committee's bulletin *True and Fair* (in recent years published in *Accountancy*). Auditors are therefore guided, to a greater or lesser extent, by four different classes of document. It is instructive to consider briefly the status of each of these documents.

Auditing standards were defined in the 1980 standards and guidelines as prescribing the 'basic principles and practices which members are expected to follow in the conduct of an audit' (APC, 1980, para. 3). Standards apply to all audits (unless otherwise indicated) and are the most general level of guidance given to auditors. Although standards are held to apply generally, the APC has taken great pains to point out that the auditor must 'exercise his judgement in determining both the auditing procedures necessary . . . to afford a reasonable basis for his opinion and the wording of his report' (op. cit., para. 4). Thus, the standards are to be thought of as establishing a framework within which the auditor will be expected to exercise judgement.

Although auditors are expected to follow standards, the standards in fact have no authority in law. Thus, the only penalties that can be imposed upon an auditor who violates a standard are those which can be imposed by the professional bodies, such as fine, suspension or expulsion. Thus, the authority of standards rests upon acceptance of those standards by auditors; if there were an *en masse* refusal to adhere to a standard, the profession would have little choice but to amend the standard. However, this situation is not necessarily undesirable, since a voluntary code of behaviour can include moral and ethical considerations, whereas a statute must be more objective if it is to be accepted as a basis for legal decisions.

Auditing guidelines give the auditor guidance as to what procedures should be adopted, how to apply auditing standards, what current audit techniques are available, and how to approach specific problems in particular industries (op. cit., para. 5). Guidelines are different from standards in that guidelines do not attempt to establish 'basic' principles and practices. Accordingly, they are not generally relevant, and auditors are not expected to apply the guidelines in all cases. Guidelines can be thought of as a second tier of the framework within which auditors are required to exercise judgement.

Audit briefs have been adopted by the APC as a means of raising controversial issues, explaining the purpose of an audit to interested parties, issuing guidance on the audit implications of legislation and providing guidance which is too detailed to be included in a guideline. These briefs are issued on the authority of the APC and do not carry the weight of full approval by the accountancy bodies which are members of the CCAB. It appears that they are the vehicle by which ideas developed by the APC are first exposed to interested parties for consideration and comment. Thus, they are a testing ground for concepts which could eventually appear in a guideline or in a standard. Of course, briefs carry no real authority and auditors are not required to follow them.

The APC's *True and Fair* bulletin is little more than a news sheet which indicates the current activities of the APC and advises auditors of areas of current concern. For example, the bulletin has been used as a newsletter advising of recent developments in legislation which have implications for auditors. Like audit briefs, the bulletin carries no real authority.

At the date of writing (spring 1990), two standards and thirty-three guidelines are in force. This represents a considerable achievement on the part of the APC. The publication of these standards and guidelines accounts for a significant part of the original programme of work set down by the APC. This programme comprised a matrix of issued documents which divided the APC's proposed work into three areas:

1. a basic framework of documents concerned with general principles and issues which are relevant to most audits;
2. a second classification for documents which are relevant only in some cases, but which are nevertheless significant; and
3. a third class of documents dealing with matters which are of concern only in specific industries.

The current status of this work programme is shown in Figure 7.1.

It will be noticed that the documents issued so far do not include a statement on personal standards to be adopted by the auditor, despite the APC's original programme of work. This is because the APC has accepted the contents of ethical guides (published by the different professional bodies) ·as containing personal standards relevant to the work of the auditor (APC, 1980, para. 12). If Figure 7.1 is to be interpreted as representing the important areas of audit pronouncement, rather than only the work of the APC, the ethical guides would have to be included.

The programme of work published by the APC is important for a number of reasons. First, it indicates that the APC's programme is well under way and that the idea that auditors should be guided by the profession is well accepted. It is therefore clear that the profession feels there are significant advantages to be gained by the issue of standards and guidelines. The nature of these advantages will be explored in the next section.

Second, there is little indication that the APC's original objectives have been satisfied. This is not to suggest that the APC has been unsuccessful, but rather that much remains to be done before the APC can claim to have completed its work. By establishing the matrix, the APC has structured its future activities in such a way as to focus attention on fundamental matters and to organize priorities for the work to be done. This suggests that the APC is consciously moving away from a haphazard 'fire-fighting' approach to audit regulation.

Third, an established, structured work programme indicates that the APC sees itself as generating a series of documents which are interrelated and which together constitute a coherent structure. The fact that some documents have been classified as belonging to a basic framework suggests that the APC has identified areas of fundamental importance to auditing. It is not difficult to deduce from this that the APC could be well on the way to constructing a 'conceptual framework' for auditing. This issue of the relationship between auditing standards, auditing guidelines and a conceptual framework will occupy us for the remainder of this chapter.

THE ROLE OF PROFESSIONAL PRONOUNCEMENTS

Although the APC has distinguished between 'standards' and 'guidelines', both classes of statement are included in the area of the matrix concerned with 'framework' issues. Accordingly, both types of pronouncement are seen to be of central importance by the APC, and both act together to regulate the audit process.

Whether professional regulation of auditing (and accounting) is desirable has proved to be a controversial issue, with both supporters and detractors. Those who support the promulgation of standards have identified a number of possible roles to be fulfilled by professional recommendations. In very general terms, these roles fall into two distinct classes: those which result in an improvement in the practice of auditing and those which result in an improvement in the public image of auditors.

Improvement of practices

When the APC was first created, its objective was to improve the quality of audits by disseminating information about audit practices (Davison, 1976). Information was to be provided in order to guide the auditor in making decisions and to ensure that auditors were fully aware of modern audit techniques. With a large enough body of information, guidance to auditors would ensure a narrowing of the areas of difference and variety in audit practices.

Information provided in professional pronouncements was to improve audit practice by providing a framework for audit decisions. Both standards and guidelines specify practices which are to be carried out, either in all circumstances or in specific circumstances. Where circumstances are encountered for which no specific guidance exists, the auditor must exercise judgement in choosing appropriate practices. The standards and guidelines which do exist provide a set of parameters within which the auditor's judgement can be exercised.

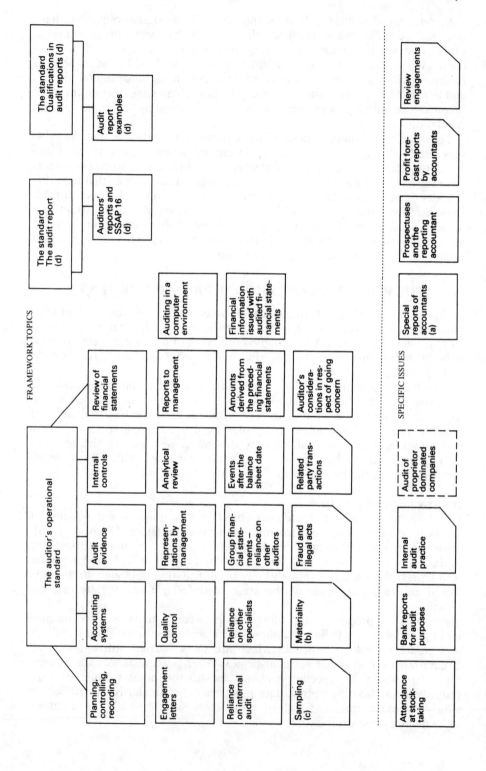

FRAMEWORK TOPICS

The standard
Qualifications in
audit reports (d)

The standard
The audit report
(d)

Audit
report
examples
(d)

Auditors'
reports and
SSAP 16
(d)

The auditor's operational
standard

Planning,
controlling,
recording

Accounting
systems

Audit
evidence

Internal
controls

Review of
financial
statements

Engagement
letters

Quality
control

Representations by
management

Analytical
review

Reports to
management

Auditing in a
computer
environment

Reliance
on internal
audit

Reliance
on other
specialists

Group financial statements –
reliance on
other
auditors

Events
after the
balance
sheet date

Amounts
derived from
the preceding financial
statements

Financial
information
issued with
audited financial statements

Sampling
(c)

Materiality
(b)

Fraud and
illegal acts

Related
party transactions

Auditor's
considerations in respect of going
concern

SPECIFIC ISSUES

Attendance
at stocktaking

Bank reports
for audit
purposes

Internal
audit
practice

Audit of
proprietor
dominated
companies

Special
reports of
accountants
(a)

Prospectuses
and the
reporting
accountant

Profit forecast reports
by
accountants

Review
engagements

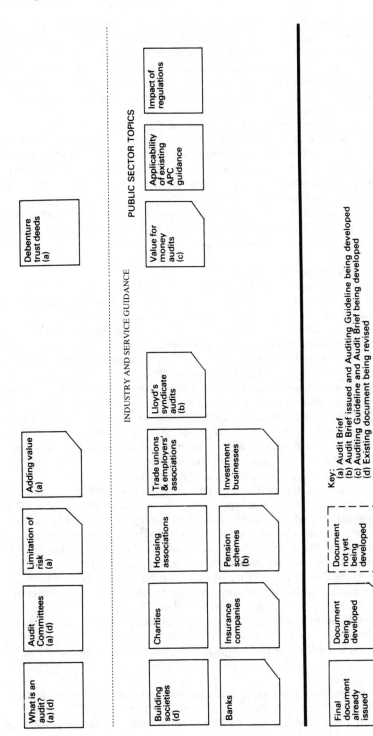

Figure 7.1 Matrix of present and prospective auditing standards and guidelines. Reproduced by permission of the Secretary of the Auditing Practices Committee

Despite the avowed intention of 'providing information', the APC has issued statements which go much further than merely informing: they also regulate audit behaviour by requiring that certain standards be adhered to in virtually all circumstances. Such standards set out what is believed to be 'best practice', acceptable to all who are involved in the audit process. As a result, uniformity of audit practice, to the extent that it exists, has been imposed by standards as well as encouraged by guidelines.

Professional pronouncements also improve audit practices by strengthening the hand of the auditor in negotiations with management. In a situation where a manager is attempting to compromise the auditor's independence, the auditor will be in a stronger position if he or she can point to a document issued by the profession and say 'this is what must be done'. Thus, narrowing the scope of the auditor's judgement can help to ensure independence. Moreover, such rules are now a necessity for professional accounting bodies to be granted recognition as supervisory bodies under the regime for regulation of auditors introduced in the Companies Act 1989.

Improvement of the public image

From the point of view of the receiver of audit reports, professional regulation results in a series of documents that provide criteria against which the performance of auditors can be judged. So informed, users are in a position at least to question the actions of auditors and to interpret replies to those questions within a framework of knowledge derived from professional pronouncements. Seen in this light, auditing standards and guidelines inform users about the purpose of auditing and about the nature of audit practices.

Armed with knowledge about the role and responsibilities of the auditor, users will be better able to interpret the audit report. Auditing standards and guidelines contain much information which facilitates consistent interpretation of concepts such as 'true and fair' and 'sufficient relevant and reliable evidence', both of which appear within auditing standards. And, of course, they give substance to the phrase 'in accordance with approved auditing standards', which is a required part of every audit report.

It is also argued that the publication of standards and guidelines enhances the public image of the profession. (Some would take this argument to extremes, suggesting that the whole of the APC's programme could end up as a 'cosmetic whitewash' (Woolf, 1978.) This suggestion that standards and guidelines enhance the public image is based on the assumption that the general public considers that such documents indicate the profession to be seriously concerned with the quality of service provided by its members. As such, self-regulation is thought to improve the credibility of the profession.

While for many years the APC concerned itself almost exclusively with issues to do with audit practice, in recent years broader aspects of the image of auditing have been considered. For example, there is currently a working party of the APC looking at the 'expectation gap' surrounding audit roles.

Other roles

In addition to improving practice and the public image of the profession, professional regulation can be said to fulfil other roles. For example, standards can assist the auditor to convince a client of the necessity for implementing certain procedures. In turn, this could be used to justify an increase in the audit fee.

A less cynical argument might be that standards indicate to the outside world that the profession is capable of generating and enforcing its own standards, thus helping to counter those who suggest that the state should control auditors. Seen in this light, self-regulation becomes part of the self-defence mechanism of professional organizations.

A final, and important, role of standards is to introduce cohesion and regularity to the whole audit process. Thus, audit procedures become more predictable and it is less easy to justify inappropriate or unnecessary procedures. This notion of cohesion and regularity brings to mind once again the matrix prepared by the APC, which seems designed to introduce cohesion and regularity to the standard-setting process.

To summarize the observations above, professional regulation can be said to fulfil at least seven roles.

1. It ensures consistent high quality of audit practice.
2. It promotes development and improvement in audit practice.
3. It aids users in understanding and interpreting the audit process.
4. It enhances the public image of the profession.
5. It discourages state regulation of the profession.
6. It assists auditors in negotiations with clients.
7. It introduces cohesion and regularity to the audit process.

It is clearly beyond the scope of this chapter to become involved in determining whether the existing standards and guidelines successfully fulfil these roles (although this would be an interesting exercise). Suffice to say at this point that there have been a number of criticisms of the standards and guidelines which cast some doubt on the claim that those pronouncements do adequately fulfil those roles.

For example, standards and guidelines have been criticized for failing to specify the extent of audit responsibility, for failing to consider independence, integrity and impartiality, for being based on an insecure foundation, for being so general as to gloss over the real issues, for being difficult to interpret and for failing to take account of the position of the small company audit.[3]

Whether such claims are justified or not, it is important that the profession (in the form of the APC) develops a strategy for answering its critics. Unless unjustified criticism can be successfully countered, and justified criticism can be taken into account, it is unlikely that any of the above objectives will be achieved in the long term. For example, unjustified criticism is likely to undermine public confidence in self-regulation, and a failure to change in the light of justified criticism is likely to result in hidebound procedures which cannot adapt to changing circumstances. A successful future for the whole process of professional self-regulation depends upon the development of the means to ensure adaptation and development of pronouncements. The recent changes to the Companies Act have strengthened the position of the APC. The 1989 Act has established an accounting standard-setting structure which, among other things, gives the power to the Review Panel to investigate contentious departures from accounting standards by large companies.

In order to ensure continuing improvements in the consistency, appropriateness and justifiability of audit practices, it is necessary to look at the overall picture represented by professional pronouncements. Thus, although a guideline on charities may not seem to have much in common with a guideline on attendance at stocktaking, there will inevitably be areas of overlap. Drafting of new pronouncements must allow for the content of existing documents and must not be issued before inconsistencies are resolved. This approach extends the idea of a matrix of audit documents further into the notion of a 'conceptual framework', a structure of logical arguments deriving appropriate procedures which has for so long eluded the best efforts of accounting standard-setters.

CONCEPTUAL FRAMEWORKS AND THE FUTURE OF PROFESSIONAL SELF-REGULATION

I have suggested above that the principal role of a conceptual framework in the context of auditing is to provide a means of looking at professional pronouncements as components of a larger structure, rather than as discrete entities in their own right. Seen in this way, the publication of a standard or guideline can be said to extend and improve the conceptual framework.

This approach is rather different from that which frequently appears in the literature. There, a conceptual framework is seen as a coherent system of interrelated objectives and fundamentals that can lead to consistent standards (FASB, 1976). That is, a conceptual framework is seen as a precursor to the generation of standards. The approach adopted in this chapter is that the standards (together with other pronouncements) actually constitute the conceptual framework, and that the publication of further pronouncements amounts to the further development of the conceptual framework.

Equating the development of professional pronouncements with the development of a conceptual framework has a number of implications for the profession. First, a major advantage of this approach is that the preparation of standards and guidelines will not be held up by unsuccessful attempts to establish a 'conceptual framework'. This has been a notorious source of difficulty in accounting, with a report prepared by Professor MacVe on behalf of the ICAEW stating that 'it . . . seems unlikely that searching for an agreed conceptual framework . . . will be successful' (MacVe, 1981, p. 14). The heated debate surrounding the recent publications by Solomons (1989) and the ICAS Research Committee (1989) indicates that agreement on a conceptual framework for financial reporting is still a long way off.

Second, as part of a larger structure, professional pronouncements can be seen as components of a theory. That is, statements within professional pronouncements will explain and justify the recommended practices. Those explanations and recommendations can be said to constitute statements within a deductive theory, in the sense that a theory is a 'set of statements . . . ordered by the relation of deducibility . . . [so that] no statement . . . remains isolated: every statement is either an assumption or a conclusion (Bunge, 1972, p. 227). By considering the body of auditing standards and guidelines to constitute a theory, the APC will have taken an important step towards ensuring that derived practices are consistent, justifiable and appropriate.

Third, such a structure will provide the basis for research efforts designed to identify inconsistencies and gaps in the standards and guidelines so far issued. There is little doubt that the APC has only recently hit upon the idea of considering the various statements as components in a larger entity, and it is extremely likely that existing statements are, in the context of that larger entity, incomplete, inconsistent or both.

Fourth, attempts to isolate and remove inconsistencies and gaps will require that relationships between statements be made explicit. In particular, all propositions on which recommended practices depend will have to be made explicit. As a result, attention will be focused on hitherto unstated assumptions, and guidance will be provided for the future development of the theory.

Finally, a re-examination of existing standards and guidelines will result in the identification of assertions used in arguments deriving practices. If those assertions are not supported by available empirical evidence, there will be grounds for doubting the justifiability of recommended practices. Thus, researchers will be encouraged to undertake empirical projects designed to refute or confirm assumptions made. Empirical research in auditing will be better directed than it is at the moment.

A STRUCTURE FOR STANDARDS AND GUIDELINES

If attempts are to be made to restructure existing standards and guidelines, it is necessary to have some criteria by which the restructuring can be carried out. That is, it will be necessary to have a model which will specify the role to be played by specific statements within the standards and guidelines. Thus, we need a 'structural ideal' according to which the standards and guidelines can be reorganized so as to form a conceptual framework.

A primary attribute of this structural ideal is that it should provide for the explicit identification of the roles of statements within the structure and of relationships between statements. For example, it will be necessary to judge whether a statement is a proposition or a rule, and whether it is a premise, a conclusion or both.

A suitable structure for our conceptual framework will also need to facilitate the subsequent improvement of standards and guidelines. This is essential if professional pronouncements are to adapt to changes in the business or legal environment of auditing. Thus, the framework should be seen as a foundation for change, rather than as a final concrete structure.

A further important attribute of our ideal structure is that it should enable the identification of those statements which are considered to be of fundamental importance to the entire structure. For example, statements concerned with an explanation of the reason for audits would probably be of fundamental importance since any errors in those statements could result in claims that the entire audit function is unjustified. This attribute is important if we are to be convinced that the programme of professional self-regulation is built upon a secure foundation.

These observations suggest that the structure will consist of a central core of fundamental propositions which will, for example, explain the role of the audit function and derive the major objectives of the auditor. In addition to this central core will be a subsidiary, more flexible, series of propositions which derive recommended audit practices in the context of overall objectives. As with the existing series of pronouncements, derived practices would not be seen as an attempt by the APC to eliminate the auditor's judgement. Rather, these derived procedures would provide a framework within which judgement could be exercised.

To summarize, the necessary restructuring (but not necessarily the re-writing) of auditing standards and guidelines should be preceded by the identification of a blueprint for an ideal structure which:

1. provides for the specification of relationships between component statements in the conceptual framework;
2. provides a basis for further development of standards and guidelines;
3. enables the specification of a central core of fundamentally important statements; and
4. provides the means of identifying inconsistent, unjustified or inappropriate audit procedures.

CONCLUSION

Although exploratory, this chapter has suggested a significant development in the APC's thinking. With its efforts at specifying a structure for auditing standards and guidelines, the profession has taken a major step along the path to the conversion of professional pronouncements into a body of theory. All it would take now is to go one step further and organize individual components of professional pronouncements (i.e. individual sentences) into a similar structure. By so doing, a detailed series of logical arguments could be derived explaining and justifying all recommended practices in terms of stated objectives.

I suspect some critics may claim that there can never be agreement on objectives (as in accounting), so that the process of theory construction cannot begin. I would counter by arguing that the objectives are already established. All that is necessary is to look at the existing standards and guidelines; although objectives may not be specifically stated, they are clearly implied. These objectives, once made explicit, can form the basis of our conceptual framework.

Nor will the further development of the framework present great difficulty, since it, too, already exists within the standards and guidelines. The problem at the moment is that the statements lack organization (in a wider sense), and that it is impossible to discern the gaps and inconsistencies which exist in the overall structure. It is necessary only for the APC to reorganize its existing pronouncements to create a true conceptual framework.

NOTES

1. For a discussion of the various roles of the auditor, see Wallace (1980).
2. As reported in 'Notes and Comments', *The Accountant's Magazine*, June 1974, p. 198.
3. See, for example, Woolf (1980, 1986), Davison (1979).

REFERENCES AND FURTHER READING

APC (Auditing Practices Committee) (1980) *Auditing Standards and Guidelines*, ICAEW, London.

APC (1986) *The First Ten Years*, ICAEW, London.

Auditing and Reporting (ICAEW, annual) reproduces all current standards, guidelines and draft statements.

Bunge, M. (1972) Metatheory, in UNESCO, *Scientific Thought: Some Underlying Concepts, Methods and Procedures*, UNESCO, Paris, pp. 227–52.

Davison, I.H. (1976) Standards – where do we go from here? *Accountancy*, April, pp. 26–8.

Davison, I.H. (1979) The new auditing standards and the smaller company, *Accountancy*, April, pp. 60–2.

de Paula, F.C. and Attwood, F.A. (1982) *Auditing Principles and Practice*, 2nd edn, Pitman, London.

FASB (Financial Accounting Standards Board) (1976) *An Analysis of Issues Related to Conceptual Framework for Financial Accounting and Reporting: Elements of Financial Statements and their Measurement*, Stamford, Conn.

Gough, B. (1978) Just how necessary are auditing standards? *Accountancy*, July, p. 118.

ICAS Research Committee (1989) *Making Corporate Reports Valuable*, Institute of Chartered Accountants of Scotland, Edinburgh.

MacVe, R. (1981) *A Conceptual Framework for Financial Accounting and Reporting: The Possibilities for an Agreed Structure*, ICAEW, London.

Solomons, D. (1989) *Guidelines for Financial Reporting Standards*, ICAEW, London.

Wallace, W.A. (1980) *The Economic Role of the Auditor in Free and Regulated Markets*, Touche Ross, London.

Woolf, E. (1978) Are the new auditing standards the answer to a major problem? *Accountancy*, September, pp. 68–9.

Woolf, E. (1980) How vague words mask dissent behind the audit standards, *Accountancy*, November, pp. 61–4.

Woolf, E. (1986) *Auditing Today*, 3rd edn, Prentice-Hall, London.

DISCUSSION QUESTIONS

1. Discuss the possible undesirable consequences of the Auditing Practices Committee's programme for the development of auditing standards and guidelines.

2. If the Auditing Practices Committee were to decide to develop a conceptual framework for auditing, how would you suggest it goes about it?

3. Identify and discuss some gaps or inconsistencies in the present auditing standards and guidelines.

4. For what purposes was the Auditing Practices Committee created? Have these purposes been achieved?

5. What is the difference between an auditing 'standard' and an auditing 'guideline'? To what extent do existing pronouncements comply with the definitions of 'standard' and 'guideline'?

6. 'Auditing standards and guidelines eliminate the need for professional judgement.' Discuss.

7. To what extent are the provisions of the Companies Act 1989 consistent with the auditing profession's current practices for issuing its own standards and guidelines?

Part II
Forming an Audit Opinion

8
Audit Reports

David J. Hatherly and Peter C. B. Skuse

INTRODUCTION

> Auditors tell each other that an audit report indicates that they have obtained reasonable, though not absolute, assurance that the financial statements are free of a material mis-statement and, further, that the level of reasonable assurance must depend on the perceived risk of the hypothetical mis-statement in question. It would seem useful to inform the readers of this interpretation.
>
> (Anderson, 1977, p. 439)

There are many, like Anderson (1977), who question whether the present approach to audit reporting is sufficiently informative of what an audit involves and what an audit opinion really means. Given the overriding requirement for informative reporting, the first part of this chapter explores the fundamental questions: what the audit report should say and how it should say it. The second part of the chapter gives the authors' own preferences and explains how they would resolve these fundamental issues. In particular, the first part of the chapter identifies ten suggestions as to what the audit report should contain and the second part discusses and analyses each of these ten suggestions in turn.

The auditor's objective to communicate his or her results based on the planning, evaluation and collection of audit evidence is governed in law in the UK by the Companies Act 1985. This requires the audit report to state whether, in the auditor's opinion, the company's balance sheet and profit and loss account are in accordance with the provisions of the Companies Act *and* whether a true and fair view is given of the state of affairs at the year-end and of the profit or loss for the year. Various other reporting duties are also imposed on the auditor by statute and they will be discussed in more detail later.

It can be argued that these statutory requirements should be extended. The auditor could have a legal duty to give an opinion as to whether the company's management is efficient, whether the company's personnel have been involved in fraud, bribery or other illegal activity, and whether management decisions have been economically, efficiently and effectively made and implemented. Some such extensions may come in the next decade;

David J. Hatherly, B.Sc. (Econ.), M.Acc., F.C.A., is Head of the Department of Accounting and Business Method at the University of Edinburgh. Peter C.B. Skuse, LL.B., F.C.A., is a partner with Peat Marwick McLintock. The views and opinions expressed in this chapter are those of the authors and do not necessarily reflect those of Peat Marwick McLintock.

they will certainly lead to problems in both fieldwork and reporting for the auditor of the limited company. However, this chapter limits its ambition to a discussion of the reporting problems that arise from the auditor's present statutory responsibilities.

WHAT SHOULD THE AUDIT REPORT SAY?

There have been many suggestions as to what the audit report should contain, and some of these argue that it should:

1. identify for whom the audit report is written;
2. explain that the financial statements are prepared by the directors and that the main purpose of the audit is to provide an independent opinion on the reliability of those financial statements;
3. identify the financial statments to which the audit report relates and explain the nature of any auditor responsibility for information in the annual report but outside the financial statements;
4. explain the limits of the auditor's responsibility for detecting fraud and irregularity;
5. give an indication of the fact that evidence available to support any audit opinion is persuasive rather than conclusive;
6. describe the audit work performed on the financial statements and in particular the role of internal control;
7. positively state all audit opinions;
8. as regards the true and fair view opinion, indicate the basis on which the true and fair view is judged;
9. make clear that the true and fair view opinion relates to the financial statements as a whole rather than to individual figures within those financial statements;
10. clearly explain the nature of, reasons for, and effect of, any qualified audit opinion.

The UK accountancy bodies have issued auditing standards and guidelines which, among other things, explain the nature of the audit. If the audit report were to incorporate all the ten suggestions, however, it would be largely 'free-standing' of the standards and guidelines since the report would itself go much of the way to explaining the responsibilities of the auditor and the nature of the audit. In the free-standing approach, therefore, there is no assumption that the audit report reader is familiar with, or even has access to, the standards and guidelines or other explanatory documents. The audit report itself is taken as the principal means of communication of the auditing profession with the 'financial public'.

The alternative to the free-standing approach is to limit the audit report to audit opinions and surrounding circumstances which are, or could be, specific to the particular company under audit (the 'client-specific' approach). The audit report would therefore concentrate on elements 1, 7, the first part of 3, and possibly 6, of the free-standing approach. Those features of the audit that are common to all company audits are covered in the auditing standards and guidelines and similar widely available documents, but not in the audit report itself.

Current position in the UK

The current unqualified audit report in the UK for a company without subsidiaries reads as follows:

Auditor's report to the members of XYZ Limited

We have audited the financial statements on pages——to——in accordance with Auditing Standards.

In our opinion the financial statements give a true and fair view of the state of the company's affairs at 31 December 19— and of its profit and source and application of funds for the year then ended and have been properly prepared in accordance with the Companies Act 1985.

The current UK reporting standard (ICAS, 1989) requires the report to identify those to whom it is addressed (element 1) and the financial statements to which it relates (element 3). The audit opinions with regard to the 'true and fair view' and 'compliance of the financial statements with legal requirements' must be positively stated (element 7) although certain other opinions, notably with respect to the maintenance of proper accounting records, are reported by exception only. Where the report is qualified it should include a brief recital of the reasons and quantify the effects on the financial statements if relevant and practicable (element 10). The current UK report does not, however, indicate the actual audit work performed in any detail (element 6). All that is included is a statement that the audit has been conducted 'in accordance with Auditing Standards'. It can be seen from this brief discussion that the current UK audit report follows the client-specific approach more closely than the free-standing approach.

At the time of writing, a working party of the Auditing Practices Committee is examining the current client-specific report. It is considering a number of options including the possibility that the client-specific report remain unchanged but with a requirement for a supplementary explanation of the audit and the auditor's report to be given alongside every published auditor's report. This idea, effectively a hybrid of the client-specific and free-standing approaches, originated in the USA (see Mednick, 1986).

HOW SHOULD IT SAY IT?

The Department of Trade Inspectors (1979, p. 156) in the Peachey Property case, accused the auditors of reporting in 'hieratic' language, which they defined as 'language which is neither comprehensible as ordinary speech nor adequately defined to a specialist'.

Audit reports may not need to be understood by every person who 'travels on the Clapham omnibus', but they should be comprehensible to the vast majority of individuals who buy and sell shares, to bank managers, tax inspectors, those in business who give credit to companies, and to the financial journalist. The potential 'user' or 'reader' of audit reports may not have received any formal accountancy or audit training but it can be hypothesized that such a person has had a sound general education, has some knowledge of the way business works and can accordingly be defined as a 'reasonably competent' reader.

To be comprehensible, therefore, either the audit report must use language in its natural sense or, if it uses technical language, that language must itself be capable of clear definition in non-technical terms to the reasonably competent reader. The use of natural language is consistent with the free-standing philosophy referred to earlier, in the sense that the language used in the report should be readily comprehensible and need no further explanation for the reasonably competent reader. A report that uses brief technical terms – specialized symbols serving as coded messages – must use definitions which are widely available to reasonably competent readers. Examples of coded messages are the use of the 'subject to' and 'except for' wordings in qualified audit reports, and these are more fully explained in the relevant standard. The advantage of using a properly explained code is that the audit opinion on any particular company's financial statements can be quickly identified by those who are familiar with the code. The disadvantage is that such people are not the only ones who read audit reports.

Taken to the extreme, the codification process reduces the entire audit report to a single symbol or 'seal of approval'. There is some evidence (Epstein, 1976) that this is what shareholders want, but there is a danger in shareholders placing unjustified reliance on the 'seal of approval' if they are unfamiliar with the nature of the audit process and the auditor's responsibilities.

Standardized v. non-standardized wording

Where coded messages are to be employed the audit report must use the standardized wording of the chosen code. Where the report seeks to explain itself in terms of natural language, however, there is a choice between the profession laying down standardized wording – albeit in terms of natural language – and allowing the auditor to use natural language of his or her own choosing. Estes (1982) argues strongly in favour of non-standardized wording:

> The hypothesis of investor conditioning is based on the standardization of audit report wording and format. The wording of the standard unqualified audit report is prescribed by the American Institute of CPAs and most CPA firms follow this wording precisely. Even qualified reports are made as uniform as possible. By standardizing the audit report, the accounting profession may have insured that it will be uninteresting. The reader has apparently been conditioned to expect no surprises and so does not read the audit report.
>
> (Estes, 1982, p. 91)

He continues (op. cit., p. 93): 'All standardized wording should be dropped; the auditor's report should be composed anew, "from scratch", for each audit. This will be recognized as a proposal for a return to something akin to the long form report.'

Estes is attempting to explain his own, and some other, research results which suggest that neither the standard unqualified audit report nor the various qualified reports issued in the USA have much effect on investor behaviour. He explains this in terms of the so-called 'investor conditioning hypothesis', which suggests that the investor loses interest in audit reports because of their excessive standardization. His explanation is only a hypothesis, however, and is not itself established by experimental research. Estes's views are in stark contrast to those of the accounting professions of the UK and USA. The UK accounting profession believes that standardized wording promotes a more consistent understanding of whether or not the auditor has any reservations and of the nature of any such reservations. However, these professions recognize that certain elements within the report which are client-specific can never be subject to standardized wording. For example, the current UK 'reservation paragraph' in which the reasons for any qualification are recited is not subject to standardization since these reasons can and do vary from client to client.

Estes may in fact be overstating the extent to which there is evidence that audit reports do not affect investor behaviour. After a recent comprehensive review of research in the area, he writes (1982, p. 29), 'despite substantial research effort, we still do not know with any degree of confidence the effect of the auditor's report on its intended audience'. Such empirical research is generally either market-based or experimental. Market-based studies examine the impact of qualified audit reports upon stock market prices. In an experimental study some participants in the experiment are given a company's financial statements with an unqualified audit report whilst other participants are given the same financial statements accompanied by a qualified audit report. All the participants are asked to evaluate the company with respect to, say, management performance, share price and as a potential investment. The impact of the audit report qualification is assessed by comparing the evaluations of those who were given a company's financial statements with a qualified audit report with the evaluations of those who were not.

Gwilliam (1987), after an extensive survey of the literature, confirms the inconclusive nature of the research results. His conclusion from the experimental studies is that although users value audit qualifications, in most cases it is difficult to identify a significant economic impact or user decision arising from the qualification. As regards market-based studies he concludes that whilst some studies suggest that a qualification may directly provoke a significant price reaction, others suggest that the price reaction is indirect, since the movement in share prices takes place some time before the qualified report is issued.

The US experience

In 1988, as a result of SAS 58 (AICPA, 1988), audit reports in the USA moved from a short, client-specific format to an explanatory style of report incorporating most, if not all, of the elements of a free-standing report. SAS 58 retained standardized wording, as follows:

Independent Auditor's Report

We have audited the accompanying balance sheet of X Company as of December 31, 19xx, and the related statements of income, retained earnings, and cash flows for the year then ended. These financial statements are the responsibility of the Company's management. Our responsibility is to express an opinion on these financial statements based on our audit.

We have conducted our audit in accordance with generally accepted auditing standards. Those standards require that we plan and perform the audit to obtain reasonable assurance about whether the financial statements are free of material misstatement. An audit includes examining, on a test basis, evidence supporting the amounts and disclosures in the financial statements. An audit also includes assessing the accounting principles used and significant estimates made by management, as well as evaluating the overall financial statement presentation. We believe that our audit provides a reasonable basis for our opinion.

In our opinion, the financial statements referred to above present fairly, in all material respects, the financial position of X Company as of December 31, 19xx, and the results of its operations and its cash flows for the year then ended in conformity with generally accepted accounting principles.

(AICPA, 1988, SAS 58, para. 8)

The new style of report has been accepted quietly by the financial community in the USA. There have not been the high levels of criticism (Dillard and Jensen, 1983) that accompanied a previous and unsuccessful attempt in 1980 to introduce a free-standing report (AICPA, 1980). The 1980 exposure draft (subsequently withdrawn), however, differed from SAS 58 in one crucial respect. In the USA the auditor does not give true and fair view opinion but rather an opinion as to whether the financial statements fairly present . . . in accordance with generally accepted accounting principles. The 1980 exposure draft suggested the word 'fairly' be omitted so that the auditor appeared to have no overriding responsibility for the 'fairness' of the presentation but merely reported whether generally accepted accounting principles had been applied. This was correctly perceived to be an attempt by the profession to limit liability, since it appeared to be out of line with US case law. For example, in the Continental Vending case, *United States* v. *Simon* (1969) 425 F2d 796, the judge stated: 'the first law for accountants was not compliance with generally accepted accounting principles but rather full and fair disclosure, fair presentation'. It is possible that the attempt to remove the audit responsibility for fairness will have generated much of the unfavourable reaction in 1980.

THE AUTHORS' PREFERENCES

The early part of this chapter has identified three interrelated issues.

1. Should the audit report be 'free standing'?
2. Should the report use 'natural' language?
3. Should the report use 'standardized' language wherever possible?

We have a strong preference for the free-standing philosophy toward audit reporting. There is evidence (Lee, 1970; Beck, 1973; Arthur Andersen, 1974) that the nature and function of the statutory company audit are not well understood by the actual or potential readership, and we believe that in this respect more use than at present can be made of the audit report as an educational medium. Moreover, we consider that the audit report should generally use words in their natural sense and avoid technical language. Based on the Lee and Tweedie (1977) studies, the understanding of technical language by audit report readers is unlikely to be high. Finally, we prefer each audit report to use the same natural wording whenever it is describing the same situation or state of affairs. In this way the natural wording can also serve as a code and avoid the confusion which can result from using different messages to describe essentially similar situations.

The remainder of this chapter discusses in further detail each of the ten elements previously suggested for inclusion in the free-standing audit report.

ELEMENTS OF A FREE-STANDING REPORT

Element 1   Identify for whom the audit report is written

As previously stated, the UK reporting standard (ICAS, 1989, para. 2) expressly requires the auditor to identify those to whom the report is addressed. The effect of this requirement is that, in the UK, the audit report is addressed to the shareholders. The US auditing profession also recognized the need for the report to be addressed to someone, and paragraph 9 of SAS 58 (AICPA, 1988) states: 'The report may be addressed to the company whose financial statements are being audited or to its board of directors or stockholders.' However, it is important to remember that in both countries the identification of the addressees of the report does not of itself limit the extent of the auditor's liability to third parties for negligent work. For further discussions of this topic, see Chapter 5.

Element 2 ᐧ Explain that the financial statements are prepared by the directors and that the main purpose of the audit is to provide an independent opinion on the reliability of those financial statements

It is a fundamental auditing concept that the auditor is independent of the persons responsible for the preparation of the financial statements. In the UK, however, unlike the USA, there is no express reference in the audit report to the fact that the financial statements were prepared by the directors. We consider that, at the same time as pointing out that the auditor does not prepare the financial statements, the audit report should explain what the auditor does do, i.e. provides an independent opinion on the reliability of the financial statements.

Element 3   Identify the financial statements to which the audit report relates and explain the nature of any auditor responsibility for information in the annual report but outside the financial statements

The UK reporting standard (ICAS, 1989, para. 2) expressly requires the auditor to identify the financial statements to which the audit relates, and this is done by use of the phrase 'the financial statements on pages——to——'. The Companies Act 1985 recognizes the need for the directors' report to be consistent with the financial statements and imposes an obligation on the auditor to comment if this is not so. The problem is that the annual report may contain, as well as the financial statements and directors' report, further information such as a chairman's report, statistical information relating to a number of years, value-added reports and reports to employees. Much of this information is expressed in financial terms. As a result, the reasonably competent reader may be unsure about which pieces of information have been subject to audit. The auditor's express identification of the parts of the annual report to which the audit report relates considerably reduces the possibility of such doubt.

In most cases the auditor will review the unaudited information in the annual report for consistency with the financial statements. It might be helpful for the audit report to explain the nature of the work performed by the auditor in respect of the directors' report and, where appropriate, any other unaudited information.

Element 4   Explain the limits of the auditor's responsibility for detecting fraud and irregularity

Responsibility for fraud detection is a highly sensitive topic for the practising auditor. The professional accountancy bodies' interpretation of the current legal requirement is some way from the 'popular' view of the auditor as someone whose job it is to track down fraud. The UK profession's view is that auditors should design their tests to give a 'reasonable expectation' of detecting material misstatements in the financial statements resulting from irregularities or fraud. The profession's position is that auditors should apply the same standard of materiality and the same standard of care (reasonable expectation) when seeking to detect misstatements caused by fraud or irregularity as they do when seeking to detect misstatements caused by inadvertent error. The implication of the 'popular' view is that auditors should work with a stricter materiality concept and/or a higher standard of care in respect of errors caused by fraud or irregularity. It was suggested by Jack (1983), at least in respect of frauds or irregularities perpetrated by company officials, that the present statutory position following the Companies Act 1980 (now consolidated into The Companies Act 1985) is closer to the 'popular' view than it is to the interpretation of the profession. Clearly Jack believes that the law has moved on from Lord Denning's dictum in *Fomento (Sterling Area) Ltd* v. *Selsdon Fountain Pen Co. Ltd* ([1958] 1 WLR 61): 'to perform this task properly he must come to it with an inquiring mind – not suspicious of dishonesty – but suspecting that someone may have made a mistake somewhere'.

Assuming that the auditing profession's view, as supported by Denning, is a correct interpretation of current law, it is desirable for the audit report to indicate to the reasonably competent reader that the auditor's responsibility for the detection of fraud is a part of his or her responsibility to detect *any* material misstatement, whatever the cause.

Element 5   Give an indication of the fact that evidence available to support any audit opinion is persuasive rather than conclusive

According to a study by Arthur Andersen (1974), a substantial minority of shareholders (37 per cent) erroneously thought that the auditor determines the accuracy of financial statements by going through all financial records. This study was conducted some time ago but its implication is that many report readers may have an exaggerated impression of the quality of the evidence which can realistically be obtained by the auditor. In reality, the evidence available to the auditor can be only persuasive, rather than conclusive, for a number of reasons, especially the need to sample the financial records and the subjective nature of any evaluation of the system of internal control. In our opinion, the way of indicating the persuasive nature of audit evidence is to preface the audit opinion(s) with words such as 'we have obtained reasonable assurance that in our opinion'.

Element 6   Describe the audit work performed on the financial statements and in particular the role of internal control

The present UK audit report refers to the audit being carried out in accordance with approved auditing standards – but should the report go on to explain the key points contained in those standards? The issue is brought into focus by looking at the guideline on engagement letters (ICAS, 1984). This says that in an engagement letter the scope of the audit should be explained and it should be indicated that:

(a) auditor will obtain an understanding of the accounting system in order to assess its adequacy as a basis for the preparation of the financial statements;
(b) the auditor will expect to obtain relevant and reliable evidence sufficient to enable him to draw reasonable conclusions therefrom;
(c) the nature and extent of the tests will vary according to the auditor's assessment of the accounting system and, where he wishes to place reliance upon it, the system of internal control.

(ICAS, 1984, para. 11)

The question arises that, if such a description is included in the engagement letter to help directors understand the audit process, why then should it not be included in the audit report to help the shareholders and others understand the audit process? Of course, if such as description were included it might lead to demands to know whether an evaluation of the internal controls had been carried out and, if so, the results. The auditor could not divulge the results of any internal control evaluation in the formal report without a statutory change in the objectives of the audit. The necessary statutory change might, however, lead to more value for money from audits since the auditor is in many cases making an internal control evaluation for purposes of assessing the reliability of the financial statements.

Element 7 Positively state all audit opinions

Positive reporting can be contrasted with reporting by exception, in which the auditor includes his or her opinion in the audit report only if that opinion is unfavourable. For example, section 237 of the Companies Act 1985 requires that, if the auditors are of the opinion that proper accounting records have *not* been kept, or that proper returns have *not* been received from branches not visited by the auditors, or if the balance sheet and profit and loss account are *not* in agreement with the accounting records, they shall state that fact in their report. Similarly, if the auditors *fail* to obtain all the information and explanations necessary for the purposes of the audit, they are to state that fact in their report, and, as previously mentioned, if the auditor is of the opinion that any of the information in the directors' report is inconsistent with the financial statements that too must be stated. Unlike reporting by exception, positive reporting requires the auditor to express his or her opinion in the audit report whether the opinion is favourable or unfavourable.

Positive reporting can also be contrasted with negative reporting, in which an auditor is prepared to say that he or she has no reason to believe there is anything wrong, but never positively states that he or she believes things to be *right*. There is no statutory requirement for the auditor to use negative reporting in connection with the annual statutory audit of a limited company's financial statements. Section 173(5) of the Companies Act 1985 does, however, require a negatively worded report from the auditor in special circumstances where a company purchases its own shares. The problem with negative reporting is that the less work the auditor does, the more confidently can he or she voice on opinion that he or she 'knows of no reason . . . '. This is in stark contrast to positive reporting where, generally, the more work the auditor does, the more confidently he or she can give an opinion.

It is reasonable to assert that positive reporting provides less potential for misunderstanding than either reporting by exception or negative reporting.

Element 8. As regards the true and fair view opinion, indicate the basis on which the true and fair view is judged

The Companies Act 1985 sets out statutory accounting principles, but it also provides that these principles and the format and disclosure requirements of the Act should be overridden, if necessary, in order to provide a true and fair view:

(a)   if the balance sheet or profit and loss account would not otherwise provide sufficient information to give a true and fair view; or

(b)   if, owing to special circumstances in the case of any company, the balance sheet or profit and loss account would not otherwise show a true and fair view.

Thus, the Act appears to link the 'true and fair view' with both the sufficiency of the information provided by the presentation and disclosure of the financial statements and the appropriateness of the accounting principles to the particular circumstances of the business.

Skerratt (1982) has drawn attention to the fact that the phrase 'true and fair' is inappropriate for audit reporting unless the purposes for which the accounts will be used are specified. Although it may not be practical at the present time to state the assumed purposes of the accounts in the audit report (possibly they should be stated in the accounts?), the fact remains that any judgement regarding a true and fair view is linked to an assumed purpose or set of purposes for the financial statements.

On the basis of these discussions we venture the following definition of a true and fair view:

> Financial statements of an enterprise give a true and fair view if they, together with related notes, are sufficiently informative of matters that affect their use, understanding and interpretation by those for whom they are intended, and they are prepared in accordance with accounting principles appropriate to the circumstances of the business.

Such a definition gives at least some guidance as to the basis on which the true and fair view should be judged.

In considering the use of the words 'true and fair view' in UK audit reports, the question needs to be asked whether the words constitute natural language, readily understandable to the reader without further definition. It seems to us that the phrase 'fair view' might be more natural language than 'true and fair view' since truth in accounting is based upon a concept of materiality and so is very different from the non-expert's concept of truth. However, whether the report opted for 'fair view' or 'true and fair view' we doubt that the nature of the concept is sufficiently familiar to the reasonably competent but inexpert reader for the words to be left in the report without any indication of the basis on which the true and fair view is judged. We suggest for example, the following wording for the opinion paragraph:

In our opinion, the financial statements give a true and fair view [or fair view] of [. . .], based upon the sufficient presentation and disclosure of the information contained in the financial statements in accordance with accounting principles appropriate to the circumstances of the business.

The continuing use of historical cost statements during periods of inflation provides a particular and difficult problem for audit reporting. Clearly, historical cost accounting principles are inappropriate in an inflationary environment and yet the current position in the UK is for the auditor to report that the historical cost statements give a 'true and fair view' without drawing attention to the limitations of the historical cost convention. In our opinion, this limitation should be emphasized in the audit report by including a separate paragraph warning that 'the financial statements do not attempt to reflect the impact of changing price levels upon the financial position and performance of the company'. A paragraph such as this, which draws attention to important aspects of the financial statements, is known as an 'emphasis of matter' paragraph and is discussed later.

Element 9   Make clear that the true and fair view opinion relates to the financial statements taken as a whole rather than to individual figures therein

Present practice in the UK is to report on whether 'the financial statements give, in our opinion, a true and fair view of the state of affairs, profit for the year, and sources and application of funds for the year'. It might be helpful to stress that the true and fair opinion does not relate to individual figures in the financial statements by reporting whether 'the financial statements, taken as a whole, give, in our opinion, a true and fair view of . . . '.

In this connection, it is interesting to note that the US Fourth Reporting Standard (AICPA, 1988, p. 6) states: 'the report shall contain an expression of opinion regarding the financial statements, taken as a whole'.

Element 10   Clearly explain the nature of, reasons for, and effect of, any qualified audit opinion

The wording of qualifications introduced by the reporting standard (ICAS, 1989, para. 8) is as follows:

Nature of circumstances	Material but not fundamental	Fundamental
Uncertainty	'Subject to'	Disclaimer
Disagreement	'Except for'	Adverse

The rows represent two different categories of circumstance, either of which might *cause* a qualification. The columns represent two possibilities for the extent to which the underlying problem *affects*, or potentially affects, the view given by the financial statements. Thus, each of the four possible permutations represents a different cause/effect combination.

The end product is a coding system, with the efficiency of the code depending partly upon the extent to which different auditors, faced with exactly the same set of circumstances and the same actual or potential effect on the financial statements, would apply the same coded message to communicate their qualified opinion. There is some evidence (Dillard, Murdock and Shank, 1978) that such coding schemes may not in this sense be effective. Only 53 per cent of the CPAs participating in the Dillard study agreed with the disclosure and opinion form used by other CPAs in a selected set of cases. The effectiveness of the code is also conditional upon it being understood by the reader of audit reports, who would also have to understand the meaning of words such as 'material' and 'fundamental'. Doubts about the code make it doubly necessary to support the opinion paragraph with a 'reservation' paragraph explaining both the circumstances and the effect on the financial statements. Readers are thus allowed to draw their own conclusions as to the extent to which the true and fair view is impaired.

In this way the reader of the report receives both a coded message, which places the particular problem in one of four broad categories, plus a paragraph explaining the situation in more detail. In general, we support the approach of communicating a qualified opinion by such as combination.

There is, however, a particular debate in respect of qualifying the audit report because of inherent uncertainty relating, for example, to major litigation or doubts about the enterprise's ability to continue as a going concern. It can be argued (CICA, 1980) that if a sensible method of accounting for uncertainty can be recognized – for example, full disclosure of any potential litigation or of the nature of any going concern problems – then, provided that such a sensible method has been employed in the financial statements, an unqualified audit opinion should be given. If such an approach were adopted in the UK it would result in the deletion of the 'disclaimer' and 'subject to' opinions. Investors would not necessarily be distressed by this. For example, Estes (1982, p. 89) found that the investors in his experiment did not react to either the 'subject to' opinion or the disclaimer. He reports (p. 89) that 'once the uncertainty is explained in a middle paragraph, the investor does not appear to care about the auditor's opinion itself; it could just as well be unqualified'. It is our view that an 'emphasis of matter' paragraph is ideally suited to those circumstances involving uncertainty where the auditor agrees that the financial statements give full disclosure of the facts and likely outcomes.

Emphasis of matter
An emphasis of matter paragraph draws attention to the relevant disclosures in the financial statements. It is particularly important to draw attention to any circumstances which could affect the validity of the going concern assumption on which the financial statements are based. An emphasis of matter is not a qualification of the true and fair view opinion. Not all commentators support the use of emphasis of matter paragraphs. Some argue that a set of financial statements should be self-contained and that if the auditor feels the need to draw attention to any aspect of those statements, that is itself indicative of a deficiency. If the statements are deficient, so these commentators argue, a qualification rather than an emphasis of matter is necessary. At the other extreme there are those who consider that the audit report should develop into a commentary upon the key features of the financial statements in order to make the audit report more interesting and informative to its readers. The emphasis of matter paragraph can be viewed as a modest step in this direction.

WORDING FOR THE FREE-STANDING REPORT

This chapter has discussed the basic issues of whether or not a report should be 'free standing', whether it should use natural language and whether the language of the report should be 'standardized'. The authors have a personal preference for the free-standing report and the chapter has discussed the possible different elements of such a free-standing report in some detail. We do not, however, venture any specimen examples of such reports in this chapter, although one of the discussion questions asks students to comment critically on the hypothetical wording of an audit report which goes some way toward the free-standing approach. There is one particular facet of this hypothetical report to which attention is drawn, and that is the use of headings. Free-standing reports tend to be longer than conventional reports and the use of headings helps to break up the report and enhance clarity of presentation. To those outside the company the audit report is the only visible product of the audit. It must be as well expressed, as presentable and as informative as possible.

REFERENCES

AICPA (1980) *Proposed Statement on Auditing Standards: The Auditor's Standard Report*, Exposure Draft (since withdrawn), Auditing Standards Board, American Institute of Certified Public Accountants, New York.

AICPA (1988) *Reports on Audited Financial Statements*, Statement on Auditing Standards 58, American Institute of Certified Public Accountants, New York.

Anderson, R.J. (1977) *The External Audit*, Pitman, London.

Arthur Andersen & Co (1974) *Public Accounting in Transition: American Shareholders View the Role of Independent Accounants and the Corporate Reporting Controversy*, Arthur Andersen, Chicago.

Beck, G.W. (1973) The role of the auditor in modern society: an empirical appraisal, *Accounting and Business Research*, Spring, pp. 117–22.

CICA (1980) *CICA Handbook*, Canadian Institute of Chartered Accountants, Toronto, sections 5510.51–3.

Department of Trade Inspectors (1979) *Inspectors' Report on Peachey Property Corporation Limited*, HMSO, London.

Dillard, J.F. and Jensen, D.L. (1983) The auditor's report. An analysis of opinion, *The Accounting Review*, October, pp. 787–98.

Dillard, J.F., Murdock, R.J. and Shank, J.K. (1978) CPAs' attitudes toward 'subject to' opinions, *The CPA Journal*, August, pp. 43–7.

Epstein, M.J. (1976) The corporate shareholder's view of the auditor's report: conclusions and recommendations, reported in AICPA (1978) *Appendix B of the Commission on Auditors' Responsibilities: Report, Conclusions and Recommendations*.

Estes, R. (1982) *The Auditors' Report and Investor Behaviour*, Lexington Books, Lexington, Mass.

Gwilliam, D. (1987) *A Survey of Auditing Research*, ICAEW/Prentice-Hall, London.

ICAS (1984) *Engagement Letters*, Auditing Guideline, Institute of Chartered Accountants of Scotland, Edinburgh.

ICAS (1989) *The Audit Report*, Auditing Standard 102, revised March 1989, Institute of Chartered Accountants of Scotland, Edinburgh.

Jack, R.B. (1983) Shareholder protection and the auditor, *Symposium on Auditing Research 1982*, University of Glasgow Press.

Lee, T.A. (1970) The nature of auditing and its objectives, *Accountancy*, April, pp. 292–6.

Lee, T.A. and Tweedie, D.P. (1977) *The Private Shareholder and the Corporate Report*, Institute of Chartered Accountants in England and Wales, London.

Mednick, R. (1986) The auditor's role in society: the auditor's report, the public's expectations: a crisis in communication, *Journal of Accountancy*, February, pp. 70–4.

Skerratt, L. (1982) Auditing in the corporate sector: a survey, in A.G. Hopwood, M. Bromwich and J. Shaw (eds.) (1982) *Auditing Research: Issues and Opportunities*, Pitman, London, pp. 69–79.

PRE-READING

The Auditing Standard, *The Audit Report*, The Institute of Chartered Accountants of Scotland, issued April 1980 and revised March 1989.

FURTHER READING

AICPA (1988) *Reports on Audited Financial Statements*, Statement on Auditing Standards 58, American Institute of Certified Public Accountants.

Estes, R. (1982) *The Auditor's Report and Investor Behaviour*, Heath, Lexington, Mass.

Flint, D. (1982) *A True and Fair View in Company Accounts*, Gee & Co. for The Institute of Chartered Accountants of Scotland, Edinburgh.

Gwilliam, D. (1987) *A Survey of Auditing Research*, Prentice-Hall, pp. 111–33.

DISCUSSION QUESTIONS

1.   Mednick (1986, p. 74) has suggested that the following explanation of the audit and auditor's report be included alongside every published audit report:

EXPLANATION OF THE AUDIT AND AUDITOR'S REPORT

The operation of the US securities markets is based on the concept of full and fair disclosure. Although it is up to individual investors to reach their own investment conclusions, it is important to ensure that these decisions can be made intelligently – through the availability of reliable financial and other information.

The audit plays an important role in this process. Basically, the auditor stands between management, which is responsible for preparing statements on a company's financial position and results of operations, and the investors who use these statements, along with other information, in making investment decisions. This is why independence is such an important element of the audit process.

An audit is intended to provide reasonable, but not absolute, assurance as to whether financial statements, taken as a whole, are free of material misstatements. It includes a study and evaluation of a company's accounting system and related controls, as well as tests of selected balances and transactions, focusing on significant areas and carefully probing for weak spots. It is not a 100 percent check on all transactions and balances; nor is it a guarantee of the complete accuracy of financial statements.

The auditor's report indicates whether the audit was performed in conformity with professional standards and whether, in the auditor's opinion, management's representations contained in the financial statements are stated, in all material respects, in conformity with generally accepted accounting principles.

An auditor's report is not an opinion on the viability of a company or on the quality of a specific investment. The success of any enterprise depends on many factors that lie beyond what the auditor directly reports on in the financial statements – for example, new products and competitive developments, international political conditions and the vitality of the economy.

In short, the auditor's opinion is a vital piece of information in the investment decision, but it is only one piece. Prudent investors will try to gather all the information they can, often with the help of professional investment advisers, and base their decisions on whether, in their view, the potential profits outweigh the risks of a specific opportunity.

(a) Discuss whether the UK should adopt Mednick's idea of an explanatory statement as a supplement to the current audit report.

(b) Discuss Mednick's proposed wording for the explanatory statement.

2. 'The audit report should be of great interest to investors, but it is not. It appears instead to be widely ignored' (Ralph Estes, 1982, p. 90).

(a) Why should the audit report be of great interest to investors?

(b) If Estes's and others' research results are correct and the audit report is largely ignored by investors, what could be the reasons for the lack of interest?

3. Discuss the advantages and disadvantages of the audit report consisting of a series of short coded messages. How much of the current UK qualified audit report do you consider to consist of coded messages?

4. Consider the following audit report wording:

AUDITOR'S REPORT TO THE MEMBERS OF AB LTD

Scope of audit
We have audited the financial statements on pages——to——in accordance, with approved Auditing Standards and have obtained all the information and explanations we considered necessary in the circumstances. In accordance with company law, the overall responsibility for the preparation of the financial statements is that of the directors. The audit is an independent examination of, and expression of opinion on, these financial statements.

The audit process
Auditing Standards require:

(1) that we obtain an understanding of the accounting system in order to assess its adequacy as a basis for the preparation of the financial statements, and that we

(2) vary the nature and extent of our tests according to our assessment of the accounting system, and where appropriate, our assessment of the system of internal control, so as

(3) to obtain relevant and reliable evidence sufficient to enable us to draw reasonable conclusions therefrom.

Unqualified opinion
We have obtained reasonable assurance that in our opinion the financial statements, referred to above, taken as a whole:

    (1)   give a fair view of the financial position of AB Limited at——19——and of the results of its operations and sources and applications of its funds for the year then ended, based upon the sufficient presentation and disclosure of the information contained in the financial statements in accordance with accounting principles appropriate to the circumstances of the business;

    (2)   comply with the Companies Act 1985.

(a)   Does the above report comply with the present UK Companies Act reporting requirements?

(b)   In what way does it differ from the present style of audit report used in the UK, and do you consider it to be an improvement?

(c)   To what extent does the report fail to take up all ten suggestions made in the chapter as regards the content of a 'free-standing' audit report?

9
Evidence and Judgement

Robert Gray

The auditor should obtain relevant and reliable audit evidence sufficient to enable him [*sic*] to draw reasonable conclusions therefrom. . . . The sources and amount of evidence needed to achieve the required level of assurances are questions for the auditor to determine by exercising his [*sic*] judgement.

(Auditing Practices Committee, 1980, p. 1)

INTRODUCTION

The culmination of the process of an annual statutory audit of a company is the expression of an expert opinion on the truth and fairness of a set of financial statements.[1] This opinion lends credibility to those statements by, among other things, reducing the risk and uncertainty inherent in financial numbers. If the opinion is to be worthy of a professional and an expert, not only must the judgement process which leads to that opinion be sound, reasoned and expert, but the evidence upon which it is based must be an appropriate foundation on which to base such a judgement. In this chapter we will scratch the surface of these ideas in order to see what they mean in practice. We start by assuming that audit judgements do not present a problem in themselves and, taking a 'textbook' view of the systems-based audit process, we undertake a 'stylized' examination of the nature of audit evidence and how it is collected. Then, adding some realism, we consider some recent changes in firms' audit processes. Following this, it is possible to take a brief look at what we know about auditors' judgements. The conclusion is that there is a great deal contained by the term 'auditors' professional judgement' of which we are relatively ignorant.

EVIDENCE

The word 'evidence' describes the whole range of 'things', such as documents, reports, guesses, inferences and calculations, upon which the auditor exercises his or her expert judgement in evaluating whether or not the accounts show a true and fair view. More formally, evidence is 'the facts presented to the mind of a person for the purpose of enabling him to decide a disputed question' (Mautz, 1958, p. 208). Now, obviously, different facts will have different influences on different persons. We cannot examine individual

Robert Gray, BSc (Econ), MA (Econ), F.C.A., M.B.I.M., is Mathew Professor of Accounting and Information Systems, Department of Accountancy and Business Finance, University of Dundee.

differences here, but, assuming a homogeneity of auditor judgement for the time being, we can examine how 'compelling to the mind' different categories of facts are. Two caveats must be stated at the outset. First, not all 'facts' are equally 'true' of a given situation. For example, an auditor's best estimate of, say, a client's likely business environment will be one of the things upon which the auditor will base judgement. Such an estimate is only loosely a 'fact' in the normal sense. Second, it is rare indeed (in any activity) that a fact or series of facts can compel absolute certainty in the mind of a person making a complex judgement. This uncertainty is known in the audit as 'audit risk', and, outside statistical sampling, is difficult to quantify.[2]

Audit evidence as a whole must possess a number of qualitative criteria; it must be relevant and of good quality, there must be enough of it and it must be corroborative. The relevance of evidence is determined by its appropriateness to the matter in hand and by the extent to which the evidence of a thing is truly evidence of *that* thing and not evidence of something else. Relevance is therefore determined largely by the quality of the auditor's judgement (of which more later) and, to a lesser extent, by the quality of the evidence. We will continue to assume for the moment that audit judgement is always sound and move on to consider the quality of the evidence.

Quality of evidence is determined by (a) the closeness of the evidence to the thing being evidenced, (b) the directness of the correspondence between the evidence and the thing being evidenced, and (c) the reliability of the source of the evidence.

The first of these was considered by Mautz and Sharaf (1961). They identified three broad classes of evidence: natural evidence, created evidence, and rational argumentation. These classes are descriptions of the 'things' upon which judgement is based. *Natural evidence* exists when the physical presence of a thing or event is itself evidence of that thing or event. Natural evidence derives from our physical senses. The evidence and the thing being evidenced are one and the same. The auditor, in physically inspecting a building, a machine, a warehouse full of inventory, acquires natural evidence. *Created evidence* is that which has been 'brought forth' from the thing or event. It is evidence which, in some sense, describes the thing to be evidenced. Goods delivery notes describe deliveries, a sales invoice describes a sale. They are surrogates of the thing to be evidenced and are thus examples of created evidence. Most documents and records with which the auditor deals fall into this category. *Rational argumentation* is evidence which has been derived by the application of logic. It is used a great deal in the audit process. Statistical sampling, for instance, produces evidence of this type. Thus, through the application of the rules of statistics, evidence about, for example, whether or not a particular control has been operating adequately is derived from a sample of examples of that control. Another example relates to the ownership of a motor vehicle. The auditor cannot prove beyond all doubt that a vehicle is owned by the client but can reason, from other evidence about its existence, such as the registration document or certificate of insurance, that title of the asset rests with the client. Furthermore, as we shall see later, most of the evidence relating to the 'accounting decisions' is of this form.

These three classes of evidence, natural, created and rational argumentation, are shown diagrammatically in Figure 9.1.

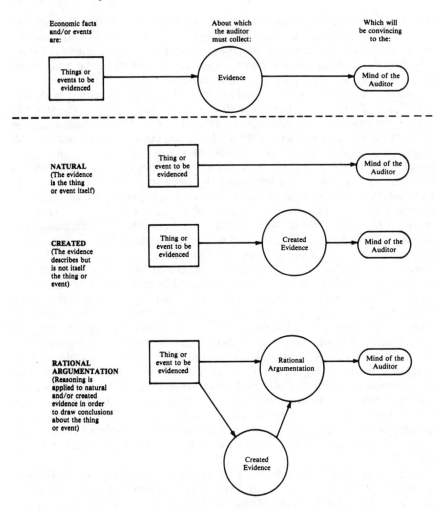

Figure 9.1 Mautz and Sharaf's classes of audit evidence

Natural evidence will always be the most compelling to the mind of the auditor and, generally speaking, created evidence may often be more compelling than rational argumentation. It is a measure of the imprecise 'science' of auditing that rational argumentation will frequently consititue the greater part of evidence upon which the audit opinion is based.[3]

The 'directness' of evidence was discussed by Keenan in an article in 1979.[4] He considered the classes of evidence to be found in law and identified these as: primary evidence, secondary evidence (both are forms of 'direct evidence') and indirect or circumstantial evidence. Primary evidence was defined as 'evidence which is the best that exists'. A moment's thought will reveal that the very best evidence that *could* exist, frequently does *not* exist as far as the auditor is concerned. Natural evidence is the very best evidence but to acquire such evidence would require that the auditor observed each delivery of goods, each payment of wages, each agreement of a contract and so on. Apart from the physical impossibility of this, at the time of an audit the physical evidence of many of these events is in the past and thus no longer exists. Primary evidence is thus more usually considered to be the best record of such events. As a general rule, where natural evidence is not available to the auditor, the primary evidence will come in the form of created evidence. In each case, there is only one piece of evidence which can be considered as the primary evidence; all other direct evidence is *secondary* evidence. The most obvious examples of secondary evidence are copies of documents, bank statements or oral or written statements from, say, a director or third party which have been derived from or describe some other record of the thing to be evidenced. There are occasions when the auditor has no choice but to rely on secondary evidence, as for example when the top copy of a sales invoice is dispatched to the customer, but in general he or she will seek to employ primary evidence whenever direct evidence is available. The third category discussed by Keenan (1979) is *indirect* or *circumstantial* evidence. This arises when there is no direct support for one fact and its existence must thus be inferred from another fact. Thus if the system of control is adequate the auditor may infer that the information produced by it is also adequate. In the case of direct evidence there is a close or direct correspondence between the evidence and the thing or event being evidenced. This is not the case with circumstantial evidence and it thus bears a very strong similarity to rational argumentation. For our purposes the terms may be treated as corresponding and thus synonymous. It should be noted that there is an element of contrivance in this categorization. There will be many cases when rational argumention or inference provides the *only* evidence available to the auditor. Such cases arise when, for example, accounting records are destroyed, or when we try to prove the ownership of a vehicle or assess the propriety of the depreciation figure. In these instances, although we have only a weaker grade of evidence, it must be considered as primary evidence as no better evidence exists.

The final element in the quality of the evidence relates to the reliability of the source of the evidence. This issue was addressed in some detail by Hatherly (1980). Hatherly identified three sources of evidence: processes largely under the control of the auditor, processes largely under the control of the directors and processes largely under the control of third parties. Again the categories are not always discrete. While natural evidence is collected directly by the auditor, evidence from statistical sampling, for example, is based both on processes under the control of the auditor (the selection and processing of the evidence) and on processes under the control of the directors (the information on which the sampling is based). The importance of the categories lies in the extent to which (a) the source of evidence can be manipulated and (b) the quality of the evidence can be reliably assessed by the auditor. Hatherly summarized the situation as shown in Figure 9.2.

Taken together the three classifications provide a fairly detailed description of the qualitative characteristics of any evidence which the auditor has collected. By preference, the auditor will always employ natural primary evidence from sources under his control. Such very best evidence is rarely to hand. The Committee on Basic Auditing Concepts (American Accounting Association (AAA, 1973) emphasized this problem:

	Evidence created largely under the control of:		
	Auditor	*Directors*	*Third party*
Susceptibility to director manipulation	Low	High	Medium
Susceptibility to quality assessment by the auditor	High	Medium	Low

Figure 9.2 Degree of susceptibility to director manipulation and auditor assessment of three classes of evidence
Source: Hatherly (1980), p. 16.

> The auditor can and does perceive the physical consequences of events. These physical consequences include the existence of cash, securities, inventory and plant. On the other hand, only a few operating events (e.g., payroll distribution and transactions in the cut-off period) are directly observed. . . . operating events are far more significant in the accounting model than the physical consequences of such events. Thus the auditor must depend on the perception of others (particularly the client's personnel) for most of the information on the financial statements.
>
> (AAA, 1973, p. 31)

Thus much of the audit opinion will be based on created evidence, from sources under the control of the directors, and will frequently involve an important degree of inference. These qualitative characteristics are summarized in Figure 9.3.

Closeness (Mautz and Sharaf, 1961)	*Directness* (Keenan, 1979)	*Source* (Hatherly, 1980)
Natural	Primary	Auditor control
Created	Secondary	Director control
Rational argumentation	Circumstantial	Third-party control

Figure 9.3 The qualitative elements of evidence

The other two criteria that were identified earlier related to the corroboration of evidence and the quantity of evidence. We have seen that the auditor can rarely acquire the very best possible evidence and has to make do with evidence which is less compelling. As far as possible, however, the auditor must try to overcome the weaknesses inherent in that evidence. This is done by acquiring further evidence which provides corroborative support for the original evidence. If the sources are independent the auditor gains a greater increase in confidence from additional evidence than if the evidence comes from the same source as the original evidence. Thus, for example, the auditor will have a degree of assurance about the stated creditors' figure from an analysis of the client's records, purchase invoices and cash payments. While the auditor may increase his or her confidence by increasing the tests on these records, the additional comfort gained from each additional piece of evidence collected from this source will not be as great as that gained from, say, an examination of creditors' statements (an 'independent' source), provided of course that the two sources furnish evidence which is consistent. Evidence from two or more sources which was inconsistent and pointed to different conclusions would naturally reduce audit confidence.[5]

The quantity of evidence neccessary for a sound audit judgement can rarely be determined with precision. We know that the auditor can never achieve certainty on an issue (a point recognized in law by the imprecision of the term 'true and fair view'), but what degree of imprecision or audit risk is acceptable? This is another matter in which the auditor must rely on his or her expert professional judgement. Outside the field of statistical sampling there are few guidelines in this area. The *quantity* of evidence is not a particularly significant issue. We know that much audit evidence is rather low-grade stuff and so there is not much comfort to be derived from having vast quantities of it. Those audit firms which prefer to keep samples at the very lowest level presumably recognize this. After all, auditing *is* more of an art than a precise science, and overemphasis on apparently rigorous hypothesis testing may simply be distracting one from this fact.

THE AUDIT PROCESS

Figure 9.4 shows, in simplified form, the five steps in the audit process and the corresponding elements of the accounting system from economic events to published accounts. The columns are made up of the elements of the accounting and audit process which one will traditionally find in standard auditing textbooks. There is thus no need for detailed explanation here.[6] What such texts do not emphasize, however, is that the audit process may be seen as having two distinct stages. Stage A, or the 'technical' stage, is where the accounting records (usually summarized in an initial trial balance) are investigated to ensure that they correspond with economic events of the accounting period. The systems-based audit represents current best practice on how this should be achieved. Stage B, or the 'accounting decisions and analytical review' stage, makes an assessment as to, among other things, the adequacy of depreciation and bad debts, the propriety of the accounting policies adopted and disclosure made, the propriety of the reported profit figure and whether the firm is a going concern. These two stages are crucially different. The accuracy of the figures that are being audited in Stage A *could* be determined with a very high degree of precision. That the auditor may not do so because of time and cost is not the issue; each item in the accounting records has some direct correspondence with an economic event that actually occurred and which can be precisely described and recorded under current accounting conventions. Thus, for example, each creditors figure consists of a series of contracts, deliveries, indebtedness and payments, each of which happened (one hopes) and can be verified in some way. The whole range of audit evidence is potentially available to the auditor, and the critical audit judgement is deciding how much of the primary evidence can be ignored. In Stage B none of this is true. Most of the accounting decisions relate to the future in some way and are almost entirely a matter of judgement. Natural and created evidence which might support these decisions rarely, if ever, exists. Usually the best evidence is inference about the business environment now, and in the future, based upon information from the directors, third parties and the auditor's experience. Precision is not a word with much significance in Stage B. It is the judgement of the auditor and directors which determines the figures that emerge from this stage and not hard, tangible, precisely measurable economic events. The evidence acquired in Stage B is unlikely to be very compelling.

Both Stages A and B are required for an audit opinion. Each is a necessary but not sufficient condition for a 'good' audit opinion. No amount of precision in Stage A can be relied upon to offset mistakes in Stage B. The effort at Stage A has, therefore, two results. First, it provides the essential foundation upon which Stage B rests, and second, because of the greater precision possible, it reduces the overall audit risk in the one place where such risk can be at least partly controlled. These are obviously important issues and auditing textbooks reflect this, concentrating almost entirely as they do on the techniques of Stage A. But no amount of effort at this stage can ensure a 'correct' audit opinion. That is, even if the bookkeeping in Stage A has been 100 per cent accurate and the trial balance completely reflects this, there will be a profound difference between this trial balance and the final accounts. The directors of the company must take this 'basic' information and take decisions on how they will value items (like fixed assets and long-term contracts), how prudent they should be (on creditors and stock, for example), how to treat and present certain items (such as extraordinary items, deferred taxation and leases) and so on. It should be apparent that it is these difficulties at Stage B which have led to many of the controversies surrounding accounting standards. Therefore all the effort exerted in Stage A on the evidence-collection techniques with which we are all so familiar must be seen in context: important, yes; essential, yes; the 'be-all-and-end-all', most certainly not.

DEVELOPMENTS IN THE AUDIT EVIDENCE-COLLECTION PROCESS

Whilst the systems-based audit approach shown in Figure 9.4 remains the model of 'best practice' it is too mechanistic a description of what actually happens in the audit process. Until recently, very little was known about the detail of audit firms' methods (Turley, 1985; Gwilliam, 1987) but recent research suggests that whilst the systems-based approach *was* employed throughout the 1970s and into the early 1980s it was badly or incorrectly applied (Higson, 1988a, 1988b). Recognition of this, coupled with the increasing pressure on audit fees in the 1980s and the escalating employment costs, as well as the growing concern that the mechanistic and procedural nature of the approach camouflaged the essential role of professional judgement, have led firms to reappraise their audit evidence-collection procedures (Turley and Cooper, 1990).

This has manifested itself in a trend towards more integration of the evidence-collection process, namely, an increased emphasis on planning; a more sophisticated approach to the assessment of audit risk; and the reappraisal of the role of analytical review (see, for example, Taylor, 1985). In effect, this is a move away from the 'bottom up' approach suggested in Figure 9.4 towards a more 'top down' approach in which professional judgement is constantly to the fore (Higson, 1988b). The changing role of analytical review perhaps best illustrates this.

The analytical review is shown in the systems-based approach as a sort of reassurance and checking process carried out at the end of an audit in order to provide comfort that no significant trends or particularly unusual figures in the financial statements have been missed. The more usual practice now is to bring the analytical review to the start of the audit as a mechanism for articulating initial audit judgements as a means for guiding the structure of the audit and the work to be undertaken.

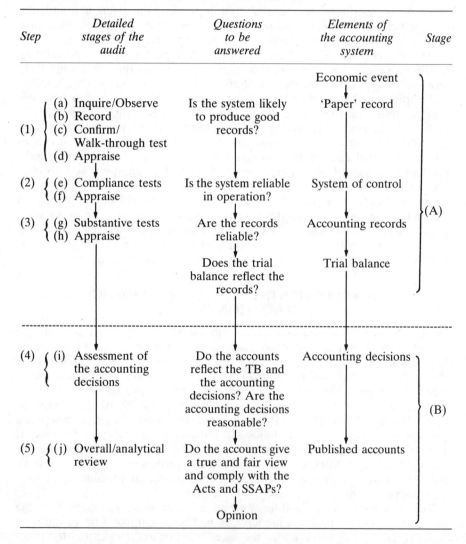

Figure 9.4   Major elements of the auditing and accounting process

The analytical review is defined as

> a substantive auditing procedure that examines the accuracy of accounting balances without considering the details of individual transactions which make up the accounting balance. [It relies] upon an auditor's ability to generate an expectation of an account based upon knowledge of a company's business and operating environment.
>
> (Knechel, 1988, pp. 74–5)

In practice, it involves the review of the current and previous financial statements in the light of operating conditions, and may be assisted by the use of financial ratios and regression techniques. No amount of statistical technique in the analytical review or in the estimation of audit risk can camouflage that the audit plan, the areas of emphasis in the audit, the size of samples, the amount and type of evidence to be sought are matters of professional judgement – all of which must be set into the context of the firm's professional judgement of the levels of materiality that must be applied (Flint, 1988, pp. 108–9); for a more detailed discussion of analytical review, see Chapter 12).

In the terms we used in our earlier discussion on the nature of evidence, we see a more realistic emphasis, from the very start of the audit, on rational argumentation and circumstantial evidence. That is, an emphasis on the 'lowest grade' of evidence. This is a more apposite emphasis in a judgemental activity such as auditing than was the case in the earlier apparent emphasis on the seemingly more 'scientific' and systematic procedures.

The result of this is that whilst the systems-based approach may provide a useful pedagogic model for the audit process, it incorrectly reflects the processes that firms increasingly adopt and improperly suggests that evidence collection (and thus the judgements made upon that evidence) is a systematic, controllable, even arithmetic activity.

AUDIT JUDGEMENT

Judgement is the central activity of the audit. Although 'judgement' and 'decision' can be synonymous terms, the use of 'judgement' rather than 'decision' has the advantage of emphasizing both the imprecision of the criteria against which the choice or conclusion must be made (e.g. the 'truth and fairness' of the financial statements) and the inconclusiveness of the evidence which supports that choice or conclusion. And judgement runs right the way through the audit. It begins when the firm decides to accept an appointment as auditor and continues through the analytical review, the assessment of audit risk, the determination of levels of materiality, the areas of the company's activities on which to concentrate, the size of samples, the form of evidence to be sought, the decision to accept or not the directors' choice of accounting treatment and disclosure and culminates in the conclusions of whether or not the financial statements do show a true and fair view and whether or not to sign off a clean audit report.

It is not possible to establish precise normative criteria against which to assess these judgements and, as we have seen, it is not possible to collate wholly persuasive evidence on these matters. Therefore the audit is an essentially imprecise and impressionistic process. It is a process in which the application of rigorous mathematical and statistical techniques and apparently systematic procedures may have an important role to play but such seemingly 'scientific' mechanisms cannot and must not be used to camouflage the central position that professional judgement must hold.

There is, though, a negative side to this in so far as 'professional judgement' suggests arcane connotations that auditors somehow gain and possess superhuman powers – certainly powers which should not be questioned or investigated (Gambling, 1977, 1985). These powers, if ever they existed, are increasingly seen as fallible because mistaken or poor judgements by accountants – in their role as auditor or not – become more visible, frequent and dramatic. As a result, the last few years have seen a quite dramatic increase in investigations into the audit judgement process as researchers, legislators and auditors alike seek to cast light on to this little-understood but absolutely crucial activity.

'Audit judgement' is the way in which an auditor somehow or other comes to a conclusion on:

1. which evidence to collect;
2. how to collect that evidence;
3. how to evaluate the evidence; and
4. whether or not the financial statements show a true and fair view.

The problem is that 'judgement' is a very big issue and virtually impossible to research successfully. Schandl (1978, p. 188) considered 'judgement' to have five elements: the validity, completeness and communicability of the judgement as well as the competence and the independence of the judge. The process of obtaining and evaluating evidence is an extremely complex and little-understood process in itself (Akresh, Loebbecke and Scott, 1988) and furthermore, as Ashton *et al.* (1988) argue, an audit decision is not determined just by the evidence but by the nature of the audit, the nature of the auditor and the audit environment.

If that is the complexity of the thing we need to understand, our tools for understanding it would need to be appropriately sophisticated. Unfortunately, the research into audit decision-making has tended to focus on the simpler (and therefore less important) issues because they are easier to research. A recent survey by Johnson, Jamal and Berryman (1989) of research into audit decision-making through the usual mechanisms of the Lens model, the assessment of heuristics and biases, and verbal protocols concluded that research had really provided very little insight into audit judgement. This was due principally to the unrealistic settings in which the research methods have been applied, the simplicity of the 'judgements' investigated and the unrealistically mechanistic assumptions made by the researchers about the nature of complex judgements. Furthermore, the most promising (but most subtle and difficult) line of research – called 'process tracing' – has yet to be seriously explored by researchers.

The result of all this is that the central issue within the audit process – the audit judgement – is one about which very little is known. The term 'professional judgement' will continue to be waved around like a magic wand until some serious investigation into its content and import is undertaken.

CONCLUSION

In the simpler, stabler world (with no audit fee pressure) that we find in the auditing textbooks, an auditor can undertake the systematic collection of persuasive evidence in order to conclude Stage A of the audit. For Stage B, the auditor must, even in a simple world, move away from the apparent regularity of the systems-based audit approach and enter a world of speculation, guesswork and best estimates in order to reach a conclusion on the accounting decisions and their impact on the financial statements. The more constrained the auditor and the less stable and simple the world, the more the apparent regularity of Stage A is illusory. It makes sense therefore for the auditor to recognize this explicitly and bring the role of judgement to the fore. This is what the audit procedures of (at least the larger) audit firms seek to do. There is, however, something comforting about being able to emphasize aspects of an audit which are researchable and understandable – statistical sampling, regression analysis and so on – and this has been the charm of the systems-based model shown in Figure 9.4. Recognition that this is a misleading picture has thrown us back on to an emphasis on judgement, and 'professional judgement' is something about which we know very little indeed.

NOTES (AND SUGGESTED FURTHER READING)

1. This chapter specifically concentrates upon audits of UK companies governed by the Companies Acts. Any audit, as an independent attestation to information, will normally involve some final judgement on, e.g., accuracy, efficiency and completeness. All such judgements will be based, to some degree or another, on evidence. Therefore the principal themes of this chapter should be applicable to audits of organizations other than UK companies
2. For an example of the quantification and calculation of audit risk see two articles by Roger Adams (1989a, 1989b) in *Accountancy*. The third article in the series is also interesting in the context of this chapter (Adams, 1989c).
3. Mautz and Sharaf (1961, chap. 5) remains a classic introduction to the subject of evidence and should be read by anyone with a serious interest in the subject. Many of Mautz and Sharaf's ideas have been adopted and developed, albeit eccentrically, by Schandl (1978), who has many interesting ideas on the subject.
4. See also a subsequent article by Keenan and Anderson (1979) which deals with some of the more practical implications of 'directness'.
5. Hatherly (1980) deals with this issue in some depth.
6. Standard texts like Sherer and Kent (1983), Lee (1986) and Woolf (1986) more than adequately cover the detail of the systems-based audit and its relationship with the accounting system.

REFERENCES

Abdel-khalik, A.R. and Solomon, I. (eds.) (1988) *Research Opportunities in Auditing: The Second Decade*, American Accounting Association, Illinois.

Adams, R. (1989a) Risks in the foreground, *Accountancy*, March, pp. 101–4.

Adams, R. (1989b) Risk: a model approach, *Accountancy*, May, pp. 120–2.

Adams, R. (1989c) Risk and the role of the APC, *Accountancy*, December, 1989, pp. 130–3.

Akresh, A.D., Loebbecke, J.K. and Scott, W.R. (1988) Audit approaches and techniques, in Abdel-khalik and Solomon (1988).

American Accounting Association (1973) *A Statement of Basic Auditing Concepts*, Studies in Accounting Research No. 6, AAA, Illinois.

Ashton, R.H., Kleinmuntz, D.N., Sullivan, J.B. and Tomassini, L.A. (1988) Audit decision making, in Abdel-khalik and Solomon (1988).

Auditing Practices Committee (1980) *Audit Evidence*, Auditing Guidelines – Operational, ICAEW, London.

Flint, D. (1988) *Philosophy and Principles of Auditing*, Macmillan, London.

Gambling, T. (1977) Magic, accounting and morale, *Accounting, Organizations and Society*, Vol. 2, no. 2, pp. 141–51.

Gambling, T. (1985) The accountants' guide to the galaxy including the profession at the end of the universe, *Accounting, Organizations and Society*, Vol. 10, no. 4, pp. 415–25.

Gwilliam, D. (1987) *A Survey of Auditing Research*, Prentice-Hall International/ ICAEW, London.

Hatherly, D.J. (1980) *The Audit Evidence Process*, Anderson Keenan Publishing, London.

Higson, A. (1988a) An examination of auditors' philosophies and approaches to the conduct of limited companies audits, Working Paper No. 196, Department of Management Studies, University of Loughborough.

Higson, A. (1988b) Developments in auditing methods, Working Paper No. 197, Department of Management Studies, University of Loughborough.

Hopwood, A.G., Bromwich, M. and Shaw, J. (eds.) (1982) *Auditing Research: Issues and Opportunities*, Pitman, London.

Johnson, P.E., Jamal, K. and Berryman, R.G. (1989) Audit judgement research, *Accounting, Organizations and Society*, Vol. 14, nos. 1/2, pp. 83–99.

Keenan, D. (1979) Evidence and the auditor, *Accountancy*, August, pp. 96–7.

Keenan, D. and Anderson, J. (1979) Evidence and the auditor (part 2), *Accountancy*, September, pp. 119–20.

Kent, D., Sherer, M. and Turley, S. (eds.) (1985) *Current Issues in Auditing*, Harper & Row, London.

Knechel, W.R. (1988) The effectiveness of statistical analytical review as a substantive auditing procedure: a simulation analysis, *The Accounting Review*, Vol. LXIII, no. 1, pp. 74–95.

Lee, T.A. (1986) *Company Auditing*, 3rd edn, Gee, London.

Mautz, R.K. (1958) The nature and reliability of audit evidence, *Journal of Accountancy*, Vol. 105, reprinted in J.H. Brasseaux and J.D. Edwards (eds.) (1973) *Readings in Auditing*, South-Western Publishing, Cincinnati, Ohio.

Mautz, R.K. and Sharaf, H.A. (1961) *The Philosophy of Auditing*, American Accounting Association, New York.

Schandl, C.W. (1978) *Theory of Auditing*, Scholars Book Co., Houston, Texas.

Sherer, M. and Kent, D. (1983) *Auditing and Accountability*, Pitman, London (reprinted 1988, Paul Chapman, London).

Smith, D. (1982) Statistical sampling and analytical review, in Hopwood, Bromwich and Shaw (1982).

Taylor, G. (1985) Audit judgement: risk and materiality, in Kent, Sherer and Turley (1985).

Turley, S. (1985) Empirical research in auditing, in Kent, Sherer and Turley (1985).

Turley, S. and Cooper, M. (1990) *Auditing in the UK – Developments in the Audit Methodologies of Large Accounting Firms*, Prentice-Hall, London.

Woolf, E. (1989) *Auditing Today*, 4th edn, Prentice-Hall, London.

DISCUSSION QUESTIONS

1. The audit process is designed to enable the auditor to build up a body of evidence from which he or she can derive an expert opinion. Explain this process and discuss the worth of this evidence.

2. 'In a "perfect world" all auditors would follow the systems-based audit and thus collect the best quality evidence available to them.'
   (a) Carefully explain the extent to which the systems-based audit can produce the best available evidence.
   (b) Carefully explain the role that 'professional judgement' plays in the systems-based audit.
   (c) Why have the larger audit firms moved away from the systems-based audit? What effect has this had upon the quality of evidence?

3. Discuss the extent to which a *profession* such as auditing should respond to market pressure on audit fees when this must reduce the quality of the evidence and thus the judgements that professional auditors will make, and thereby reduce the value to society of the auditors' privileged position.

4. Speculate upon the extent to which an auditor's judgement is less to do with how best to serve the client (the company and the shareholders) and more to do with protecting the auditor's reputation and being able to defend a decision should the auditor be taken to court.

5. Imagine that you are considering a villa holiday in Sardinia. You have in front of you a brochure with a glowing description of your chosen villa and environs. How would you set about coming to a judgement on the 'truth and fairness' of this description without actually leaving the UK? What type of evidence would you seek? What quality would it be? How would you choose what evidence to seek? How confident would you be in your final judgement?

6. You are the senior in charge of the audit of a company's financial statements for the year ended 31 December 19X8. What evidence would you look for to verify the following amounts appearing in the balance sheet?
   (a) Leasehold buildings stated at £85,000.
   (b) Rates of £18,500 paid in advance.
   (c) Treasury bills £30,000.
   (d) Salemen's commissions £19,500.
   (e) Interest receivable £4,150

7. 'Evidence consists of information and data that can be verifed, is relevant to the matter under consideration, and can influence the auditor in arriving at an opinion. Auditors rely on documentary evidence more than any other type of evidence.' Describe and compare the reliability of the following types of documentary evidence, so far as the auditor is concerned, giving one example of each:
   (a) confirmations received directly by the auditor from third parties;
   (b) documents produced by the client to the auditor which have been prepared by outsiders;
   (c) documents produced by the client to the auditor which have been prepared by personnel within the client company;
   (d) documentary evidence calculated by the auditor from company records.

Questions 6 and 7 are adapted from the examinations of the Association of Certified Accountants and are reproduced by permission of the Education Officer.

10
Audit Risk

Roger Adams

INTRODUCTION

A dictionary definition of the word 'risk' is: 'hazard; chance of bad consequences, loss etc.'. We all face risk every day – when we cross the road we face the risk of being hit by a car, when we buy shares in a privatization issue we face the risk of a Black Monday on the stock market decimating our hard-earned savings. We can minimize the first risk by remembering our highway code; the second by diversifying our investments – not putting all our eggs into one basket.

Entrepreneurs face risks as well: the two most common being that you don't sell enough in the first place to create the potential for sufficient cash flow and that, if you do, your debtors fail to pay. Entrepreneurs can also minimize risk. In the first instance market research would help by providing the best estimate of sales for this particular product. In the second instance there are a variety of possible solutions: factoring (selling for a discount), your debtors, insuring overseas exports sales by the government's Export Credit Guarantee Scheme, and so on.

Auditing firms rarely face any of the risks mentioned above and yet they do face risks. By law auditors are required to form an opinion as to the truth and fairness of a set of financial statements. Various approaches have been devised to discharge this duty but none has yet been invented which eliminates the possibility that the auditor's opinion, delivered through the medium of the annual report to shareholders, might be incorrect because of an undetected error in the financial statements.

Thus audit risk can be defined as: *the probability that the audited financial statements contain a significant error or misstatement.*

If audit risk materializes and the audited accounts are subsequently found to contain a significant misstatement which is not reflected in the auditor's report, the consequence is often financial loss or exposure for the audit firm concerned. The firm is presumed to have delivered a negligent audit opinion, an aggrieved party sues, the auditor may be judged guilty of negligence and will suffer financially both directly (in terms of the costs awarded) and indirectly (through adverse publicity and the opportunity cost of time spent fighting the case).

A final introductory comment concerns the relationship between perceived levels of risk and the related level of preparation which accompanies the activity concerned. Clearly, a mountaineer intent on scaling a hitherto

Roger Adams, M.A., F.C.A., F.C.C.A., is Head of Technical Services for the Chartered Association of Certified Accountants.

unclimbed peak in the Himalayas will undertake a considerable amount of research, will attempt to be at the peak of physical fitness and will have state-of-the-art equipment to hand. The middle-aged climber of Snowdon on a spring Sunday needs to carry out little of this activity – the personal risks are much less.

An auditor undertaking the first audit of a newly floated company specializing in high-technology research and development is engaged in a high-risk activity comparable to that of the Himalayan mountaineer. The reappointed auditor of a private family company with a turnover of £35 million, a known and efficient accounting and control system and a helpful and concerned board of directors may be going for the audit equivalent of the Sunday stroll up Snowdon as far as risk is concerned.

SYSTEMATIZED APPROACHES TO AUDITING

Since prevention is always better than cure, auditors have sought to reduce audit risk to a minimum. In doing so they lessen their own exposure to loss. It is as well to point out from the outset, however, that audit risk can never be completely eliminated and thus auditors will always be exposed to the damaging consequences of a negligence action.

Auditing is a process carried out by human beings who are called upon to make a series of related, but nevertheless subjective, judgements in the course of fulfilling their statutory duties of forming and delivering an opinion on the financial statements. The possibility must always remain that a significant fraud or error remains undetected even by the most meticulous audit procedures carried out by the most conscientious auditor.

Systematizing the audit approach has become the preferred method of minimizing audit risk. The planning, controlling, reviewing, testing, record- ing and reporting aspects of the audit process have all been standardized. The Auditors' Operational Standard issued by the Auditing Practices Committee (APC) in 1980 prescribes the recommended framework for an audit intended to result in the delivery of an opinion as to truth and fairness.

The auditing guidelines issued by the APC provide more detailed descriptions of how each of the individual elements of the Operational Standard should be approached in practice. The audit manuals issued by all sizeable auditing firms complete the standardization picture, containing explicit guidance on planning procedures, sampling approaches and documentation (to name but three areas covered by all audit manuals).

One way of approaching the audit of financial statements would be to adopt a 'top-down' approach: obtain copies of the financial statements and audit downwards (or backwards) to the underlying audit evidence. The problem with this approach is that the auditor focuses on only a defined population of transactions – those that appears on the face of the balance sheet or profit and loss account – and can say little about the completeness of the accounts, or about their freedom from deliberate or accidental misstatement, since top-down audit tests will not be, and could not be, designed to elicit this type of audit assurance.

If a top-down approach to gaining audit assurance is not appropriate for the majority of cases, a 'bottom-up' methodology offers more possibilities because it can start with a non-transaction-based area of investigation: accounting systems and internal controls.

The systems approach to auditing is based on the premise that by studying and evaluating the internal control systems the auditor can form an opinion as to the quality of the accounting system – in particular the completeness of the records and their susceptibility to deliberate or accidental error. This opinion will in turn determine the extent of detailed substantive testing performed upon financial statement items. Recall the mountaineering analogy: the higher the risk that the control systems will fail to detect or prevent error or manipulation, the greater the amount of detailed audit testing required to reduce audit risk to an acceptable level.

The core of the systems approach can be illustrated as follows:

1. ascertain, record and evaluate systems of internal control – by interview, flowchart, internal control questionnaire and evaluation;
2. confirm initial evaluations of internal control systems – programme compliance tests and carry them out;
3. programme balance sheet (substantive) audit work based on results of compliance tests – the weaker the controls the more extensive the substantive testing.

In recent years, however, auditors have become aware that the systems approach, whilst providing a useful framework, does not deal directly with the issue of audit risk. Audit evidence can come from many sources – a knowledge of the organization, its environment and its past history, an assessment of its control systems, analytical review procedures and detailed substantive testing, all play their part in accumulating the totality of audit evidence required to form an opinion. The systems approach as traditionally carried through lacks a means of linking these various sources together in an acceptable quantitative way.

Additionally, it is argued that the systems approach is inflexible in that it may require the auditor to carry out unnecessary compliance testing. It may be quite clear from a review of past history, the 'control environment' and the controls themselves that little assurance can be gained from compliance testing, in which case the auditor should move directly to detailed substantive testing without delay, thus concentrating audit resources in the areas where they are most needed.

Thus the established systems approach of internal control ascertainment, compliance testing and substantive work has given way to a *risk-centred methodology* which provides the auditor with an overall measure of risk whilst at the same time providing a quantitative articulation of each stage of the audit process.

The modern auditor approaches the problem of determining the extent of detailed testing from a purely risk-based perspective. This chapter explains the nature of the risk assessments involved and provides some quantified illustrations of the risk-based approach now recommended by both UK and US standard-setters, and increasingly used in practice by British accounting firms.

Figure 10.1 illustrates how the risk-based approach looks and shows how the material described in the rest of this chapter links into audit sampling procedures.

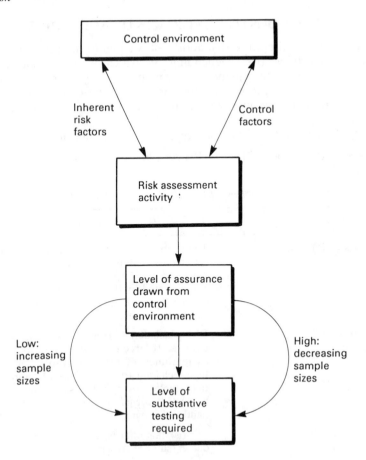

Figure 10.1 An overview of the risk-based approach

AUDIT RISK ASSESSMENT

The first category of risk which is usually considered is the overall level of acceptable audit risk. This is usually defined as the probability that the audited financial statements contain a significant error or misstatement.

Auditors recognize that it is impossible to eliminate audit risk entirely and set a maximum level to the amount of risk they feel able to tolerate. There are no fixed guidelines here, but many auditing firms indicate in their audit manuals that they set tolerable audit risk at the 5 per cent level. Whether or not this really means that they are happy to accept that five out of every hundred audit reports they sign may be incorrect is a moot point – but, as will be shown below, it is difficult to see how they could reduce audit risk to (say) the 1 or 2 per cent level and still remain competitive. One of the quid pro quos for keeping the audit function out of the hands of government is the acceptance of a certain degree of risk, and 5 per cent seems, currently, to be the level most generally accepted by auditors.

THE CONSTITUENT PARTS OF AUDIT RISK

It is argued in the literature that audit risk is equal to the product of various types of underlying risk. Depending on which audit manual or which professional body's recommendations you are looking at you will find slight variations on the definitions and the formulae to be employed. Table 10.1 shows the most commonly encountered definitions of the sub-elements of audit risk.

Using these definitions, the following audit risk models have been derived:

$$AR = IR \times CR \times DR \quad \text{(AICPA, 1983, p. 123; APC, 1987, p. 28)}$$

Table 10.1   Risk definitions

Type of risk	Definition
Audit risk (AR)	The probability that the audited financial statements contain a significant error or misstatement. (An alternative formulation is: the risk accepted by the auditor that an invalid conclusion will be drawn after completion of all audit procedures.)
Inherent risk (IR)	Risk which derives from the characteristics of the entity and of its environment prior to the establishment of internal controls. For example, high-tech industries are inherently more risky than stable ones, and stocks and work in progress are usually considered more risky than cash in hand and at bank.
Control risk (CR)	The risk that internal controls will not prevent or detect material errors.
Detection risk (DR)	The risk that the auditor's substantive procedures and review of the financial statements will not detect material errors.
Analytical review risk (ARR)	The risk that analytical review procedures will not detect material errors (thus a subset of detection risk).
Substantive tests risk (STR)	The risk that material errors will not be detected through the use of detailed substantive testing procedures (also a subset of detection risk.)
Sampling risk (SR)	The risk that the conclusion drawn by the auditor from the results of testing a particular characteristic of a sample of items differs from the conclusion he or she would have drawn had the entire population been tested in like fashion.
Non-sampling risk (NSR)	All those risks of drawing an incorrect conclusion from an audit test that are not due specifically to sampling. This includes, for example, the risk that an auditor will draw an incorrect conclusion about an individual item in the sample tested.

This definition can be expanded by recognizing that detection risk (DR) can be broken down into several sub-categories:

$$AR = IR \times CR \times ARR \times STR \quad \text{(Robson Rhodes, 1988, section 6.1)}$$

A variation on this expanded form is:

$$AR = IR \times CR \times DR \times SR \quad \text{(APC, 1987, app. 1)}$$

Table 10.2 provides an illustration as to the way in which risk percentages can be subjectively attached to some of the risk categories identified above.

Table 10.2 Illustration of risk percentages

Qualitative assessment of assurance	Inherent factors (IR)	Risk percentages Internal control (CR)	Analytical review (ARR)
High	80%	30%	50%
Moderate	90%	60%	70%
Low	100%	80%	90%
None	100%	100%	100%

The objective of this approach is to determine the level of assurance (assurance being the converse of risk) required from the detailed substantive tests, given that the auditor has already gained some assurance from other sources. Three numerical examples will demonstrate how the models outlined above might be used in practice: note that for the purposes of these examples risk is simply classified as high or low – we will examine the underlying factors which give rise to these classifications in a later section.

Example 1 Low-risk company client
- Audit risk (maximum tolerated) = 5 per cent
- Inherent risk (a successful continuing client in a stable industry) = 80 per cent
- Control risk (strong internal control systems and no prior-year adverse audit comments: no recent changes) = 30 per cent

$$AR = IR \times CR \times DR$$

$$DR = \frac{AR}{IR \times CR}$$

$$DR = \frac{0.05}{0.8 \times 0.3}$$

$$= \frac{0.05}{0.24}$$

$$= 0.2083$$

Thus the level of audit assurance (or minium confidence level) required from substantive testing is relatively low:

$$100\% - 20.83\% = 79.17\%$$

Remember: the lower the level of assurance required, the smaller the sample size required for the substantive tests.

Example 2 High-risk company client
- Audit risk (maximum tolerated) = 5 per cent
- Inherent risk (new client, young business, high-tech industry) = 100 per cent
- Control risk (preliminary assessment indicates weak systems with strong possibility of management override) = 70 per cent

$$AR = IR \times CR \times DR$$
$$DR = \frac{0.05}{1.0 \times 0.7}$$
$$= \frac{0.05}{0.7}$$
$$= 0.0714$$

Thus the level of audit assurance (minimum confidence level) required from substantive testing is much higher:

$$100\% - 7.14\% = 92.86\%$$

and the sample size will be correspondingly higher.

Example 3 High-risk company – reduced audit risk
- Audit risk (maximum tolerated) = 2 per cent
- Inherent risk as in Example 2 = 100 per cent
- Control risk as in Example 2 = 70 per cent

$$AR = IR \times CR \times DR$$
$$DR = \frac{0.02}{1.0 \times 0.7}$$
$$= \frac{0.02}{0.7}$$
$$= 0.0285$$

Thus the level of audit assurance (minimum confidence level) required from substantive testing rises yet again, to:

$$100\% - 2.85\% = 97.15\%$$

and the sample size will rise accordingly.

Summary
From the three examples illustrated it can be seen that the more reliance an auditor can place on systems of internal control, and the more assurance he or she can obtain from alternative sources (a review of the industry/environment/client background and a full analytical review) the less he or she need rely upon detailed substantive audit work. The weaker the systems and the less reassuring the review of inherent factors proves, the more the auditor must focus upon detailed substantive work as a mechanism for reducing audit risk to the maximum amount considered tolerable.

Thus: 'Substantive testing is, in a sense, the balance of audit evidence and assurance required in order to fulfil the acceptable level of audit risk' (Robson Rhodes, 1988, section 6.1).

'MAGIC NUMBERS' – HOW TO ASSESS THE VARIOUS CATEGORIES OF RISK

Audit risk

As has already been stated, audit (or ultimate) risk is often arbitrarily assessed at the 5 per cent level. Why 5 per cent? It is a statistical fact that when carrying out a two-tailed hypothesis test, something in the region of 95 per cent of the population lies between plus and minus 1.96 standard deviations from the mean. Perhaps as a consequence of having always been taught that 95 per cent is a 'magic number' auditors have never been able to shake off its supposed importance. As has already been shown in the quantitative examples above, audit risk is an important input into the determination of substantive or detection risk.

The lack of any theoretical justification for using a 95 per cent level of confidence as the audit risk benchmark and the wholly subjective nature of the other risk assessments described below should not be seen to undermine the risk-based approach. Modern audits require a sample-based approach to be taken and thus audit judgements have to be made concerning the nature, timing and extent of the substantive tests.

It is a fact of life that these judgements cannot be made until the auditor has considered what assurance has already been provided by alternative sources of audit evidence. The consistent and intelligent application of the risk-based approach must be seen as an improvement on the traditional systems approach, which lacked any unifying theory and forced individual auditors into increasingly arbitrary decisions as to how much of what should be tested when.

Inherent risk

Table 10.2 showed that only a limited amount of reassurance can be gained from background knowledge about the client, its management and its past history. For many smaller clients the knowledge that managerial override of controls is a possibility will mean that the auditor refuses to accept any assurance from inherent factors. In other cases the client's past audit history may have justification for accepting at face value the Mautz and Sharaf (1961, p. 48) postulate that 'in the absence of evidence to the contrary what has held true for the enterprise in the past will hold true in the future'.

Reworking Example 1 above to exclude the limited amount of assurance which may be gained from inherent factors shows that the amount of assurance required from substantive testing increases as a result:

Data as per Example 1 except that inherent risk is omitted entirely from the equation:

$$DR = \frac{0.05}{0.3}$$
$$= 16.67\%$$

Thus the substantive assurance required rises from 80 per cent with some inherent assurance to 83.33 per cent without.

Control risk

In the determination of the timing, extent and nature of the substantive tests, the auditor continues to derive much of his assurance from the knowledge that there either does or does not exist a properly functioning system of internal control. To that extent it can be argued that the central pillar of the traditional systems-based audit approach remains intact (although considerably embellished and woven into a more complex design).

Once again it will be clear from Table 10.2 that the wider range of values attributable to control risk demonstrates the continued importance attached to this measure in assessing the amount of assurance to be derived from substantive testing procedures.

Analytical review risk

As the fully expanded audit risk formula suggests, and as all practitioners are intuitively aware, audit evidence comes from many sources. Analytical review techniques (ARTs) have been around for many years but it is only comparatively recently (1988) that the Auditing Practices Committee has issued formal guidance on the topic. It seems likely that there remain some small firms which do not use ARTs at all and many which fail to document them adequately. The guidance offered by the APC is partly to blame for this latter shortcoming as it does not offer any detailed advice on what ARTs to use when, or how to interpret the results.

Auditors can draw more comfort from ARTs than they can from inherent factors simply because when interpreting the results of ARTs they are at least focusing on the current period of real trading activity, although often relying on summarized information and internally generated management accounts. As a result, the range of values shown in Table 10.2 attributable to analytical review assurance is wider than that permissible for reliance on inherent factors.

Substantive tests

Substantive tests risk represents the balancing figure in the audit risk equation. By knowing how much overall risk the auditor is prepared to assume, by gaining some reassurance from knowledge of the client's background, from evaluating the internal control system and from analytical review procedures we are able to determine just how much detailed substantive testing is required and what degree of assurance must be gained from it.

INPUTS TO THE AUDIT RISK MODEL

Figure 10.2 shows diagrammatically the sources of inputs to the various elements in the audit risk model (ARM). It will be observed that whilst some of the input techniques are familiar, many are sufficiently contemporary for there to be no authoritative guidance available at present from the APC. This means that actual practice is bound to be fragmented, with larger auditing firms attempting to use *all* the techniques identified but setting unique limits

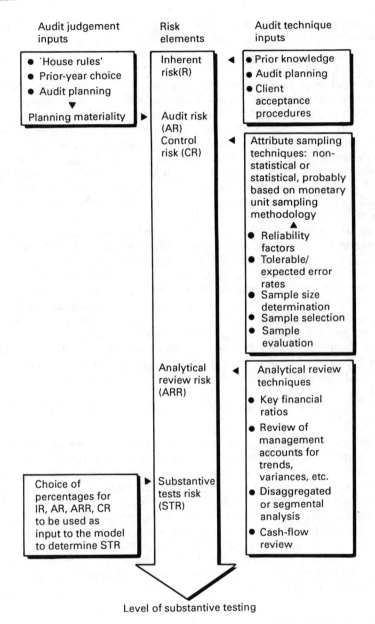

Figure 10.2 Elements of the audit risk model (reproduced by permission of *Accountancy*)

to their application, whilst smaller firms pay lip service to the more well-known techniques and ignore the others.

Audit risk and 'house rules'

Although Figure 10.2 indicates the possibility of a degree of flexibility in the choice of an acceptable overall level of audit risk, the reality is (as was pointed out above) that 5 per cent is still the level everyone is trying achieve. Prior-year experience of the audit engagement in question seems to be of little relevance, as does knowledge gained from audit planning activities.

'House rules', as set out in the audit manuals of the major auditing firms, provide the only important input to the decision as to where to pitch the audit risk level. In effect both prior-year experience and audit planning knowledge would seem to fit much better on the other side of the diagram as inputs into 'inherent risk'.

Should the level of overall risk a firm is prepared to accept vary from year to year and from client to client or should it remain steady? The advantage of the ARM is that one can actually bake one's cake *and* eat it – audit risk can be held at a uniform rate across all audits and all years because the specific data relevant to a particular audit can be manipulated across the right-hand side of the ARM. The greater the initial assurance from inherent factors, the control system and analytical review, the less is required from detailed substantive testing, and the less time is spent on substantive work.

Alternatively, if preliminary assessments of IR, CR and ARR are very poor then there is not a lot of point in delaying and carrying out masses of redundant compliance tests. Just move straight on into detailed substantive work.

So house rules on the acceptable level of audit risk exposure have several advantages.

1. Standardization at a given percentage must reduce the risk that individual auditors will have momentary aberrations and equate an audit client with low or minimal inherent risks as one where the firm can accept a much higher level of audit risk. The result of this might be to reduce compliance or substantive testing to an unacceptably low level.
2. By focusing on the three or four terms on the right-hand side of the equation and allowing them to vary whilst holding the left side constant, the auditor relates those audit judgements which *have* to be made to practical audit techniques and allows for an easy, understandable and justifiable transfer of audit resources based upon the outcome of the underlying audit work.

Planning materiality

The judgement concerning an overall level of audit risk that can be accepted is quite different from the decision concerning 'planning materiality' – a measure which will be an important input into the sampling plan used later, at the compliance and substantive stages of the audit. Like audit risk, however, planning materiality represents a positive choice by the auditor – and once the choice is made, subsequent changes of heart need a great deal of justification.

'Planning materiality' refers to the extent to which the true value of a population (in either monetary or pure numeric terms) can vary from the stated 'book figures' before the divergence becomes significant enough to warrant adjustment. It is that amount of variation which, if known to the investor/lender/third party, would cause the relevant decision-maker to arrive at a *different* decision – presumably a different decision regarding the optimal allocation of resources.

Table 10.3 demonstrates the range of possibilities which underlie the planning materiality choice; the table is similar to that presented by Chandler (1985).

It is usually regarded as highly important that the planning materiality level should be both set *and* approved before the audit commences. Later judgements concerning the acceptability or otherwise of sample results must then be taken in the context of an agreed, predetermined materiality level.

Inherent risk and knowledge of client

The practical audit procedures which underlie the formation of an audit opinion as to the level of inherent risk were indicated in Figure 10.2 and are discussed in more detail below.

1. *Prior knowledge of client* is really the province of the engagement partner and the audit manager – audit seniors and juniors tend to move on too quickly for them to build up a body of knowledge concerning a particular audit client.
2. *Audit planning material* will differ according to whether or not the engagement is a new or continuing one. The difference between the inputs in item 1 above and this item is likely to be a matter of detail about industry, technology, product, management, employees, financial ratios, cash flow, deadlines, parent and related companies, and so on. Audit planning material will, or should, encompass all these points in some detail – simple 'prior knowledge' may be too personalized and indefinite.
3. *Client acceptance procedures* are increasingly becoming standardized – with forms to fill in which must be placed on the permanent audit file. Many of the items mentioned in 2 above will be included but it is likely that there will be some attempt at risk assessment – Table 10.4 incorporates a number of points concerning the inherent risk of a new client.

By taking inherent risk into account the auditor is simply saying that some clients *are* more risky than others – the factors identified in Table 10.4 are typical. By making a small reduction, in the case of a less inherently risky client, from 100 per cent assurance demanded, the auditor is saving time and money. The assumption that control and analytical review risks are also reduced from the maximum implies that the amount of detailed substantive work can be reduced by a small amount.

It is clear that many auditors are, however, unwilling to make any allowance for apparently satisfactory inherent risk reviews. The choice is entirely subjective and the impact on overall sample size at the substantive testing stage of the audit is probably marginal. Keeping the inherent risk factor at 100 per cent in the equation allows auditors to feel that they are erring on the side of caution (which is true) in the belief that the internal control review is a more reliable pointer to the degree of assurance required from detailed substantive testing (which may not be quite so true).

Table 10.3   Examples of practice-based materiality guidance levels

Bases for estimation of materiality	Firm A (%)	Firm B (%)	Firm C (%)	Firm D (%)
Profit and loss items:				
Turnover	0.5–1	2–4	0.5–1	1
Gross profit	— not disclosed —			5
Pre-tax profit	5–10	5–10	5–10	10
Balance sheet items to:				
Total assets	1–2		0.5–1	1 (net assets)
employed				5 (working capital)

Table 10.4   Client acceptance procedures – criteria for inclusion in an audit checklist

Risk factor	Level of business risk	
	Lower	Higher
The state of the economy in which the company operates	Healthy	Depressed/stagnant
The type of industry within which the company is located	Established/mature stable; relatively uninfluenced by external conditions	Relatively new – susceptible to external changes
The company's management philosophy	Conservative	Aggressive
The company's control environment including possibility of management override	Strong administrative controls; control-conscious	Weak controls; highly centralized management structure

	Unqualified opinions from prior audits; no disagreement; few recorded adjustments	No prior audit history; previous adverse/qualified opinions; unusually high auditor turnover
The company's previous audit history		
Rate of turnover for top management and board	Low	High
Company's financial and operating position	Strong	Weak
Company's existing or potential litigation	Insignificant	Significant
Business reputation of managers and owners	Good	Poor
The experience of the managers and principal owners	High level	Low level
Ownership status	Non-public	Public
Client understanding of auditor's role/responsibilities	Clear	Vague
Conflicts of interest, regulatory problems	Insignificant	Significant
Location of company	Large city	Small community
Level of business acumen in community where company operates	Low	High

(Reproduced by courtesy of *Accountancy*.)

Control risk and attribute sampling

Although the next section assumes that the auditing firm uses a formal statistical sampling plan, involving attribute sampling at the compliance test stage and monetary unit sampling for variables at the substantive stage, it is worth noting that not all audit firms use such highly formalized approaches. Indeed, the draft auditing guideline *Audit Sampling* (APC, 1987) makes clear reference to both statistical and non-statistical sampling approaches.

Compliance testing for attributes (i.e. correct/incorrect conditions rather than monetary variances) should, ideally, leave the auditor in a position to say something constructive about the risk that errors will not be picked up by the systems of internal control which have just been reviewed (i.e. the 'control risk'). There are various ways of phrasing the results of such tests. Systems could be weak (high risk), moderate (moderate risk) or strong (low risk). For any of these categories the auditor's evaluation might be phrased: we are 95 per cent confident that the error rate in the population will not exceed, say, plus or minus 3 per cent. To fit into the ARM format, however, the audit assessment must be translated into percentage terms, as shown in Table 10.5.

The outcome of the attribute sampling process will thus directly affect the final element in the ARM by determining the extent to which the auditor feels able to rely on the controls systems, and in doing so can reduce the extent and severity of his or her detailed substantive tests.

Analytical review risk: the APC guideline

The APC guideline on analytical review procedures (APC, 1988) points out that analytical review should not be restricted to a simple financial ratio analysis towards the end of the audit. On the contrary, it is an important tool in the audit planning stage (getting to know the business and the industry) and should be used throughout the audit.

In the context of the audit risk model, analytical review may be recognized as a specific source of audit assurance. The reduction in other required assurance arising from a satisfactory set of analytical review procedures is a matter of audit judgement. Earlier in this chapter it was suggested that a highly satisfactory result could lead to a 50 per cent reduction in the degree of other assurance demanded as compared with only 20 per cent for inherent factors.

Whatever figure one eventually settles upon, it is important that it emerges from a *structured consideration of analytical review opportunities* which is sufficiently portable to be of use across a range of audit clients. Analytical review should not remain, as still seems common, an *ad hoc* audit technique used by keen, recently qualified auditors to impress (and confuse?) their elders.

Table 10.6 sets out some analytical review procedures commonly used by auditors.

THE NEXT STEP

The next step is to link the assurance required from substantive tests of detail to audit sampling techniques, which will determine the precise extent of the substantive testing required – this will involve a consideration of the 'materiality level' judged appropriate.

Table 10.5   Assessment of risks within the Audit Risk Model

Audit risk		Inherent risk		Control risk		Analytical risk		Substantive test risk
5%	=	90%	×	60%	×	50%	×	18.5% (residual)
Standard audit risk		Moderate degree of inherent risk		Moderate degree of assurance from testing internal control		High degree of assurance from AR procedures		The extent of final substantive tests determined by the formula

Table 10.6   Analytical review procedures

Ratio analysis	Financial and management ratios to establish trends and relationships
Segmental analysis	Disaggregating client operations in order to analyse different classes of business
Variance analysis	Comparisons of actual against budget to identify loss of control
Regression analysis	Measuring the significance of expected relationships in order to model or predict behaviour
Ageing analysis	Stratifying debtors, creditors or stocks according to age, thus enabling the audit to focus on material items which could affect profit and loss

Detection risk and monetary unit sampling

It has been demonstrated above that the outcome of manipulating the audit risk model results in a 'level of demand from assurance' from substantive testing. As can be seen, the results of the workings in Table 10.5 are that detection risk equals 18.5 per cent and that audit assurance required from the detailed substantive tests must therefore be in the region of 81.5 per cent.

It is not possible to give here a comprehensive review of sampling procedures. By way of illustration, under monetary unit sampling (MUS) the way in which the audit assurance required is fed into the determination of sample parameters can, however, be described in outline.

1. Audit assurance required (calculated from the tables) translates into a reliability (R) factor.

2. $\text{Sample size} = \dfrac{\text{R factor} \times \text{Population value}}{\text{Tolerable error (materiality)}}$

3. $\text{Sampling interval} = \dfrac{\text{Population value}}{\text{Sample size}}$

4. Evaluation of MU samples must be carried out strictly according to the sampling plan used.

The draft auditing guideline *Audit Sampling* (APC, 1987) provides clear guidance on the evaluation of this type of sample.

CONCLUSION

This chapter has attempted to related the audit risk model to the actual practical techniques auditors are using. It is demonstrated that, provided the auditor is prepared to make a series of subjective judgements concerning the extent to which risk is reduced (or assurance increased), the risk model provides a useful means of articulating what were once disparate stages of the audit.

It is suggested that the issue of subjective judgements will always remain with us and thus it will be impossible to reduce audit risk to zero. Intelligent and consistent application of risk-based techniques can, however, improve the overall quality of the audit and provide the auditor with greater assurance that the audit opinion finally delivered will be correct.

REFERENCES

AICPA (1983) *Audit Sampling* (Audit and Accounting Guide) AICPA, New York.
APC (1987) *Audit Sampling*, Exposure Draft, APC, London.
APC (1988) *Analytical Review*, Auditing Guideline, APC, London.
Chandler, R. (1985) Materiality: does it need to be a guessing game? *Accountancy*, February, pp. 84–6.
Mautz, R.A. and Sharaf, H.A. (1961) *The Philosophy of Auditing*, American Accounting Association, New York.
Robson Rhodes (1988) *Audit Manual*, Robson Rhodes, London.

ACKNOWLEDGEMENT

The author would like to thank *Accountancy* for permission to reproduce several of the figures used in this chapter.

RECOMMENDED READING

Official publications
Auditing Practices Committee (APC) (1984) *Materiality*, Audit Brief (by T.A. Lee), APC, London.
Auditing Practices Committee (APC) (1987) *Audit Sampling*, Auditing Guideline Exposure Draft, APC, London.
Auditing Practices Committee (APC) (1987) *Audit Sampling*, Draft Audit Brief, APC, London.
Auditing Practices Committee (APC) (1988) *Analytical Review*, Auditing Guideline, APC, London.
Auditing Practices Committee (APC) (1989) *Risk Management for Auditors*, Audit Brief (by E. Woolf), APC, London.
International Federation of Accountants (IFAC) (1989) *The Assessment of Inherent and Control Risks and Its Impact on Substantive Procedures*, Proposed Audit Guideline, IFAC Exposure Draft 31, February, IFAC, New York.

Other publications
Adams, R. (1989) *Auditing*, Longman, London.
Alderman, W. and Tabor, R.H. (1989) The case for risk driven audits, *Journal of Accountancy*, March, pp. 55–61.

DISCUSSION QUESTIONS

1. This chapter has discussed risk minimization from an audit testing point of view. Auditors also seek to minimize risk by instituting quality control measures in their offices. Identify five important areas where quality control might be used effectively.
2. Consider the importance of inherent risk factors in determining the level of audit testing to be carried out. How can the auditor 'maximize' the benefit to be gained from a consideration of these factors?

3. To what extent is the adoption of a risk-based auditing approach likely to affect the auditor's liability for negligence?
4. What are the implications of the risk-based approach for audit management?

11
Planning for an Effective and Efficient Audit in a Computerized Environment

Jon Grant

Today's business environment reflects accelerating technological advancement. Innovations in data processing are increasing the volumes of transactions that are being processed and developments in telecommunications are changing the way transactions are being initiated and conveyed. The 'black box' is becoming more sophisticated and businesses are becoming increasingly dependent on computerized information systems (CISs).

Effective use of technological advancements can change the way businesses operate and is often a key factor in competitive terms. For example, some manufacturers have utilized advanced inventory control and purchase order systems to facilitate just-in-time purchasing from their key suppliers. This has enabled them to reduce the costs of financing and warehousing materials inventory.

However, with the increased dependence on CIS comes a greater need for appropriate control systems to be in place to ensure that systems are operating properly and without interruption. An error created by a faulty system can be damaging to the financial well-being of a company. Looking again at the manufacturer, an error in the computerized purchase order system that goes undetected can cause significant financial damage. Breakdowns in the system could result in production dislocation and customer dissatisfaction.

THE EXPANDING ROLE OF THE PUBLIC ACCOUNTANT

Client expectations of the public accountant have increased dramatically in the last decade. The audit engagement, once seen as largely a regulatory necessity, is now being viewed as an opportunity to gain valued external advice from the public accountant on the business's operations, particularly with respect to the performance of the entity's CIS.

The increased public expectations have led authoritative bodies in countries around the world to publish pronouncements emphasizing the need to understand the client's control systems. These pronouncements, coupled

Jon Grant, B.A., F.C.A., is currently Price Waterhouse's world director of audit research and technology, based in Morristown, New Jersey, USA. Prior to this appointment he was the UK audit methods partner and was involved in a number of ICAEW activities including membership of the Research Board and the Auditing Research Foundation. The views and opinions expressed in this chapter are those of the author, and do not necessarily reflect those of Price Waterhouse.

with the frequent expectations of clients to have their auditors advise them on their CIS, have led to an expanded role for the auditor's services.

Increasingly, auditors are aware of the importance of effective planning, to develop an audit approach that addresses the client's expectations at the same time as gathering the evidence required for the audit opinion. Audit firms' methodologies, which provide the structure for planning an audit, often explicitly recognize not only 'audit risk', but also what might be referred to as 'client service risk'. Audit risk is defined as the risk the auditor accepts that the financial statements contain a material undetected error or irregularity after the audit is complete and an unqualified opinion has been issued. Client service risk is the risk that the auditor may not deliver high-quality service by failing to obtain an understanding of the client's needs and expectations.

The two main alternative strategies for gaining audit satisfaction sufficient to reduce audit risk to a low level are: a substantive audit approach and a systems-based approach, which combines reliance on the client's control system with a relatively smaller amount of substantive audit work. In today's business environment, the latter approach involves obtaining a detailed understanding of the client's CIS and a knowledge of the operating effectiveness of the controls integrated into the CIS design.

The auditor's approach therefore must be designed to be flexible, allowing for an integration of client service needs into the audit plan. Where the client has no expectations beyond that of the auditor rendering an opinion on the financial statements and where there are no persuasive reasons to adopt a systems-based approach, the audit approach can be substantive. Where the processing environment is complex or where client service expectations exist with respect to CIS and related controls, the audit strategy can be based on obtaining control satisfaction.

THE FRAMEWORK OF RISK AND SATISFACTION

Audit risk is controlled and reduced to acceptable levels by means of obtaining the appropriate amount of audit satisfaction. As is described elsewhere in this book, risk-based approaches to auditing rely on drawing satisfaction from a variety of sources in a multiplicative model where:

Overall audit risk = Inherent risk × Control risk × Detection risk

By assessing the inherent risk of error in the financial statements and the risk that such error will not be eliminated by the internal control system (control risk), the auditor can determine the amount of risk that can be tolerated (or satisfaction required) with the substantive audit procedures (detection risk) and still leave the overall risk of error at an acceptable level.

The assessment of inherent risk is cental to determining the appropriate amount of satisfaction required from audit procedures. Inherent risk is defined as the susceptibility of the financial statements to material error or irregularity, before recognizing the effectiveness of the control systems. The assessment is made by considering factors that make the financial statements more prone to error. For example, some factors relevant to the assessment of inherent risk are related to the nature of the client's business (e.g. the client's industry is subject to rapid development of new products and aggressive marketing, increasing the risk of product obsolescence), the nature of the financial statement accounts (e.g. subjectivity or complexity of accounting methods in use) and the nature of information and accounting systems (e.g. nature, extent and complexity of CIS design and capability of handling varying levels of activity). Other factors such as the extent of management's influence on decisions affecting the financial statements and its motivations to overstate or understate results are considered along with the prior occurrence of error. Consideration of these factors in detail supports the auditor's professional judgement as to the level of inherent risk and consequently the amount of audit evidence required.

The assessment of control risk is central to the determination of how much audit evidence can be obtained from relying on the client's control system to detect material error. Control risk is defined as the risk that the control systems, including internal audit, may fail to prevent or detect material error or irregularity on a timely basis. If control risk is sufficiently low, audit satisfaction can be obtained from *control satisfaction* and the amount of evidence required from substantive audit procedures declines.

CONTROL RISK IN COMPUTERIZED SYSTEMS

Over the years, the auditor's assessment of control risk has been made more complicated by rapid technological advances in CIS design, which have an impact on the way transactions are executed, processed and accumulated. This has led to the development of structured methodologies to evaluate the design and operating effectiveness of client CIS and related controls, to serve not only to evaluate control risk but to meet any client expectations regarding understanding their systems and providing valuable recommendations for improvement.

The assessment of control risk can be methodically determined as follows.

1. Identify the key activities of the client's business. A high-level under-standing of the system(s) supporting the business activities should be obtained considering both audit and client service needs.
2. Examine the design of the client's system in order to identify potentially key management and independent controls (high-level direct controls designed to detect material errors).
3. Obtain an overall understanding of the flow of transactions and related information.
4. Specify the main features of the systems relating to each business activity to aid identification of potentially key processing controls (manual and computerized) and computerized processing functions (CPFs).
5. Consider the underlying general controls to determine if reliance can be placed on direct controls and CPFs.

Incorporated into the auditor's approach to internal control and CIS are certain concepts which are critical to the effectiveness of the control evaluation.

1. Management and independent controls should be evaluated separately from processing controls and CPFs because they reflect the way management controls the business and they are detective in nature. However, consideration should be given to the extent to which these

controls are dependent on the computerized processing of transactions and directly related information.

2. The identification of the main features of the control systems is an important aspect of understanding the flow of transactions. They incorporate the main features of the CIS, with respect to the flow of transactions, namely:

   (a) *Access*: Access to the transaction processing functions and related data records should be restricted to authorized persons.

   (b) *Input*: Transactions and related data should be entered for processing accurately, completely and only once.

   (c) *Rejection*: Rejected or unmatched transactions and related data should be isolated, analysed and corrected in a timely manner.

   (d) *Processing*: Transactions and related data should be completely and accurately processed in the proper accounting period, including the transfer of data to other systems.

   Specifying each system's features provides a comprehensive framework for assessing the adequacy of processing controls and CPFs.

3. General controls (segregation of incompatible duties and CIS department controls) are normally not considered in isolation; rather, they are evaluated with specific direct controls in mind (i.e. potentially key management and independent controls and/or processing controls and CPFs). CIS department controls are considered in the following categories:

   (a) *Organization*: The organization structure and operating procedures of the CIS department should provide a data processing environment that is conducive to the preparation of reliable financial information.

   (b) *Program changes*: Changes to application software should be restricted to those which are appropriately authorized and are accurately input.

   (c) *Access*: Access to data files or application programs used to process transactions, for the purpose of changing data or programs, should be restricted to authorized persons.

Within each firm's audit methodology, particular procedures will be used to facilitate the assessment of control risk. Each of the CIS control categories noted above will be evaluated in terms of the way they relate specifically to the various business activities of the client.

The auditor's primary concern is not with individual transactions and balances but with the financial statements as a whole. Accordingly, one way to approach audit planning is to start from the financial statements and work back to the business operations and the potential risks affecting the quality of information in those statements. This 'top-down' approach is illustrated in Figure 11.1.

The auditor should begin by focusing on the terms of reference for the engagement; considering client service objectives as well as the audit opinion on the financial statements in the audit plan. The emphasis can then be placed on the client's business organization and how its important *business units* function. This approach enables the auditor to focus on those aspects of the business which significantly affect the financial statements and to reduce the

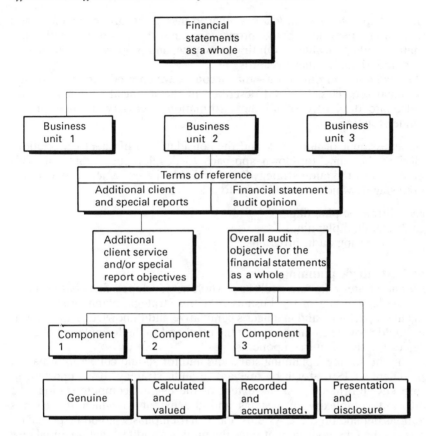

Figure 11.1 A framework for audit planning

effort in other aspects. This emphasis provides a structure for assessing risks and for determining audit engagement strategy. The business units may be subsidiaries, divisions, geographic locations or other significant segments of the business. Each business unit is then subdivided into manageable parts, which we may call 'components'. A component may be a financial statement amount, or part thereof, or a group of transactions within one or more financial statement notes. Within each component the auditor's objective is to ensure the validity of a limited number of assertions about the financial statement information. These assertions reflect the implicit and explicit representations by management regarding the financial statement accounts. Assertions can be grouped into four broad categories.

1. *Genuineness* – that transactions have occurred and balances exist, representing rights or obligations, and that transaction have been appropriately authorized.
2. *Calculation and valuation* – that transactions and balances are shown at their proper amount and reflect all events and circumstances that affect their underlying value, in accordance with applicable accounting principles.

3. *Recording and accumulation* – that transactions are completely and accurately recorded in the proper accounts in accordance with their nature and applicable accounting principles, and properly accumulated in the underlying financial records.
4. *Presentation and disclosure* – that accounts are correctly and consistently summarized, classified and described in the financial statements, with adequate disclosure of all the information necessary to their proper understanding.

The assessment of audit risk and the consideration of client expectations can follow the same top-down approach to develop the audit plan. This development of the audit strategy for an individual engagement is performed in three stages, which we shall refer to as:

Stage 1: Strategic planning.
Stage 2: Detailed planning.
Stage 3: Preparing audit programs.

Stage 1 Strategic planning
The broad strategy for the audit as a whole is developed first, based on an overall understanding of the business. At this strategic planning stage, the engagement partner's and manager's cumulative audit knowledge and experience should provide a major input to the plan, and to the formulation of audit strategies for significant components.

During the strategic planning stage and auditor should collect information on the client's CIS that will be relevant to audit strategy. It is important to capture key information on the extent of the client's computerization, the nature and complexity of systems and the extent to which the client's operations depend on these systems. Particular emphasis should be placed on changes to the CIS environment since the previous audit so that potential new risks and new opportunities for client service can be identified. Information obtained on these issues can assist in the development of audit strategy and can influence decisions as to the need for specialized CIS skills on the engagement team.

The preliminary decisions on the audit approach should be fully documented, capturing key planning information, on a component-by-component basis, including:

1. identification of inherent and control risk factors;
2. preliminary assessments of inherent and control risk levels;
3. expected audit approach; and
4. detailed instructions on work to be carried out in the detailed planning stage.

Planning information and decisions could be documented on microcomputer-based audit planning packages.

Stage 2 Detailed planning
The detailed planning stage should focus on the component level, where a more detailed analysis is undertaken of inherent and control risks as they

apply to each of the assertions. Detailed planning will typically be performed for significant components of the audit. This phase should usually be performed by senior field staff under the direction of the audit manager. The inherent and control risk assessments can be analysed in more detail using two principal approaches:

1. performance of what might be called diagnostic analysis;
2. updating the auditor's knowledge of the client's accounting systems.

Diagnostic analysis can be employed during detailed planning to enhance the auditor's understanding of the nature and volume of transactions and balances, primarily as a means of identifying components where risk may have changed. Examples of the types of diagnostic procedures which can be used during detailed planning are:

1. analyses of the nature and volume of transactions, including significant or unusual transactions;
2. analyses of account balances, including details of major elements (e.g. significant items, ageing analsis);
3. relationships (e.g. ratio analyses) between transactions, balances and external indicators (such as general economic and specific industry trends).

Any new risk factors identified from these procedures should be documented for review by the audit manger and engagement partner to update their knowledge of the client's business and to approve any modifications to the inherent and control risks assessments.

Updating the auditor's knowledge of the client's accounting systems should be an annual process, with information on systems and control being updated from the prior year using inquiry, observation and reperformance techniques. As part of the update process, some satisfaction on the adequate operation of controls may be obtained. If further evidence of control is required, specific key controls should be identified for more extensive testing.

Having fine-tuned the assessments of inherent and control risk, the senior field staff, under the direction provided by the audit partner and manager in the strategic plan, should prepare the detailed audit approach. This stage involves selecting from the available range of audit procedures those relevant to each of the typical components of the audit. The selection process must take into account the need to reduce audit risk and obtain sufficient satisfaction; that is, procedures should be selected which address the inherent risk factors identified in the audit plan. Each relevant assertion category in each relevant component must be considered. The extent of audit work will vary with the extent of inherent risk and the extent of control test procedures will vary with the assessment of control risk and the decision to rely on controls to obtain audit satisfaction. During this selection process consideration can also be given to the client service objectives and to the cost-efficiency of each procedure. It is the correlation of risk factors and audit procedures on an assertion-by-assertion basis that provides a framework for the auditor to ensure that all representations by client management embedded in the financial statements are adequately considered and that the audit effort is properly directed towards their confirmation.

Stage 3 Preparing audit programs
The third stage of the plan is to prepare the audit programs, which are designed to ensure that the audit plan is properly executed. The procedures selected should be organized into an appropriate order of execution, allocating them to different audit visits. Detailed steps should be added to procedures to clarify the requirements for execution, particularly for those procedures to be performed by the more junior, inexperienced staff. References must also be added to clarify the client staff to be contacted while performing the procedure, where client documents can be obtained and to what extent the client will assist in execution (e.g. extracting specified documents for the auditor's examination). Properly developed audit programs can help to ensure that the audit is executed in both an effective and an efficient manner.

Revising planning decisions
The structure of planning outlined so far suggests a sequential process with each element and procedure being dealt with in turn. It is also worth noting that there may also be many situations which arise during the audit when planning decisions need to be reviewed in the light of additional information which becomes available, changes in the client's circumstances and the auditor's experience in implementing planning decisions and carrying out programmed procedures. Such review could lead to changes at any of the three levels of planning identified above: strategy, choice of detailed procedures and programming their execution.

SUMMARY

This chapter has provided an overview of the planning activity in the modern audit. Planning has become increasingly important with developments in the auditing environment in recent years. Economic factors have promoted an emphasis on efficiency in the choice of audit approach and the selection of detailed procedures, changing expectation have influenced audit objectives as auditors strive to provide a service which responds to these demands, and the complexity of business systems and records has necessitated a more thoughtful and considered approach to the collection of evidence in each specific audit. Computerized accounting and information systems have a particularly important influence on what is both desirable and possible for the auditor to undertake in audit work.

In order to ensure that planned audit work is both purposeful and efficient, it is important that the auditor plans in a way which reflects identification of the audit objectives associated with the financial statements and consideration of the alternatives means by which those objectives can be met. By starting from the financial statements, the underlying business activities they report and the qualities or assertions which should hold true therein, the auditor can devise an appropriate audit strategy for each engagement. Focusing on the important assertions involves asking: what can go wrong which would affect the validity of each assertion for the financial statements? Audit planning then becomes a process of assessing the risks associated with these potential errors and making choices on the design of the audit approach and the selection of audit procedures in order to test such risks and ensure that they are reduced to a level which the auditor feels is sufficiently low to warrant the intended audit opinion.

DISCUSSION QUESTIONS

1. What influences should the auditor respond to and take account of in identifying the objectives of the audit which are to be satisfied in the work programme that results from audit planning?
2. How should the auditor go about obtaining an understanding of a client's business and operations before planning the audit approach on a new client?
3. What special problems might be encountered in audit planning as a result of a client's computerized accounting and information system?
4. What criteria would you suggest should govern the significant judgements to be made by the auditor at each stage of the planning process?

12
The Rise of Analytical Auditing Procedures

Andrew Higson

INTRODUCTION

Auditing practice is constantly evolving. Nowhere is this more apparent than in the case of analytical review. The term 'analytical review' was little used in the auditing literature of the late 1960s and very early 1970s. Its first explicit mention in the American auditing standards appears to have been in 1972, in SAP No. 54 (AICPA, 1972). The late 1970s and early 1980s saw a great increase in its use by auditors (e.g. Higson, 1987), and by 1987 the APC's publication *True and Fair* (APC, 1987) was describing analytical review as one of two techniques which were crucial in any audit approach (the other being sampling). In the USA, SAS No. 56 (AICPA, 1988), issued in 1988, placed greater emphasis on analytical procedures than the standard (SAS No. 23: AICPA, 1978) it replaced, to such an extent that analytical procedures became mandatory at the planning and final review stages of the audit. It can, therefore, be seen that in a space of less than twenty years analytical review has become one of the key components of the audit process.

WHAT IS ANALYTICAL REVIEW?

There is no concise, generally agreed definition of the term 'analytical review'. What is more, despite the mounting research conducted on this topic (e.g. see Gwilliam, 1987, pp. 272–97), Solomon and Krogstad (1988, p. 2) still considered that 'knowledge about analytical procedures is quite sparse'.

The American SAS No. 23 described analytical review procedures as 'substantive tests of financial information made by a study and comparison of relationships among data' (AICPA, 1978, para. 2, p. 1). The more recent SAS (No. 56) defined analytical procedures as 'evaluations of financial information made by a study of plausible relationships among both financial and non-financial data' (AICPA, 1988, para. 2, p. 1). In the UK the auditor's operational guideline on audit evidence (APC, 1980a, p. 11) stated that analytical review procedures include 'studying significant ratios, trends and other statistics and investigating any unusual or unexpected variations'. The auditing guideline on analytical review, which was issued in 1988, elaborated on the types of procedures which it comprises:

Andrew Higson, B.Sc. Ph.D., A.C.A., is a lecturer in the Department of Management Studies, Loughborough University of Technology.

- analysing the relationship between items of financial data ... or between financial and non-financial information ... ;
- comparing actual data with predictions derived from the analysis of known or expected relationships between items of data;
- comparing information for the latest period with corresponding information for earlier periods, other comparable enterprises or industry averages;
- investigating unexpected variations which are identified by such analysis and comparison;
- obtaining and substantiating explanations for those variations;
- evaluating the results of such analysis, comparison and investigation in the light of other audit evidence obtained to support the auditor's opinion on the financial statements.

(APC, 1988, p. 159)

Arens and Loebbecke (1984, pp. 204–5) cite the following as being the potential benefits to the auditor from the use of analytical review: it may offer a better understanding of the client and its industry by comparing its current year ratios with those of other businesses in the same industry; it may give an indication of financial difficulty, certain ratios possibly indicating a high risk of financial failure; it may bring to light errors in the financial statements; it could lead to a reduction in the levels of other substantive tests; and it may enable the auditor to make recommendations to the client if the review produces results which are significantly different from the rest of its industry. It can, therefore, be seen that many potential benefits could arise from the judicious use of analytical review – the problem facing the auditor is how to reap these benefits.

The nature of analytical review is such that it can range from a simple comparison of figures (or even just scanning the data) to the use of sophisticated statistical packages. Though the academic literature contains discussions of, for example, regression and ARIMA (integrated-autoregressive-moving-average-based predictions) by Kinney (1978), index models by Lev (1980), analytical hierarchy process by Lin, Mock and Wright (1984) and X-11 (a time series model) by Dugan, Gentry and Shriver (1985), few of these appear to have found their way into auditing practice.

While the use of the term 'analytical review' may be a relatively new phenomenon, the analytical procedure of reviewing the figures in the financial statements is well established. Stringer (1975, p. 4), when discussing its emergence in the AICPA's official pronouncements, considered: 'However, by that or some other name the process described briefly therein has probably been an accepted practice of most auditors for many years. For example, it has been a required procedure in our firm [Haskins & Sells] for at least forty years.'

In an early published version of the Coopers & Lybrand audit manual (Cooper, 1969, p. 20) mention is made of the comparison of annual profit percentages and ratios. These included gross profit on trading, gross profit as a percentage of turnover, net profit before taxation as a percentage of turnover, turnover analysed between different classes of businesses, ratios of year-end debtors to turnover and ratios of year-end stock to turnover. This data was to be kept in the client's permanent file, but it almost seems as if it was produced 'as a matter of routine' (op. cit., p. 7). The manual does make the point (op. cit., p. 40) that an 'auditor cannot adequately carry out an audit unless he has a thorough grasp of the nature of the business and the structure of the concern he is auditing', and then goes on to describe such analytical procedures as touring the factory, comparing the revenue and expenditure of the current year with that of the previous year (op. cit., p. 46) and inquiring about unusual variations, and examining trading results made up to a date before the end of the financial year so as to assist in directing attention to potential problems. Analytical procedures, therefore, have a long auditing history, even though the term 'analytical review' may be fairly modern. The major change that has come about is probably the extent to which analytical procedures are used and the greater emphasis now placed on them as a source of substantive audit evidence in an integrated audit approach.

WHEN SHOULD ANALYTICAL REVIEW BE USED?

Analytical review is generally recognized as having a potential role at three stages of an audit: planning, detailed testing and final review of the financial statements.

The auditor's operational standard (APC, 1980b) requires an auditor to obtain sufficient relevant and reliable audit evidence to be able to form an opinion on a client's financial statements. To enable this to be achieved as efficiently and effectively as possible, a key element is planning the audit. The use of analytical review procedures at the planning stage may add to the auditor's understanding of the client's business, 'but their primary purpose is to identify, and thereby to enable the auditor to direct audit resources to, areas of the financial statements where the recorded values may vary from the values the auditor would expect' (APC, 1988, p. 160). Where unusual variations are revealed the auditor is expected to plan to conduct further work in order to discover their causes. At the detailed testing stage of the audit, analytical review is classified as a substantive test. Its purpose, therefore, is to provide audit evidence as to the completeness, accuracy and validity of the data contained in the accounting records or the financial statements. Analytical review should usually be used in conjunction with other substantive tests, but may on occasions be used on its own. The extent of the reliance an auditor places on analytical review at the detailed testing stage will depend on such factors as (ibid.): the relevance, reliability, comparability and independence of the data used in the review; the adequacy of the client's internal controls over the preparation of both financial and non-financial data; the auditor's ability to predict an expected value; and the materiality of the item in question. At the final review stage, the auditor should use analytical review to assess the overall reasonableness of the audited financial figures (see Table 12.1).

The main problem associated with the use of analytical review, at any stage of the audit, is the generation by the auditor of the expected value for a particular calculation. For as Kinney (1978, p. 49) stated: 'In any analytical review, the auditor compares the client's reported balance (or ratio) with the auditor's assessment of the likely true (audited) balance.' In fact, it is this assessment which is the key part of any analytical review. Lev (1980, p. 525): 'the crucial stage of the analytical review process is the generation of expected, or reasonable, values of financial statement items'. Unless some form of statistical package is used, the expected value has to be based on

Table 12.1 The timing and objectives of analytical review

Stage	Timing	Objectives

Planning	At the start of the audit and updated throughout the audit	To see whether the preliminary figures are in line with the auditor's expectations, based on knowledge of the client's business/industry, etc
		   To identify potential financial and operational weakness
		   To direct audit resources
		   To increase the auditor's understanding of the client's enterprise

Detailed testing	During the substantive examination of the transactions and balances	To provide the auditor with a level of audit confidence that, when combined with reliance on the client's internal controls and evidence obtained from other substantive tests, satisfies the auditor that the overall audit risk is reduced to an acceptable level
Final review	At the end of the audit	To assess the overall reasonableness of the financial statements

Developed from Smith (1983, p. 16) and APC (1988).

professional judgement. Even if a computer-based package is employed, professional judgement still has to be used in specifying the relationship between the variables. In either case, judgement then has to be used to decide when the difference between the client's figure and the auditor's expected figure is unusual.

POSSIBLE REASONS FOR THE RISE OF ANALYTICAL REVIEW

The economic climate of the late 1970s and early 1980s, combined with increased threats of litigation, as well as technological developments, resulted in auditors becoming not only very cost conscious but also extremely mindful of the quality of their work. Auditors have, therefore, looked for ways of reducing their audit costs in order to contain their audit fees (Sherer, 1985, p. 8) whilst maintaining the quality of their work. Burton and Fairfield (1982) saw the possible consequences as follows:

> Pressures on prices should lead to greater audit efficiency as firms strive to reduce costs to remain competitive . . . . Thus audit efficiency will likely occur primarily at the level of stage hours committed to an engagement. These are hours that can best be replaced by increased use of analytical techniques and modern computer technology . . .
>
> (Burton and Fairfield, 1982, p. 4)

Accountancy firms admit that changes have been made: 'auditors have made many alterations to their methods and procedures in a continuing drive for efficiency and economy, in an increasingly competitive market' (Spicer and Pegler, 1985, p. v). In view of the threat of litigation, it is not surprising that auditors have placed greater emphasis on identifying risk areas. This, coupled with the publication of the auditing standards and guidelines in 1980, would help to explain some of the increased emphasis on analytical review at the planning stage of UK audits. Westwick's (1981) examination of analytical review was also intended to increase the profession's awareness of it. The effectiveness of analytical review at signalling errors in the financial statements was highlighted in a study by Hylas and Ashton (1982). This study examined how auditors discovered errors requiring adjustment, and found that more errors were signalled by analytical review procedures than by any other single category of initial events.

Turley (1989, p. 111) makes the point that 'the concept of audit risk has been one of the most significant influences on the development of audit methodology in the last decade'. So at the substantive test level, the development of risk-based approaches may mean that auditors try to obtain the overall assurance they require by quantifying the individual risk elements. For example, Cushing and Loebbecke (1983, p. 27) include analytical review as a specific element in the audit risk model:

$$UR = IR \times IC \times AR \times TD$$

where:

UR = the allowable ultimate risk that the auditor will fail to detect a monetary error equal to the maximum tolerable amount.

IR = the inherent risk of error in the financial statement generation process.

IC = the auditor's assessment of the risk that, given that errors equal to tolerable error occur, the system of internal accounting fails to detect them.

AR = the auditor's assessment of the risk that analytical review procedures and other relevant substantive tests would fail to detect errors equal to tolerable error.

TD = the sampling risk of incorrect acceptance for substantive tests of detail.

The use of a risk-analysis model would enable an auditor to integrate the audit approach so that confidence obtained from, say, analytical review could then directly lead to a reduction in other substantive tests of detail, so long as the allowable ultimate risk was tolerable. As analytical review is a relatively inexpensive means of increasing auditor confidence in the validity of reported balances, it is not surprising that its use as a substantive test has increased. Though it may require less time than the detailed testing of a sample, it does need to be conducted by a person who has the experience and ability to interpret the results.

ANALYTICAL REVIEW IN PRACTICE

Perhaps the best way of assessing the use of analytical review is to consider the result of a number of research studies which have attempted to document the effect of these procedures on audit practice. There has been much discussion of analytical review in the academic literature, yet little of its use in practice. In 1980 Lev was of the opinion that

In fact, the whole subject of analytical review appears to be shrouded in mystery. Accounting firms have allegedly been conducting analytical reviews for some time. Yet judging from the literature, no established, widely known procedures have emerged from this long practice . . .

(Lev, 1980, p. 525)

STAR (Stringer, 1975) was perhaps an exception to this. This was a statistical method to assist in analytical review which was introduced into practice in 1971 by Haskins & Sells. It was a form of step-wise regression which was used to establish norms from which deviations in financial data could be measured. The firm considered that regression analysis increased the objectivity of the review process, hence its desirability. The data required for a STAR analysis usually consisted of thirty-six monthly observations which were then used to produce projections for the time period in question. The acccount item under investigation was classified as the dependent variable, whilst the independent variables were chosen by the auditor based on an assessment of the factors likely to have a significant relationship with it. It was stressed that this relationship had to be plausible, otherwise, even if a statistical relationship was found to exist, it would be nonsense to use it. Once a logical relationship was specified, judgement was still required to decide when a fluctuation was unusual. In discussing Stringer's article, Warren (1975) made the point that if a client was aware of the form of the regression equations, it could adjust its book figures to agree with the regression prediction and thus not arouse the auditor's suspicions. The firm's policy was not for its mandatory use, but rather to encourage its use. In a follow-up article, Stewart (1978) stated that by 1978 it had been used 30,000 times worldwide in audit engagements.

Ernst & Whinney's risk analysis framework was described by Grobstein and Craig (1984). This placed great emphasis on analytical review. The firm provided extensive guidance for using analytical review as a substantive test so as to lessen the amount of detailed testing that might otherwise have been required. The Ernst & Whinney approach appears to be essentially judgemental in nature, however, and so it is in stark contrast to the Haskins & Sells approach.

Smith (1983) studied the use of analytical review by Canadian firms of accountants. He found that there was a wide diversity in the amount of reliance placed on analytical review procedures, ranging from it being the main source of audit evidence to hardly being used at all. Analytical review was still predominantly performed at the end of the audit in order to check the reasonableness of the figures in the financial statements. Some firms were using it in their planning process, so as to highlight problem areas, and it was also used as a source of substantive evidence. The most common analytical review calculations performed by the sample of firms were: gross profit percentages, stock levels and turnover, operating expenses as a percentage of sales and administrative expenses compared to the figure for the previous year. Smith found that little use was made of industry statistics and surprisingly 'comparison of reported data to management expectations or budgets is rare' (op. cit., p. 12). Only one of the firms interviewed integrated, in a mathematical way, the confidence obtained from analytical review to the overall confidence required. A common problem was the determination of what constituted an unusual variation: 'determining the significance of fluctuations is a complex decision requiring a good deal of professional judgement, knowledge of the business and experience' (ibid.). For this reason all the interviewees believed that analytical review should be performed only by a senior member of the audit team. Smith's overall conclusion, based on his limited study, was that 'there is little evidence of any consistent approach to analytical review' (op. cit., p. 14).

Biggs and Wild (1984) conducted a survey in the USA to provide evidence of analytical review practices. They found that judgemental procedures appeared to dominate, i.e. ratio analysis and scanning were preferred over regression and time series modelling. However, less experienced auditors tended to prefer the quantitative procedures.

Higson (1987) conducted a study of developments in auditing methods, by interviewing members of accountancy firms, focusing on changes in the late 1970s and early 1980s. Twelve of the fourteen interviewees felt that during this period their firms had increased their use of analytical review procedures. One of the interviewees described it as 'a phenomenal increase', whilst another thought there was 'much greater reliance [on it] now' (op. cit., p. 308). A possible reason for this is the increase in both quality and quantity of management information available to the auditor. One person expressed the view, however, that the best type of analytical review procedure was simply walking around a client's premises, or in fact doing anything that helped create in the auditor's mind a picture of the way the business had developed. It was felt very strongly by this person that just looking at the accounting systems did not disclose what was really happening in the business. A number of firms, in fact, describe their audit approaches as 'business oriented', in that if the auditor understands the client's business, it should be apparent when things are wrong. This appears to be going back to the time when the partner was closely involved in the day-to-day activities of the audit. However, the auditor's drive for delegation has meant that the partner is now far removed from the mundane audit process, and so his or her special knowledge has been lost and, as one interviewee stated, 'replaced by a galaxy of ratios' (op. cit., p. 309). One partner who stated that his firm made no great use of analytical review conceded that this may have been a weakness in his firm's audit approach. He expressed concern that he was not satisfied that auditors had decided exactly what analytical review was and what it was worth. This person was worried that auditors may now be relying too heavily on analytical review without performing it at a sufficiently stringent level. It can, therefore, be seen that within the accounting profession there is some debate as to what actually constitutes analytical review and exactly how useful it is.

Akresh, Loebbecke and Scott (1988) report an unpublished study by Loebbecke (1987). This was an examination of analytical review research which covered some fifty-three studies. He was able to conclude that analytical procedures are important to auditing and are extensively but inconsistently used by auditors. These procedures tended to be fairly unsophisticated, and varied in their effectiveness. Perhaps the most important point was the conclusion that analytical procedures were probably more effective in attention directing rather than as a direct substitute for substantive testing.

It is apparent that a variety of analytical procedures are used by auditors in practice, but in the majority of audits the sophistication of these procedures is relatively low. Many firms have yet to explore fully the potential benefits of incorporating financial modelling (so as to take account of industrial and economic data) and statistical techniques (such as regression analysis) in their analytical comparisons. At the moment analytical procedures are frequently limited to basic comparisons of actual balances with prior-year and budgeted amounts.

The position of consistency of application is further compounded by the lack of acknowledged definitions as to what constitutes an 'error', or a significant variation, requiring additional audit work. Given that analytical review procedures rely essentially on the notion of the reasonableness of the figures and whether they 'make sense', considerable latitude is available to auditors to exercise subjective judgement in assessing the evidential value of an analytical review and deciding whether there is a need for further investigation.

SUMMARY

Though the term 'analytical review' may be fairly new, analytical procedures have been used by auditors for many years. The innovation has been in the way increased emphasis has been placed on it. The last ten years have seen a great increase in the use of analytical review at the planning stage of the audit. In the USA its use is now mandatory at the planning and final review stages of the audit. At the detailed testing stage of the audit, some auditors now obtain quantitative assurance from their analytical procedures in their overall integrated audit approaches. Others purely use judgement to reduce their detailed substantive testing. There is still a debate, however, in the profession as to exactly how useful analytical review is, and how meaningful its results are. In fact, it has been suggested that analytical review may be more useful for attention directing, than as a direct substitute for other substantive tests.

From the point of view of the auditing practitioners, analytical review has come a long way in the last twenty years, but considerable progress is still required before the content, role and value of these procedures in auditing can be regarded as settled.

REFERENCES

AICPA (1972) Statement on Auditing Procedure No. 54, American Institute of Certified Public Accountants, New York.

AICPA (1978) Statement on Auditing Standards No. 23, AICPA, New York.

AICPA (1988) Statement on Auditing Standards No. 56, AICPA, New York.

Akresh, A.D., Loebbecke, J.K. and Scott, W.R. (1988) Audit approaches and techniques, in A.R. Abdel-khalik and I. Solomon (eds.) *Research Opportunities in Auditing: The Second Decade*, American Accounting Association, Illinois.

APC (1980a) *Audit Evidence*, Auditing Guideline, reproduced in *Accountancy*, May, pp. 108, 111.

APC (1980b) *The Auditor's Operational Standard*, reproduced in *Accountancy*, May, pp. 102, 105, 108.

APC (1987) *True and Fair*, no. 33, Summer.

APC (1988) *Analytical Review*, Auditing Guideline, Auditing Practices Committee, reproduced in *Accountancy*, June, pp. 159–61.

Arens, A.A. and Loebbecke, J.K. (1984) *Auditing: An Integrated Approach*, 3rd edn, Prentice-Hall, New York.

Biggs, S.F. and Wild, J.J. (1984) A note on the practice of analytical review, *Auditing: A Journal of Theory & Practice*, Vol. 3, no. 2, Spring, pp. 68–79.

Burton, J. C. and Fairfield, P. (1982) Auditing evolution in a changing environment, *Auditing: A Journal of Practice & Theory*, Vol. 1, no. 2, Winter, pp. 1–22.

Cooper, V.R.C. (1969) *Manual of Auditing*, Gee, London.

Cushing, B.E. and Loebbecke, J.K. (1983) Analytical approaches to risk: a survey and analysis. *Auditing: A Journal of Practice & Theory*, Vol. 3, no. 1, Fall, pp. 23–41.

Dugan, M.T., Gentry, J.A. and Shriver, K.A. (1985) The X-11 model: a new analytical review technique for the auditor, *Auditing: A Journal of Practice & Theory*, Vol. 4, no. 2, Spring, pp. 11–22.

Grobstein, M. and Craig, P.W. (1984) A risk analysis approach to auditing, *Auditing: A Journal of Theory & Practice*, Vol. 3, no. 2, Spring, pp. 1–16.

Gwilliam, D.R. (1987) *A Survey of Auditing Research*, ICAEW/Prentice-Hall, London.

Higson, A.W. (1987) An empirical investigation of the external audit process, unpublished Ph.D. thesis, University of Bradford.

Hylas, R.E. and Ashton, R.H. (1982) Audit detection of financial statement errors, *Accounting Review*, Vol. LVI, no. 4, October, pp. 751–65.

Kinney, W.R. (1978) ARIMA and regression in analytical review: an empirical test, *Accounting Review*, Vol. LII, no. 1, January, pp. 48–60.

Lev, B. (1980) On the use of index models in analytical reviews by auditors, *Journal of Accounting Research*, Vol. 18, no. 2, Autumn, pp. 524–50.

Lin, W.T., Mock, T.J. and Wright, A. (1984) The use of the analytical hierarchy process as an aid in planning the nature and extent of audit procedures, *Auditing: A Journal of Practice & Theory*, Vol. 4, no. 1, Fall, pp. 89–99.

Loebbecke, J.K. (1987) Research opportunities in auditing: analytical procedures, unpublished working paper, cited by Akresh, Loebbecke and Scott (1988).

Sherer, M. (1985) Auditing today: opportunities and threats, in D. Kent, M. Sherer and S. Turley (eds.) *Current Issues in Auditing*, Harper & Row, London.

Smith, D.G. (1983) *Analytical Review: A Research Study*, Chartered Institute of Canadian Accountants, Toronto.

Solomon, I. and Krogstad, J.L. (1988) Integration and perspectives on substantive audit issues, in A.R. Abdel-khalik and I. Solomon (eds.) *Research Opportunities in Auditing: The Second Decade*, American Accounting Association, Illinois.

Spicer and Pegler (1985) *Practical Auditing*, 17th edn, Butterworths, London.

Stewart, T. (1978) Regression analysis in auditing, *Accountancy*, March, pp. 69–70, 71.

Stringer, K.W. (1975) A statistical technique for analytical review, *Studies on Statistical Methodology in Auditing, Journal of Accounting Research*, Vol. 13, Supplement, pp. 1–9.

Turley, W.S. (1989) Concepts and values in the audit methodologies of large accounting firms, in *Auditing and the Future*, ICAEW and ICAS, London.

Warren, C.S. (1975) Discussion of 'A statistical technique for analytical review', *Studies on Statistical Methodology in Auditing, Journal of Accounting Research*, Vol. 13, Supplement, pp. 10–13.

Westwick, C. (1981) *Do the Figures Make Sense? A Practical Guide to Analytical Review*, ICAEW, London.

DISCUSSION QUESTIONS

1. Analytical review is more than just ratio analysis. Discuss the types of analytical procedures an auditor may employ in the course of an audit.
2. Discuss the main arguments for and against the use of analytical review as a form of audit evidence.
3. Analytical review is no more, or less, subjective than any other part of the external audit. Discuss.

13
Statistical Sampling

Stuart Manson

INTRODUCTION

Although it is generally accepted today that, in arriving at an opinion, the auditor will have carried out only test checks, this was not always the case. Lee (1986) notes that the movement, in the 1930s and 1940s, from detailed checking and vouching of transactions to test-checking transactions was prompted by the emergence of larger companies and a change in the role of the auditor. Prior to this time it was the consensus that one of the prime functions of the audit and hence of the substantial checking done was to detect fraud and error. As it became accepted that company management was responsible for this the need for the auditor to carry out detailed checking was reduced. Similarly, the increase in size of businesses had the consequence that the only way an audit could be completed in a reasonable time was by test checking. In both instances the underlying motive was undoubtedly the fact that the benefit to be gained by continuing with detailed checking was outweighed by the costs.

A consequence of the reliance on test checking is that there is a possibility, however small, that the opinion may be in error. Thus, the audit should be designed in a way that minimizes this possibility. If this were not the case one could question the need for the audit function. When the auditor is determining the construction of the test checks a major concern is their effectiveness in assisting the auditor to arrive at a correct opinion. Additionally, since the auditor is operating in a competitive market and is aware that the cheaper his service the more likely it is that he or she will obtain new clients, there is an incentive to ensure that the tests are efficient. Thus, the auditor does not want to select a sample of 300 items for testing if 200, with the consequent lower cost, would be adequate to meet the objectives of the test. It is the twin pressures of effectiveness and efficiency that are usually credited with the increased emphasis on statistical methodology in audit testing (Scott, 1984). The belief is that use of statistical testing will reduce audit costs whilst maintaining or indeed improving audit quality.

A related rationale for the use of statistical sampling is the increased concern in the auditing profession with the possibility of litigation. The use by auditors of 'modern techniques' such as statistical sampling may be regarded as evidence of conformance with generally accepted best practice. It may thus

Stuart Manson is a lecturer in the Department of Accounting and Financial Management, University of Essex.

form part of the defence to be used in a court of law to prove that the auditor had not been negligent (Gwilliam, 1987).

AUDIT STRATEGY

Given the requirement that a competent audit should be carried out, but at a reasonable cost, auditors have to consider which particular test will meet their objectives. They must weigh the effectiveness of a test against the cost of performing it. Specifically, the balance between analytical review, proof in total, selection of key items, 100 per cent testing and sample testing must be determined. Within each particular audit assignment a choice must be made on how much compliance and how much substantive testing are necessary. If internal control systems are good and this has been verified by means of the compliance tests, the auditor will perhaps reduce the scope of the substantive tests performed. This decision, itself, may have implications for whether or not statistical sampling is used. Thus Elliott and Rogers (1972) imply that statistical sampling may be more applicable in substantive testing:

> Although a statistical attribute test may be of some use in examining systems and controls, it is by no means necessary. Generally, in examining systems the auditor seeks a qualitative conclusion. . . . Seldom does he need precise measurement of rates of occurrence, such as would be provided by an attribute test.
>
> (Elliott and Rogers, 1972, p. 47)

Having decided on a particular audit strategy that contains some amount of sampling the auditor has to determine when statistical sampling is more appropriate than non-statistical sampling. The draft audit brief, *Audit Sampling* (APC, 1987a), lists three benefits of statistical sampling.

1. It imposes on the auditor a more formal discipline as regards planning the audit of a population.
2. The required sample size is determined objectively.
3. The evaluation of test results is made more precisely and the sampling risk is quantified.

Against these advantages may be set a number of disadvantages. It is usually more time consuming to carry out statistical sampling, and this will lead to higher audit costs. In order to perform statistical sampling each individual item (the sampling unit) in the population must be capable of being identified in some unique way. This ability may depend on the form in which the audit client maintains its records, it being generally recognized that statistical sampling is more likely to be feasible when the records are computerized. It can also be argued that statistical sampling leads to a mechanistic audit approach and thus loses out in the use of the auditor's experience and 'gut' feeling about the likely location of errors in the company's records or when there are most likely to be problems. Audit firms may also be reluctant to implement statistical sampling because of its complexity. McRae (1982), in a study of 136 medium-sized auditing firms, found that only sixteen used statistical sampling and, of these, the majority used attribute sampling. The decision to use statistical sampling seemed to be influenced by the size of the client and whether records were computerized.

STATISTICAL SAMPLING

Sample selection
The auditor selects and evaluates a sample with a view to making inferences about the population from which it has been drawn. For these inferences to be justified certain conditions must be met.

A representative sample
The sample selected must be representative of the underlying population; only if this is the case can the auditor validly reach conclusions about the population based on the sample. The ideal of obtaining a representative sample does not apply just in cases of statistical sampling, it should also be an objective in non-statistical sampling. Various methods can be used to select a representative sample. The basic concept is the same in all methods, that is, the desire to select a random sample. A random sample is a sample where each item in the population has an equal chance of being selected for examination.

To obtain a random sample the auditor may make use of random number tables. In this procedures the auditor assigns a unique number to each item in the population and then uses random number tables to select the items which are to form the sample. Alternatively, the auditor may use a method known as systematic sampling. In this method the number of items in the population is divided by the sample size to arrive at a figure known as the sampling interval. For example, if the population consists of 10,000 items and the sample size has been calculated as 125 the sampling interval will be 10,000 divided by 125, giving 80. The auditor then determines a random start point in the population and selects every 80th item until 125 items have been selected. A criticism sometimes made of this method is that if there is some systematic characteristic in the population the sample selected may be biased. Other methods of selection such as block sampling do not ensure that every item has an equal chance of being selected and thus do not conform to a basic requirement of statistical sampling.

Is the population homogeneous?
Prior to selecting a sample the auditor has to ensure that the population is homogeneous.[1] For instance, if the auditor is checking that invoices have been properly authorized prior to payment, it is a requirement that all the invoices be subject to the same control procedure. If there were two individuals who signed or initialled invoices as authorized, one of the individuals authorizing payments greater than, say, £50 and the other payments for lesser amounts, then, effectively we have two populations of invoices and the auditor should carry out tests on both populations. If this is not done any inferences the auditor makes based on the sample could be in error.

Sample size determination
Statistical sampling which is based on sampling theory[2] enables the auditor to determine the appropriate sample size for any given population size. To do this the auditor must determine the confidence level to be used and decide on the tolerable error. The confidence level or degree of assurance required by

the auditor is simply a quantitative assessment of the reliability that can be placed on the sample results; tolerable error refers to the maximum error or deviation rate the auditor is willing to accept in the underlying population. Thus, on the basis of the sample results, the auditor can state, for a given level of confidence that the error rate in the population lies within certain bounds. The extrapolation from a sample means that the auditor can never be 100 per cent certain. This would be possible only if every single item in the population was examined,[3] which would defeat the whole purpose of test checking. The converse of the confidence level is the risk the auditor is taking that any statement concerning the population may be incorrect. Thus, when the auditor is operating at a 95 per cent confidence level there is a risk of (100% − 95%) 5 per cent that the inferences made about the population may be incorrect.

This risk can be related to the risk models outlined in Chapter 10. Thus, if the auditor is using the risk model illustrated in the draft audit brief, *Audit Sampling* (APC, 1987b), the appropriate risk level to be used can be calculated as follows:

Risk model: $AR = IR \times CR \times DR \times SR$

where:[4]

AR = audit risk, risk of incorrect acceptance of the population
IR = inherent risk
CR = control risk
DR = detection risk from substantive tests other than audit sampling
SR = sampling risk from sampling substantive tests

If the auditor has estimated the risk levels for AR, IR, CR, and DR he can derive, by rearranging the equation above, the appropriate risk factor to use in the substantive tests. Thus:

$$SR = \frac{AR}{IR \times CR \times DR}$$

As an illustration, assume that $AR = 5$ per cent, $IR = 100$ per cent, $CR = 35$ per cent, and $DR = 60$ per cent and, using the formula above, the sampling risk from sampling substantive tests is 24 per cent. This means that when carrying out audit tests on this application the auditor should set a confidence level of (100% − 24%) 76 per cent.

There is, however, some evidence to doubt the efficacy of these models. Using a case study involving debtors, Daniel (1988) asked a sample of thirty-three audit managers to specify their assessment of the total audit risk and the individual risk components involved in the assignment. She found that although total risk in isolation was commonly assessed at 5 per cent, the estimate of this provided by using three risk models was generally less than 5 per cent. There were a number of managers who estimated audit risk at 5 per cent, and gained some assurance from the system of control and the analytical review, yet who nevertheless used 5 per cent (i.e. 95 per cent confidence level) in their subtantive tests of detail. This would seem to imply that the auditors were over-auditing in their substantive tests and needlessly increasing the costs of the audit.

In statistical sampling the specification of confidence levels does not eliminate judgement but does require the auditor to quantify the amount of risk he or she is willing to bear. Risk in the audit context can be categorized into two types. The first is the risk that, on the basis of the sample results, the auditor rejects a population that is within the tolerable error; this is known as alpha risk (or Type I error). The second risk is the failure to reject, on the basis of the sample results, a population that does not meet the criteria set for tolerable error; this is known as beta risk (or Type II error). The costs associated with alpha risk are likely to be those incurred in carrying out further audit work or requesting the client to 'prove' that the particular item is not subject to material error. This type of error thus affects the efficiency of the audit as it is likely that either or both the client and auditor may have to carry out additional work involving additional financial cost. It is interesting to note that one of the main methods of statistical sampling used today, monetary unit sampling (discussed below), has been criticized by Kaplan (1975a) for not specifically taking alpha risk into account. Beta risk is usually regarded as the more serious risk, since, if this type of error is made it means that the auditor may be accepting a population that is materially in error, which may result in the financial statements being misleading. Because it may have a deleterious effect on the auditor's reputation and could result in claims for negligence it is a risk that the auditor takes most seriously and will wish to minimize.

On the basis of sample results the auditor acquires a point estimate of the error level in the population. Now, if the auditor had selected a different sample he or she may have obtained a different point estimate of the error rate. The use of sampling theory allows the auditor to make a statement at a particular level of confidence that the error or deviation rate in the population lies within a certain range. In compliance-type testing the auditor is concerned with determining at the confidence level being used if the upper limit of this range or bound exceeds the tolerable error. If this is the case the auditor may have to revise the amount of reliance that was going to be placed on the internal control systems for the determination of the extent of substantive testing. If, on the other hand, after carrying out tests the auditor finds the upper error rate is less than the tolerable error rate, this means that the level of confidence or assurance obtained exceeds that which was used in the planning stage. The implication of this is that the population has been over-audited and hence audit costs have been higher than they needed to be. Ideally, the auditor wishes to end up with an upper error rate which is equal to the tolerable error, for when this has been achieved the testing has been economical.

In substantive testing the tolerable error may be defined as the maximum monetary error in the population the auditor is willing to accept. This concept, which is related to materiality, requires the auditor to decide at the outset of the audit what level of error is acceptable in the financial statements before concluding that they are materially misstated and may require to be qualified. For example, if the auditor finds on the basis of the statistical sampling tests that debtors may be materially misstated, he or she will have to decide on an appropriate course of action. This may take the form of carrying out additional audit tests or requiring the client to adjust debtors to take into account any errors found. If the client declines to alter the debtors figure and subsequent additional tests corroborate the evidence of the original statistical sampling tests, the auditor may have to consider some form of audit qualification.

Both these concepts (confidence level and maximum acceptable error rate) are directly related to sample size. The higher the confidence level the larger the sample size must be to achieve that level, whereas, for a given expected error rate, the lower the maximum acceptable error rate the larger the sample size. The following example using tables from Guy (1981) will help illustrate these relationships.

The auditor is examining a population of purchase invoices to ensure that they have all been initialled as authorized for payment. This test is carried out as part of the procedures to verify the likelihood of the company paying for goods it has not received. The auditor believes, on the basis of past experience, that 2 per cent of the invoices will not be initialled.

Table 13.1 illustrates the sensitivity of the sample size to the confidence level chosen and the maximum acceptable error rate. Thus, if the auditor is willing to accept a maximum error rate of only 4 per cent, for the confidence levels shown in Table 13.1 the sample size can vary between 200 and 500. The large difference in these values would ultimately be reflected in the cost of the audit. The auditor may decide that to use samples as large as 300 or 500 would be uneconomical and instead obtain the required assurance from alternative tests.

In the example above no mention has been made of the size of the population. This is because sample size, as illustrated in Table 13.2, is relatively insensitive to population size.

Non-sampling risk

At this point it is important to make a distinction between sampling risk and non-sampling risk. In the discussion above we were concerned with controlling only for sampling risk. Non-sampling risk is defined by Roberts (1978, p. 233) as: 'The portion of audit risk of not detecting a material error that exists because of the inherent limitations of the procedures used, the timing of the procedures, the system being examined, and the skill and care of the auditor.'

A common example of this type of risk is where the auditor wishes to check that the client has invoiced all sales and checks a sample of sales invoices through to inclusion on the debtors account. This test, however, does not achieve the audit objective; to do this the auditor would need to check from the delivery note to the sales invoice. Another common example of non-sampling risk is where the auditor, on checking a sample, fails to recognize an

Table 13.1   Determination of sample size

Maximum error rate%	Confidence level %		
	90	95	99
4	200	300	500
5	140	200	300
6	90	140	200
7	80	90	140

Table 13.2   *Required sample sizes for different population sizes*

Population size	Sample size
50	45
100	64
500	87
1,000	90
2,000	92
5,000	93
100,000	93

Assuming the auditor is working at a 95 per cent confidence level, expects a population error rate of 1 per cent and has specified an upper error rate of 5 per cent.

Source: AICPA (1983).

error when it has occurred or misinterprets the evidence examined. Statistical sampling does not control for this type of risk, which can be reduced by proper audit planning, control, and training of staff.

METHODS OF STATISTICAL SAMPLING

Attribute sampling
Attribute sampling is typically applied in compliance testing, where the auditor is concerned to establish whether or not a particular characteristic is present. It may also be used in substantive testing when the population does not contain monetary values or these are not in a form suitable for using other forms of statistical tests. If the auditor is verifying the use of a specific control procedure, the answer will be a straightforward yes or no.

The prime aim of compliance testing is to form some estimate of the reliability of the accounting records for determining the required level of substantive testing. As discussed above the auditor is required to determine a confidence level for the application. The level chosen will to some extent reflect the importance of the particular control procedure that is being tested and the assurance either gained or expected to be gained from other audit procedures (e.g. substantive tests) which are related to the control procedure. The tolerable error is the maximum error rate acceptable to the auditor. If the error rate exceeds this level the auditor can no longer place as much reliance as planned on the control procedure and, depending on the nature of the procedure, this will lead to an increase in the level of substantive testing. The confidence level and the tolerable error, together with the auditor's estimate of the expected error rate in the population (which is likely to be influenced by past experience), are used in conjunction with suitable statistical tables to calculate the sample size.

Using the data from Table 13.1, a confidence level of 95 per cent, a tolerable error rate of 6 per cent and an estimated error rate of 2 per cent will require a sample size of 140. The evaluation of the sample results depends on the number of errors found. Thus, if two errors were found in the sample, giving an error rate of 1.4 per cent (2/140 × 100%), using appropriate statistical tables the auditor can conclude at the 95 per cent confidence level that the upper error rate is 5 per cent. As this is within the tolerable error rate the population would be accepted. If, however, five errors were found, giving an error rate of 3.57 per cent (5/140 × 100%), the upper error rate is 8 per cent, which is in excess of the auditor's predetermined tolerable error. Given this, the auditor may decide, after due consideration of the nature of the errors, to reduce (or abandon) reliance on this control procedure and increase the level of substantive testing. It is important to stress that although in the last example the upper error rate is 8 per cent, the actual error rate in the population could still be less than the tolerable error, in which case the auditor would be committing a Type I error. To aid the auditor in this position it is possible to calculate what level of confidence would be commensurate, given an expected error rate of 2 per cent and a tolerable error rate of 6 per cent, with an actual error rate of 3.57 per cent. The auditor can then decide whether to accept the population at this lower level of confidence. A criticism that is sometimes made of attribute sampling as portrayed above is the usefulness of the upper error rate. It has been argued that the crucial requirement in attribute sampling is merely to know if the population can be relied upon or not (Elliott and Rogers, 1972). This criticism can be met through a variant of attribute sampling known as acceptance sampling. In this method the decision is merely taken to accept or reject the population for the purposes of reliance in the determination of the scope of substantive tests.

Thus far, emphasis has been given to the quantitiative analysis of errors but this does not mean to suggest that consideration of qualitative factors is unimportant. The auditor should as part of the evaluation of the test results determine the type of errors that occurred in the sample. For instance, if authorizing signatures are missing from creditors' invoices but it is found that these errors occur only in invoices for negligible amounts, this may imply that individuals concern themselves with correctly authorizing only material amounts. It is also worth stressing that a missing authorizing signature does not necessarily mean that the invoice has not been authorized: it is possible that the authorizer examined the invoice but then merely omitted to initial that a check had been carried out. Burgstahler and Jiambalvo (1986), in a study that examined the treatment of errors by 109 audit firm employees, found that in their evaluation of errors they tended to consider certain errors as 'unique' and would exclude them when extrapolating the results of the sample to the population. The authors suggested (op. cit., p. 247) that this behaviour could be explained by the fact 'that failure to project a "unique" error is not often associated with a loss to the auditor'.

Alternatively, of course, there may be errors that alert the auditor to potential irregularities, which would lead him or her either to extend the tests to request the client to investigate fully the events surrounding the error(s) detected. It is clear that qualitative evaluation is a matter where individual audit firms have to decide what policy is appropriate and should be used in their attribute sampling plans. In general, the inability, in attribute sampling, to come to some conclusion about the materiality of errors has led to the suggestion that in compliance testing the rigour of statistical sampling is not required and that non-statistical sampling is adequate (Elliott and Rogers, 1972).

Monetary unit sampling[5]

In monetary unit sampling (hereafter MUS) the auditor attempts to come to some conclusion about the amount of monetary error in a population. This can, generally, be accomplished only if the population is specified in terms of £1 monetary amounts and a cumulative total of these amounts can be calculated. Thus, if the auditor is concerned with selecting debtors for circularization purposes, a monetary cumulative running total of the amounts owed will be required, and within that total the allocation of specific monetary units to particular debtor accounts. Since the population is in £1 units this means that the sample selected will consist of specific £1 units from the population. These £1 units are, however, only a hook for the individual debtor accounts that are to be audited. Based on the specific £1 units selected the auditor obtains a sample of debtors to be circularized. Assuming that no errors are expected in the population the determination of the sample size proceeds as follows.

The auditor, first, must specify the confidence level, and the tolerable error – the amount of error in the account being audited which when combined with errors in other accounts would lead to the financial statements being misleading. Corresponding to each level of confidence there is a reliability factor.[6] The appropriate reliability factor is divided into the tolerable error to determine the sampling interval. The sample size is then simply the value of the population divided by the sampling interval. Assuming the sampling interval to be n, the auditor can select the sample by first randomly choosing a start point in the first n pounds of the population, and then selecting every nth pound thereafter. The individual item, i.e. the specific debtor account, associated with each pound selected is then the subject of the audit procedures.

A problem with this approach in a situation where no errors are anticipated, is that if any error *is* found in the sample the population should be rejected. To counter this some adjustment is usually made for the possibility of error. The specification of this adjustment seems to be a matter of some judgement; for instance, on this matter the draft audit brief, *Audit Sampling* (APC, 1987a), states:

> typically, some tolerance for the possibility of finding errors in the sample is built in to the sample size (i.e. it is increased slightly) by increasing the reliability factor based on a monetary estimate of the level of error likely. (A similar effect can be achieved by reducing the tolerable error acceptable for the test.)
>
> (APC, 1987a, p. 85)

The AICPA (1983) is somewhat more specific in its guide, *Audit Sampling*. It notes that when errors are expected in the population the auditor should convert the tolerable error and the expected error into percentages of the population value and then use attribute sampling theory, as outlined in the preceding section, to calculate the sample size.

The use of MUS ensures that the probability of an item being selected is proportional to its size and, consequently, any item that has a larger monetary value than the sampling interval n is certain to be selected. The evaluation of the sample requires the auditor to calculate for each item in error the percentage in error, a percentage known as the 'level of tainting' in the item. Thus, if an invoice for £100, say, is selected and found to be in error by £20, the level of tainting is 20 per cent.[7] To estimate the most likely error in the population, the sum of the taintings must be calculated and then multiplied by the value of the sampling interval. For example, if the auditor finds three errors with taintings of 10, 60 and 40 per cent and the sampling interval is £30,000 then the most likely error is:

$$10\% + 60\% + 40\% = 110\% \times £30,000 = £33,000$$

This, however, is only a point estimate and is supplemented by calculating the upper error limit. To determine this the first step is to obtain what is known as the basic precision (the allowance for sampling risk assuming there were no errors); this is arrived at by multiplying the sampling interval by the reliability factor, assuming no errors, appropriate to the chosen confidence level. The next stage is to rank the tainting percentages from the largest down to the smallest. Each of these is then multiplied by a precision gap widening (PGW) factor (these factors which are derived from the reliability factors reflect the increase in sampling risk when errors are found in the sample), the largest tainting error percentage being multiplied by the PGW factor applicable to the finding of an error, the second tainting error being multiplied by the PGW factor applicable to a second error and so on, till all the tainting errors have been multiplied by their appropriate PGW factors. These are then summed, multiplied by the sampling interval, added to the basic precision and the total of this is then added to the most likely error, to obtain the upper error limit.[8] This procedure allows the auditor to make a statement of the most likely error and, at the confidence level being used, the upper error limit in the population. The figure calculated is then compared with the tolerable error for the item under consideration. If the upper error limit is less than the tolerable error the auditor can accept the population. If the opposite is the case he or she may adjust the upper error limit for any errors found – assuming the client agrees to the adjustment – to determine whether that reduces the upper error limit to below the tolerable error. If the upper error limit remains above the tolerable error the auditor should carry out such procedures as are laid down by the audit firm to deal with this situation. For a worked example involving MUS see the Appendix to this chapter.

Some problems with MUS

This section considers some of the problems involved in MUS. First, the earlier discussion made no mention of whether the errors are understatements or overstatements. As usually presented, it is assumed that the maximum error in any particular sampling unit, e.g. debtor account, will be a 100 per cent tainting. Thus, if the book value of the debtor account is £100 but the audit tests reveal a value of £50, there is tainting of 100 per cent. It is, however, possible that the debit balance on the debtor account should have been a credit balance of £100, thus giving rise to a tainting percentage greater than 100. Similarly, with creditors the book value of a particular account may be £200 and the audit value £220, a tainting of – 10 per cent. When over- and understatements occur in the sample the appropriate procedure to deal with them is a matter of some debate (Scott, 1984).[9]

A secondary problem involving understatements is where the population being tested is more likely to be subject to under- rather than overstatement, e.g. creditors. It should be apparent that if an item is understated its chance of being selected for audit examination is reduced. Using the example above, if a creditor had a book value of £2 it would be a hundred times less likely to be selected than if the true value of £200 were stated. At the extreme, a creditor stated at nil in the books has a zero chance of being selected for examination. It is for this reason that the draft audit brief, *Audit Sampling* (APC, 1987a, para 3.13), recommends that MUS is more likely to be a useful procedure when the auditor 'is primarily concerned with tests for overstatement and where significant understatements are not expected'.

It is stressed by some of the proponents of statistical sampling that the problems in detecting understatements are not unique to statistical sampling but are also present in non-statistical sampling, and that the auditor has to devise specific alternative audit tests to deal with those occasions where understatements are likely.

Second, it is generally recognized that the upper error limit calculated using the Stringer technique, which is basically a pragmatic way of dealing with multiple errors with less than 100 per cent tainting, gives a conservative estimate (Plante, Neter and Leitch, 1985). This may lead to satisfactory populations being rejected – a Type I error – and the auditor carrying out additional audit tests with the attendant incremental costs. Various alternatives have been suggested in the literature to calculate tighter bounds[10] (upper error limits), but these alternatives in turn tend to have their own limitations, such as problems in implementation due to lack of information on the distribution of errors in the population.

Allied with this is the general consensus that MUS is appropriate only in populations with low error rates (Akresh, Loebbecke and Scott, 1988). Hence, if high error rates are expected the auditor will have to consider using some alternative approach. This, of course, leaves open the question of what is meant by low and high error rates.

Variables estimation

This type of sampling can be used either to estimate the value of a population whose value is unknown or, more likely in the audit situation, to assess the 'accuracy' of the recorded population value. There are three main types of variables estimation: mean per unit estimation, difference estimation and ratio estimation.

In mean per unit estimation the auditor selects a sample,[11] calculates its mean value and then multiples this by the number of items in the population to obtain an estimate of the population value. In difference estimation the auditor compares the book value of the sample item with the audit value to determine the difference, if any, between the two. The differences are then summed and divided by the number of items in the sample to obtain a mean difference. This is multiplied by the number of items in the population and added to the book value of the population to obtain an estimated audit value.

Ratio estimation involves calculating the ratio of the sum of the sampled audited values to the sum of the sampled book values. This ratio is then multiplied by the (book) population value to determine an estimate of its audit value. In all three types normal distribution theory is used to obtain an allowance for sampling risk.

There are a number of disadvantages in variables estimation sampling which tend to limit its usefulness in auditing. First, in mean per unit sampling, if the population is skewed, the size of sample required to obtain a satisfactory estimate of audit value becomes very large and hence is an inefficient way of sampling. Typically, audit populations tend to be characterized by a few large-value and many small-value items, hence the distribution tends to be positively skewed. This problem can be alleviated to some extent by stratifying the population but, unfortunately, this is turn increases both the complexity of calculations involved and the time required to carry out the test. Further, if no or few differences are found between the audit value and the book value of the sample units, it is difficult for the auditor to make any statement about the precision of the population estimate. Similarly, in difference and ratio estimation *Audit Sampling* (APC, 1987a) notes that for these methods to be used successfully there must be at least fifty differences between the book value and the audit value in the selected sample. It is generally thought that these conditions are not likely to be met in samples derived from the typical audit population.

In difference estimation, ideally, errors in the audit population should be of similar value and consist of approximately equal numbers of under- and overstatements. McRae (1982), in his study of seventy-six UK audit samples, found a greater number of overstatements than understatements; that the distribution of error values was skewed, in that 5 per cent of the errors accounted for 83 per cent of the value of errors discovered; and small-value audit items (less than £2,000) tended to be associated with proportionately larger errors than large audit items (greater than £10,000). It should be apparent that these characteristics are exactly the opposite of what is required for successful difference estimation. The consequences of these are less important in ratio estimation but its value is limited by the requirement for a substantial number of errors in the sample. Overall, unless the auditor suspects the population will contain numerous errors the techniques seem to have limited application.

Bayesian sampling
This method of sampling requires the auditor to specify a prior set probability distribution for the error rates likely to arise in a population. Thus, in contrast with attribute sampling, where the auditor is merely required to estimate the expected error rate in the population, this method requires subjective probabilities to be attached to the potential population error rates. This prior probability distribution can then be used with the actual sample results to specify at a particular confidence level the expected upper error rate. The main thrust behind Bayesian sampling is the notion that if an individual has *a priori* a set of expectations about the likelihood of an event and subsequent experience (i.e. the sample results) confirms those expectations then the individual's confidence in them will be increased.

The main advantage of this method of sampling compared with other methods is that for a given confidence level the sample size is reduced; the main problem lies in assessing the prior distribution of error rates for the population. The application of this method is detailed in the *Thomson McLintock Audit Manual* (McLintock, 1983). In the method outlined, which is based on error rates rather than monetary values, the level of substantive tests is determined by the auditor's assessment of the upper limit of inherent error rate, the upper limit of detection error rate and the number of errors found in the compliance tests. Combining data from these three sources enables a prior distribution to be determined for use in the substantive testing. The auditor's assessment of the maximum error rate in the population at a specified confidence level depends on the prior distribution used and the number of errors found in the sample.

The major limitation in the use of the Bayesian method is the subjectivity involved in determining the prior distribution. Whilst this criticism may to some extent be valid, the auditor uses judgement in all varieties of statistical sampling and the Bayesian method 'merely' involves extending the judgemental process. Indeed it may be argued that as the auditor gains experience in the formulation of prior distributions it is likely that their variability will be reduced. As Smith (1976, p. 214) concludes: 'Bayes Theorem is the logical method for combining the sample data with the prior evidence.'

CONCLUSIONS

At the outset of this chapter the importance of sampling for an effective and efficient audit was emphasized. Statistical sampling is a response to the need to formalize the judgement which must take place any time the auditor draws a sample as opposed to testing the complete population. This formalization can be justified as an attempt to make more precise the determination of the sample size and the consequences of sample errors for the population from which the sample has been drawn. This formalization has led to authors such as McRae (1982) designating statistical sampling as a scientific approach to sampling, hence emphasizing its supposed objectively and neutrality. This probably overstates the case, since statistical sampling, as has been stressed in this chapter, relies on specification of a number of factors. These include confidence levels, upper error rates, estimated error rates, the ability of auditors properly to recognize and evaluate errors and, in MUS, the dependence on the spread of errors in the population. This list of underlying assumptions should raise questions about dubbing statistical sampling 'scientific'. This is not intended to devalue its use but only to emphasize that, perhaps, one of its main benefits is simply its requirement that auditors should formally consider their judgement.

Kaplan (1975b), in his synthesis of a conference on auditing, arued that statistical sampling was an area in which communication between academics and practitioners would be beneficial to the practice of auditing. Whilst this is a most laudable sentiment, it is perhaps a matter of some concern that much academic research, particularly in the USA, is centred around refining the mathematical techniques rather than more fundamental questions. In the UK very little is known about the quantity and value of errors that arise in audit populations, the ability of auditors to evaluate errors correctly, the effect of results in one audit area on another related audit area, the allocation of upper error limits to populations and the reasons for the lack of implementation of statistical sampling by all but the larger firms. It is research into topics such as these that is likely to be of most benefit to the audit process.

NOTES

1. Items in a population are homogeneous if they all possess the same characteristics, such as being subject to the same control procedures or for similar amounts. Where populations are not homogeneous it is possible – by dividing the population into sections, where each section is effectively a sub-population having similar characteristics – to improve homogeneity. This process of division is commonly referred to as stratification.
2. Typically the sampling theory is based on the hypergeometric distribution or its approximations, the binomial and Poisson distributions.
3. Even if the auditor did test the complete population the possibility of non-sampling risk (see below) would prevent the auditor from reaching a conclusion with 100 per cent certainty.
4. For a precise definition of these items see Chapter 10.
5. There are many variants and different names for monetary unit sampling, including combined attributes–variables sampling (CAV), probability proportionate to size sampling (PPS), cumulative monetary amount sampling (CMA) and dollar unit sampling (DUS). In this chapter they will all be treated as synonymous with MUS.
6. The reliability factor, which depends on the confidence level and the expected number of errors, can be obtained from suitable tables. For further details regarding the statistics involved in the calculation of the reliability factors the reader is referred to Leslie, Teitlebaum and Anderson (1980).
7. The percentage tainting is calculated as: (Book value – Audit value) ÷ Book value × 100.
8. This method of calculating the upper error limit is called the Stringer bound, named after one of the pioneers in statistical sampling, Ken Stringer.
9. Grimlund and Schroeder (1988) present details of the way twelve large accounting firms in the USA – including the 'Big 8' – plan their sample size and treat understatements.
10. Leslie, Teitlebaum and Anderson (1980) – the cell bound; Fienberg, Neter and Leitch (1977) – the multinomial bound; Garstka (1977) – compound Poisson model.
11. In variables estimation sampling, calculation of sample size and allowance for sampling risk involve mathematical formulae and calculations which are beyond the scope of this chapter. Interested readers are referred to Roberts (1978).

REFERENCES AND FURTHER READING

Akresh, A.D., Loebbecke, J.K. and Scott, W.R. (1988) Audit approaches and techniques, in A.R. Abdel-khalik and I. Solomon (eds.) *Research Opportunities in Auditing: The Second Decade*, American Accounting Association, Sarasota, Florida.

American Institute of Certified Public Accountants (1981) *Audit Sampling*, Statement on Auditing Standards No. 39, AICPA, New York.

American Institute of Certified Public Accountants (1983) *Audit Sampling*, AICPA, New York.

Anderson, R. and Teitlebaum, A.D. (1973) Dollar-unit sampling, a solution to the audit sampling dilemma, *Canadian Chartered Accountant*, April, pp. 30–9.

Auditing Practices Committee (1987a) *Audit Sampling*, Draft Audit Brief, APC, London.

Auditing Practices Committee (1987b) *Audit Sampling*, Auditing Guideline, APC, London.

Black, A.D. and Eastwood, A.M. (1980) Audit evidence – the benefits of monetary unit sampling, *The Accountant's Magazine*, May, pp. 197–200.

Burgstahler, D. and Jiambalvo, J. (1986) Sample error characteristics and projection of error to audit populations, *Accounting Review*, Vol. LXI, no. 2, pp. 233–48.
Canadian Institute of Chartered Accountants (1980) *Extent of Audit Testing: A Research Study*, CICA, Toronto.
Cosserat, G. (1983) Judgement sampling rules OK!, *Accountancy*, April, pp. 91–2.
Daniel, S.J. (1988) Some empirical evidence about the assessment of audit risk in practice, *Auditing: A Journal of Practice & Theory*, Vol. 7, no. 2, pp. 174–81.
Elliott, R.K. and Rogers, J.R. (1972) Relating statistical sampling to audit objectives, *Journal of Accountancy*, July, pp. 46–55.
Fienberg, S.E., Neter, J. and Leitch, R.A. (1977) Estimating the total overstatement error in accounting populations, *Journal of the American Statistical Association*, Vol. 72, no. 358, pp. 295–302.
Gafford, W.W. and Carmichael, D.R. (1984) Materiality, audit risk and sampling: a nuts-and-bolts approach, *Journal of Accountancy*, October, pp. 109–18 and November, pp. 125–38.
Garstka, S.J. (1977) Models for computing upper error limits in dollar-unit sampling, *Journal of Accounting Research*, Vol. 15, no. 2, pp. 178–92.
Goodfellow, J.L., Loebbecke, J.K. and Neter, J. (1974) Some perspectives on CAV sampling plans, *CA Magazine*, October, pp. 22–30 and November, pp. 46–53.
Grimlund, R.A. and Schroeder, M.S. (1988) On the current use of the stringer method of MUS: some new directions, *Auditing: A Journal of Theory and Practice*, Vol. 8, no. 1, pp. 53–62.
Guy, D.M. (1981) *An Introduction to Statistical Sampling in Auditing*, John Wiley, New York.
Gwilliam, D.R. (1987) *A Survey of Auditing Research*, Prentice-Hall International/ ICAEW, London.
Johnson, R.N. (1984) Sampling? use your professional judgement, *Accountancy*, January, pp. 70–3.
Kaplan, R.S. (1975a) Sample size computations for dollar-unit sampling, *Journal of Accounting Research*, Vol. 13, Supplement, pp. 126–33.
Kaplan, R.S. (1975b) A synthesis, *Journal of Accounting Research*, Vol. 13, Supplement, pp. 134–42.
Lee, T. (1986) *Company Auditing*, Van Nostrand Reinhold, London.
Leslie, D.A., Teitlebaum, A.D. and Anderson, R.J. (1980) *Dollar-Unit Sampling: A Practical Guide for Auditors*, Pitman, London.
Loebbecke, J.K. and Neter, J. (1975) Considerations in choosing statistical sampling procedures in auditing, *Journal of Accounting Research*, Vol. 13, Supplement, pp. 38–52.
McLintock & Co., T. (1983) *The Thomson McLintock Audit Manual*, Macmillan, Surrey.
McRae, T.W. (1982) *A Study of the Application of Statistical Sampling to External Auditing*, Institute of Chartered Accountants in England and Wales, London.
Meikle, G.R. (1972) *Statistical Sampling in an Audit Context*, Canadian Institute of Chartered Accountants, Toronto.
Plante, R., Neter, J. and Leitch, R.A. (1985) Comparative performance of multinomial, cell and stringer bounds, *Auditing: A Journal of Practice & Theory*, Vol. 5, no. 1, pp. 40–56.
Roberts, D.M. (1978) *Statistical Auditing*, American Institute of Certified Public Accountants, New York.
Scott, W.R. (1984) The state of the art of academic research in auditing, *Journal of Accounting Literature*, Vol. 3, pp. 153–97.
Sherer, M. and Kent, D. (1983) *Auditing and Accountability*, Pitman Books, London, (reprinted 1988 Paul Chapman, London).
Smith, T.M.F. (1976) *Statistical Sampling for Accountants*, Haymarket, London.

Teitlebaum, A.D. and Robinson, C.F. (1975) The real risks in audit sampling, *Journal of Accounting Research*, Vol. 13, Supplement, pp. 70–91.
Zuber, G.R., Elliott, R.K., Kinney Jr, W.R. and Leisenring, J.J. (1983) Using materiality in audit planning, *Journal of Accountancy*, March, pp. 42–54.

DISCUSSION QUESTIONS

1. During the course of an audit, the auditor attempts to obtain sufficient relevant and reliable evidence to provide the satisfaction that the financial records are complete and accurate. One of the ways that the auditor obtains such satisfaction is to select representative samples of transactions and balances for detailed testing, such samples being made using either statistical or non-statistical methods.
    You are required to:
    (a) described the main factors which influence the auditor in determining the size of the sample he or she will use for the detailed testing;
    (b) describe three areas where judgement will be exercised by the auditor when using statistical sampling;
    (c) explain the factors which the auditor must consider in making the choice between a statistical and a non-statistical sampling procedure.
2. Some major firms use 'conventional' statistical sampling, some use monetary unit sampling and some use only judgemental sampling. To what extent do you believe this knowledge should influence your interpretation of the reliability of these firms' respective audit reports?
3. Bayesian sampling, with its use of the auditor's prior knowledge of the transactions or balances being tested, seems to be the optimal form of statistical sampling. Discuss
4. Statistical sampling seems to rely as much as any form of sampling on the auditor's judgement and thus its supposed advantages are more of a myth than a reality. Discuss
5. Describe the three methods of variables estimation sampling and discuss the limitations inherent in them.

Question 1 is adapted from the examinations of the Association of Certified Accountants and is reproduced by permission of the Education Officer.

APPENDIX: MUS EXAMPLE

Data

Population value: £22 million
Tolerable error: £660,000, or 3 per cent of population value
Confidence level: 90 per cent
Expected value of errors: £110,000, or 0.5 per cent of population value

Using attribute sampling tables appropriate for a confidence level of 90 per cent, an upper error rate of 3 per cent and an expected error rate of 0.5 per cent, the sample size is 129.

$$\text{Average sampling interval} = \frac{\text{Population value}}{\text{Sample size}}$$

$$= \frac{\pounds 22,000,000}{129}$$

$$= \pounds 170,543$$

In the event, errors were found:

Error	Book value	Audit value	Difference	Sample error tainting (%)
1	430	387	43	10
2	1988	1491	497	25
3	875	525	350	40
				75

Evaluation of errors

Most likely error = Sum of taintings % × average sampling interval

$$= 0.75 \times \pounds 170,543$$

$$= \pounds 127,907$$

Basic precision

= reliability factor assuming 0 errors × average sampling interval

= 2.31 (from tables) × £170,543

= £393,954

The 90 per cent precision gap widening (PGW) factors are:

Error no.	PGW factor
1	0.58
2	0.44
3	0.36

Precision gap widening:

Ranked taintings	PGW factor	PGW
40%	0.58	0.40 × 0.58 = 0.232
25%	0.44	0.25 × 0.44 = 0.110
10%	0.36	0.10 × 0.36 = 0.036
		0.378

PGW = 0.378 × £170,543 = £64,465

Upper error = £127,907 + £393,954 + £64,465 = £586,326

Summary

Most likely error = £127,907.

There is a 10 per cent risk that the book value of £22 million is overstated by more than £586,326. As this is less than the specified tolerable error, at this confidence level, of £660,000, the population should be accepted.

Part III
Special Contexts

14
Auditing in the Financial Services Sector

John Tattersall

THE BACKGROUND

The collapse of companies in most sectors of the economy or the discovery that the financial statements of businesses are misleading has frequently triggered actions by those who were or are shareholders or proprietors of those businesses, against their auditors. The auditor's traditional responsibility is to the proprietors: it is to them that the report is addressed, and it is to them that the auditor has responsibilities enshrined in company law. However, those who suffer from the collapse of a business in the financial services sector are far more likely to be customers, depositors or clients of those businesses and it is not unnatural that they view with some frustration the limitations to their rights of action against the auditor. The 1980s saw changes in the obligations imposed upon and public expectations of auditors, which changes have been embodied in new legislation, going beyond that in company law, and which has given the auditor new responsibilities to the regulator or supervisor. Those regulators and supervisors are themselves given the job of looking after the interests of customers, depositors and clients and ensuring that financial markets remain solvent.

The financial services sector may, therefore, be distinguished from other sectors by the extent to which the businesses within it hold or take responsibility for their customers' assets. Frequently, that responsibility is actually represented by physical possession: stockbrokers often hold their clients' money while they effect transactions in securities, bankers hold their customers' cash as deposits and fund managers hold and manage their customers' investments. Investment advisers, many of whom never physically deal with their customers' funds, nevertheless have considerable responsibility to their customers to advise them when to effect changes in their portfolios, when to change their strategy or when to make various elections. It is these customers and depositors who depend upon auditors of stockbrokers, bankers, fund managers and advisers to monitor the way in which those businesses dispose of their assets and to ensure that those businesses are in a position to continue their roles.

The financial services sector covers a variety of different businesses.

John Tattersall, M.A., F.C.A., is a partner in Coopers & Lybrand Deloitte, chartered accountants, and specializes in the banking and securities industry. The views and opinions expressed in this chapter are those of the author, and do not necessarily reflect those of Coopers & Lybrand Deloitte.

Definitions almost inevitabily include banks, building societies, stockbrokers and other securities houses, investment managers, investment brokers, futures and commodity brokers, professional firms which undertake investment business as part of their services and advisers of many kinds. It is often useful to regard the sector as defined by the scope of regulatory legislation: the Financial Services Act 1986, which has introduced the concept of 'investment business' and has initiated a regulatory system for such business; the Building Societies Act 1986, which has further developed the regulations affecting building societies; the Banking Act 1987, which has updated the arrangements for authorization and regulation of deposit-takers including banks; and the Insurance Companies Act 1982, which brings within its scope both general insurance and life assurance companies. All these Acts now introduce some concept of reporting to regulators by auditors.

THE ROLE OF THE AUDITOR REDEFINED

The responsibilities of the auditor of a financial services business under company legislation have not been redefined: it is only in respect of off-balance-sheet commitments and fiduciary roles that the auditor's responsibility for such clients is in any way extended so far as accounts drawn up under the Companies Act 1985 are concerned. The major redefinition of the auditor's role is in respect of reports to regulators and supervisors (or to his or her client for onward transmission):

1. on what is normally described as an '*ad hoc* basis' on matters of which the auditor has become aware in his or her capacity as auditor and of which the regulator or supervisor should be aware;
2. on accounting records and systems of internal control, particularly where those records and systems relate to the assets of the business's clients;
3. on the disposition of client assets themselves; and
4. on the adequacy of the financial resources of the business, as defined in rule books and regulations.

Inevitably, this duty to the regulator includes a further responsibility to customer and depositor although, were action to be required against an auditor, it would in many cases fall to the regulator or supervisor to take such action where loss had been occasioned as a result of the auditor's negligence in reports which they had received. The auditor cannot undertake such responsibilities lightly.

APPROACHING THE AUDIT

The first issue which has been addressed by regulators is that of whether or not a qualified accountant or accountancy firm, properly authorized to carry out the audit of a company in the UK, should be allowed to audit businesses within the financial services sector, or whether an additional 'experience' requirement should be implemented to ensure that those charged with reporting to regulators actually understand the principles and issues involved. Following discussion, the conclusion was reached that qualifications for auditors should be in line with those for appointment as auditors under the Companies Act 1985, but the regulators appointed under the Financial

Services Act reserve the right to disqualify auditors whose performance has not matched up to expectations, and there is a further option to appoint a second auditor to re-audit the books of an investment business where the regulator believes that there is good reason to do so. Similar powers are granted to the Bank of England under the Banking Act 1987.

The implications of this for the auditor are clear: he or she must ensure that all those responsible for managing and performing the audit of a client within the financial services sector have appropriate levels of experience and are aware of their responsibilities. It must be regarded as unacceptable for an audit team not to have access, for example, to the relevant rule book or books issued by regulators or supervisors of their clients. There must be adequate training courses for such staff or alternative means of training (such as self-study packs). While audit staff have traditionally learnt 'on the job' about the industries they are auditing, the complexities of the rules and the reliance placed upon their work by regulators and supervisors means that this method alone is not sufficient. Where customers' assets and deposits are concerned, auditors must fully understand the rules which have been set up to protect investors and depositors. Not only do auditors risk being disqualified by the regulators from auditing within that sector again but they jeopardize the reputation of the whole accountancy profession, given the public expectations of the role of the auditor in this sector, however exaggerated such expectations may be. In approaching the audit, the auditor must also give considerable thought to the letter of engagement: the extra responsibilities in reporting to regulators and supervisors, and the increased scope of the audit, mean that he or she must spell out this task in rather more detail than is conventionally done in a letter of engagement, if only to ensure that the client appreciates the work that has to be done and the fact that it must all be paid for by the client, at least under the present regime.

THE RELATIONSHIPS OF THE AUDITOR WITH THE CLIENT AND THE REGULATOR

Ad hoc reporting
The first issue arising from increased responsibilities of auditors within the financial services sector is that of the strain which is imposed on their traditional client relationships. The relationship of confidentiality, established in auditors' professional bodies' ethical guides, has hitherto precluded the auditor from giving any information to third parties without the client's consent. The Financial Services Act, the Banking Act, the Building Societies Act and the Insurance Companies Act (with a section inserted by the Financial Services Act) now all set that duty aside where reports to regulators and supervisors are involved. The relevant sections provide the right for auditors to provide such information to regulators and supervisors, whether or not in response to a request from them, while also requiring auditors' professional bodies to lay down rules governing the circumstances in which auditors are expected to exercise that right; in the absence of adequate rules, the Secretary of State for Trade and Industry or the Treasury, as appropriate, is empowered to lay down rules specifying circumstances where it is the duty of an auditor to communicate to regulators and supervisors. The term

'auditor' is extended to reporting accountants appointed under sections 8 and 39 of the Banking Act 1987.

Not surprisingly, the Auditing Practices Committee has been quick to lay down rules and these have been accepted by the relevant government departments. The regulations governing investment businesses authorized under the Financial Services Act, for example, are set out in the exposure draft of an auditing guideline, *The Implications for Auditors of the Financial Services Act 1986* (APC, 1988), dated February 1988, but expected to be superseded shortly by a final guideline. For banks and building societies, the relevant rules are set out in auditing guidelines published by the Auditing Practices Committee entitled, respectively, *Banks in the United Kingdom* (APC, 1989) and *Building Societies in the United Kingdom* (APC, 1982). These guidelines, which apply with minor modifications to insurance companies, Lloyd's underwriting agents, and Lloyd's brokers, are set to establish a new pattern for the responsibility of the auditor to the regulator. What might at first have seemed to be a 'sneak's charter' is now generally accepted as a sensible solution to the requirements of regulation. Key elements of these guidelines are as follows.

1. To enable the auditor to exercise such powers, his or her action must be in good faith and not malicious: in theory, the legal profession could provide many interpretations of what the term 'good faith' means but the need for swift action if depositors' or customers' assets are to be protected requires the auditor to make the decision, speedily, whether a matter requires to be reported.
2. The right to report applies regardless of the source of the information to be reported, provided that the auditor becomes aware of the matters reported in the capacity of auditor or reporting accountant of the specific institution concerned.
3. This *ad hoc* reporting line does not replace the normal primary sources of information for the regulator or supervisor, which come directly from the institution's management and directors, and become relevant only when that normal, primary, source is in question or fails to respond.
4. The obligation imposed in practice does not require extra work by auditors or reporting accountants but only extra vigilance to report those matters of which they become aware in the ordinary course of their audit work or reporting accountants' examinations.
5. The obligation applies not only to the auditing division or audit team: it would apply also to work done by any department of an accounting firm, including their taxation team, or their management consultants.

The critical guidance is on when to report: again, the guidance for different parts of the financial services industry varies slightly, but the key principles are that the auditor or reporting accountant must take the initiative:

1. when there has been an advance occurrence or a change in the auditor's or reporting accountant's perception of an existing situation, which may include an adverse change in the circumstances of his or her client;
2. where the adverse occurrence has given rise to material loss or indicates with a reasonable probability that material loss may arise; and
3. where the position is such the interests of customers or depositors might

be better safeguarded if the matter were reported to the regulator or supervisor.

If the actual relationship between auditor and client is to be preserved, quite apart from the duty of confidentiality, the auditor's first action on discovering something which might jeopardize customers' or depositors' interests should be – in almost all circumstances – to encourage the client to report the matter: failing the chief accountant, financial controller or financial director, then chief executives, chairmen or non-executive directors need to be approached. It is only when all those routes fail (which must be unlikely given the implications for those individuals if the auditor's concerns prove to be right) that the auditor must go direct to the regulator or supervisor. In practice, there are certain circumstances where the auditor would be obliged to go direct, for example where he or she had lost confidence in the integrity of directors or senior management or possibly where he or she believed that they had committed or were about to commit a fraud or other misappropriation, or where he or she had lost confidence in their competence to conduct business in such a way as to protect the interests of their customers or depositors.

Tripartite meetings

The second area where the traditional relationship is potentially strained is in the requirement on reporting accountants of authorized deposit-taking institutions (such as banks) to attend joint meetings involving the supervisor, the client and the auditor or reporting accountant. This is a route which is regularly followed by the Bank of England in respect of bank auditors, although in practice other regulators have the power to gain the equivalent information from auditors. The main advantage of this approach for supervisor and auditor is that both are aware of each other's understanding of specific circumstances, without the need to embarrass clients in any way by following matters through to auditor or supervisor directly. In practice, the Bank of England's experience of the first year's meetings suggests that they have gone well.

Caveats

A final issue arising from this relationship is that of the use to which the regulators and supervisors put opinions issued by auditors: inevitably, where auditors are required to comment upon accounting records and systems of internal control over such records, the recipient might feel justified in concluding that if, when the report was issued, the systems and records were in proper working order, they might continue to be so, in the absence of an adverse occurrence, for some time. However, the auditor's role is to report on systems and records during a particular financial year or period, and this potential confusion has led to the insertion of additional paragraphs in auditors' reports to regulators setting out the limitations on their work where any projection of their opinions to future periods is involved, and the following are typical paragraphs used by some auditing firms:

> The directors of the company are responsible for establishing and maintaining adequate accounting and other records and internal controls systems. In fulfilling

that responsibility, estimates and judgements must be made to assess the expected benefits and related costs of management information and of control procedures. The objective is to provide a reasonable but not absolute assurance that assets are safeguarded against loss from unauthorized use or disposition, that transactions are executed in accordance with established authorization procedures and are recorded properly, and to enable the directors to conduct the business in a prudent manner.

Because of inherent limitations in any accounting and internal control systems, errors or irregularities may nevertheless occur and not be detected. Also, projection of any evaluation of the systems to future periods is subject to the risk that management information and control procedures may become inadequate because of changes in conditions or that the degree of compliance with those procedures may deteriorate.

It is interesting to note that the use of such paragraphs is not uniform among all the major auditing firms, although it is strongly recommended in what will almost certainly become the standard work on the subject, *Auditing Investment Business*, by Christopher Morgan and Matthew Patient (1989).

THE SCOPE OF THE AUDIT

Reports to the regulator or supervisor

The contents of reports to regulators and supervisors are laid out in detail in their regulations and in notices issued by them. The essential requirements are for the audit report to cover the following additional areas:

1. a statement of financial resources for businesses authorized under the Financial Services Act, stating whether or not the business has complied with financial resource requirements;
2. an opinion on the reconciliation of the annual return to quarterly returns submitted earlier during the financial period, particularly as regards income but also the balance sheet in the last quarterly return of the year;
3. an opinion on accounting records and, in certain cases, systems of control thereon not only as to whether proper accounting records had been kept as defined in company legislation, but also as to whether the more detailed requirements laid down by the relevant regulatory organizations had been followed: in the case of building societies this extends specifically to systems of inspection and report;
4. an opinion on whether the business had adequate systems throughout the financial year to comply with the various rules governing client money and client property (such as share certificates) and, specifically , whether they were in compliance with those requirements at the year-end and (in certain cases) on certain other dates.

For members of the Securities Association, these requirements are extended quite significantly to cover systems and procedures for the agreement and reconciliation of balances and securities positions with counterparties, banks and clearing houses; procedures and controls for reporting and investigating the ageing and analysis of balances with counterparties; and procedures for monitoring the member's position risk and counterparty risk exposures and providing appropriate levels of management with the information necesssary for them to make relevant, timely and informed decisions to control such risks. In the case of banks and other deposit-taking institutions, requirements for reports on accounting and other records and internal control systems are determined from year to year, normally on a cyclical basis so that all areas of the bank are covered over a certain number of years, but for smaller deposit-taking institutions such reports tend to cover all significant accounting records and controls; in addition, reports are requested from time to time by the Bank of England on specific prudential returns made, rather than on specified annual prudential returns.

The systems-based audit becomes mandatory

The main impact of this requirement is to extend the scope of the audit to require positive opinions on systems and controls. Whereas many auditors have, for many years, based their audit approach on an understanding of and testing of systems of internal control, many smaller audits have consisted largely of substantive tests of year-end balances and transactions, particularly where systems of internal control were not deemed to be sufficiently reliable. That approach is now no longer acceptable for companies which hold client money or other assets, or which accept deposits from customers. The audit has to be structured in such a way as to enable the auditor to assess whether or not sufficient controls have been in place throughout the period under audit. Almost inevitably, it raises further the experience level and ability expected of audit staff.

The extension of the report to cover the financial resources of the institution and whether it met the regulator's financial resource requirements also demands a detailed knowledge of precisely what the business did during the year, in order to assess what category of membership or which set of requirements applied. In particular, an investment adviser which may or may not have held client money during the year will be in a substantially different category depending on whether or not it did. It falls to the auditor to be satisfied that the business did not hold client money before he or she can accept that reduced financial resources requirements applied. In many cases, auditors spell out the fact that they have relied on representations from the client or that they have carried out only limited testing to determine whether or not client money was held, thereby indicating the scope of their work in their audit report.

The compliance function

A further area which has demanded increased attention from auditors is that of the compliance function: all investment businesses are required to appoint a compliance officer who is responsible, *inter alia*, for confirming to the regulator at least annually that the business has complied with the relevant regulations. Although the auditor's report is limited to accounting records, internal controls, financial resources and controls over client property and assets, the penalties which could be imposed upon an investment business that failed to comply with all the other regulations, particularly the conduct of business rules governing relationships with clients and customers generally, could have a significant impact on the future of the business itself. If, for example, the result of a breach of conduct of business rules was that an investor was able to claim substantial compensation under section 62 of the

Financial Services Act 1986 (which in certain circumstances allows restitution of an investor's losses by the investment business concerned) the breach could either significantly change the state of that business's affairs or mean that its viability in the future was in question. Further, if that same breach of rules meant that the regulator was likely to remove authorization as an investment business, it could jeopardize the going concern status.

This mean that the auditor must extend the review of the company's affairs in order to be satisfied that adequate compliance procedures are in place including, for example, tests carried out by the compliance officer or by someone delegated by him or her to ensure that regulations are being followed. The auditor should also be concerned with the personnel department, and in particular with the question whether or not adequate checks are made of those employees who will deal with clients before they are taken on. Investment businesses themselves take responsibility for ensuring that their employees are fit and proper and for notifying the regulatory authorities accordingly, and any failure to follow proper practices could also have severe consequences.

Client assets

The underlying principle behind client asset protection is that money held or securities of any sort held by investment businesses on behalf of their clients should be protected from the claims of those businesses' creditors and from rights of set-off which might be established by their bankers. A further principle, effectively amplifying what was already contained in the law of agency, is that investment businesses should be required to seek the best return available for their clients on money which they hold from time to time, taking into account also the risk and inconvenience involved, and to pass on such return to those clients unless they have specifically (and not under duress) agreed otherwise.

For banks, the application of such rules is rather different, given that the opening of a specific account for a customer in a bank (or a building society) means that such account is itself protected by the Banking Act 1987 and the Deposit Protection Fund established under that Act. Accordingly, most of the specific requirements which relate to clients' money are waived where the businesses are also authorized deposit-taking institutions, provided that client funds are immediately credited to an account opened in the name of the client concerned rather than being left in a general suspense account.

The main areas of attention in respect of client assets for auditors become:

1. making sure that client money or other assets received are immediately identified and channelled into appropriate accounts or classifications;
2. checking that such accounts or classifications thereafter remain separate and satisfy the regulations which protect such assets from claims by creditors or bankers: this extends to the titles of client money accounts, undertakings required of the banks at which such accounts are held and the arrangements with custodians that physically hold client securities for another investment business;
3. reviewing the regular carrying out of reconciliations between statements from third parties (banks or custodians) and summary accounting

records, and those same summary accounting records and the detailed underlying accounting records;
4. testing procedures to ensure that interest is paid at appropriate intervals on clients' funds held; and
5. testing procedures governing the withdrawal of client funds and assets and restricting such withdrawals to appropriately authorized officers and circumstances.

While the rules for the protection of client assets sometimes appear simple to administer, this is the area of greatest temptation for the unscrupulous manager of an investment business: clients' money or assets become particularly tempting when the business itself is under financial strain. The trust placed with such managers could be easily abused by fraudsters. Accordingly, this is a specific area which auditors ignore at their peril.

CONCLUSION

The scope of auditing within the financial services sector has undoubtedly been redefined over the past decade: much of it is in response to legislation, itself triggered by the major banking and commodity business losses of the 1970s. However, the rising regulatory expectations of auditors and, indeed, the increasing prominence of the accountancy profession have heightened public expectations of the auditor. Whatever the auditor's legal responsibilities, themselves substantially increased, the experience and training required of and the application necessary from auditors have increased dramatically.

REFERENCES AND FURTHER READING

Association of Futures Brokers and Dealers (1988) *Rules and Handbook* (regularly updated), AFBD, London.

Auditing Practices Committee (1982) *Building Societies in the United Kingdom*, Auditing Guideline (revised 1989), APC, London.

Auditing Practices Committee (1988) *The Implications for Auditors of the Financial Services Act 1986*, Exposure Draft of an Auditing Guideline, APC, London.

Auditing Practices Committee (1989) *Banks in the United Kingdom*, Auditing Guideline, APC, London.

Bank of England (Banking Supervision Division) (1987) *Guidance Note on Accounting and Other Records and Internal Control Systems and Reporting Accountants' Reports Thereon*, notice to institutions authorized under the Banking Act 1987, Bank of England, London.

Bank of England (Banking Supervision Division) (1987) *The Bank of England's Relationship with Auditors and Reporting Accountants*, notice to institutions authorized under the Banking Act 1987, Bank of England, London.

Bank of England (Banking Supervision Division) (1987) *Guidance Note on Reporting Accountants' Reports on Bank of England Returns Used for Prudential Purposes*, notice to institutions authorized under the Banking Act 1987, Bank of England, London.

Banking Act 1987, HMSO, London.

Building Societies Act 1986, HMSO, London.

Building Societies Commission (1986) *Relationships between Auditors and the Commission*, Prudential Note 1986/2, BSC, London.

Financial Intermediaries, Managers and Brokers Regulatory Association (1988) *Rules* (regularly updated), FIMBRA, London.

Insurance Companies Act 1982, HMSO, London.

Investment Management Regulatory Organization Limited (1988) *Rules* (regularly updated), IMRO, London.

Morgan, C. and Patient, M. (1989) *Auditing Investment Business*, Butterworths, London.

Penn, G. (1989) *Banking Supervision – Regulation of the UK Banking Sector under the Banking Act 1987*, Butterworths, London.

Securities Association (1988) *Rules* (regularly updated), Securities Association, London.

Securities and Investments Board (1988) *Rules and Regulations*, Vol 1, 2 and 3 (regulatory updated), SIB, London.

DISCUSSION QUESTIONS

1. What sort of experience should be expected of audit staff responsible for the audits of businesses within the financial services sector?
2. What sort of consideration should be given by an auditor before reporting directly to a self-regulating organization, the Bank of England or the Building Societies Commission on matters concerning his or her client?
3. How does an auditor decide what constitutes 'good faith'?
4. Should an auditor be willing to give to a regulator an opinion on records and systems which is unencumbered by specific caveats or should he or she specify that his or her opinion should not necessarily be relied upon as to the soundness of systems and records in the future? Why?
5. What sort of work should an auditor do to establish whether or not a client has accepted 'client money' during the year?
6. What work might an auditor be expected to do to establish whether or not an investment business client has complied with conduct of business rules during the period under audit or, indeed, the period between the year-end and the date on which the auditor signed his or her audit opinion?

15

The Auditor and the Smaller Company

Michael J. Page

INTRODUCTION

There are two broad questions to be discussed in this chapter: Should small companies be required to have their accounts audited? And: If an audit is required by the operation of company law or otherwise, what special problems do auditors of a small company face and how should they resolve them? The first question is a matter of public policy and in practice needs to be answered by government; the second question is about the conduct of auditing engagements and is a matter upon which members of the accounting and auditing professions need to form a view.

Before discussing these questions, it may be helpful to state what is meant by the term 'small company'. Unless otherwise specified in this chapter a small company is defined as in the Companies Act 1989. The essence of the definition is that the company satisfies two of the following three criteria:

1. Turnover – not exceeding £2 million;
2. Total assets (balance sheet total) – not exceeding £975,000;
3. Number of employees – not exceeding fifty.

The definition is derived from a permissible rounding-up of the criteria provided by the European Community (EC) Fourth Directive on Company Law; the monetary totals are updated for inflation from time to time.

SHOULD AN AUDIT BE REQUIRED OF SMALL COMPANIES?

The UK is unusual in requiring small companies to prepare full audited accounts. In nearly all other countries small companies are not required to disclose comprehensive accounts to the public, and only in a few countries (for example Belgium, Denmark, Sweden and Switzerland) are small companies required to have an audit. Compare the difference between the situations in the UK and in the USA.

In the UK the full audited accounts for a period must show a true and fair view of the results of the period and of the state of affairs at the balance sheet date. Until recently, small companies were required to make public their full accounts, but the Companies Act 1981 (now consolidated into the Companies

Michael J. Page, M.A. F.C.A., is Halpern and Woolf Professor of Accounting at Portsmouth Polytechnic.

Act 1985) permitted small companies to file with the Registrar of Companies so-called 'modified' accounts which contain much less information than the full accounts. Modified accounts comprise a balance sheet in abbreviated form, a statement of accounting policies and little else.

In the USA only public companies are required to disclose audited financial statements which 'fairly present' a view of the enterprise in accordance with 'generally accepted accounting principles'. Non-public companies need neither disclose information to the world at large nor, unless they so choose, have their accounts audited. This means they are free to prepare accounts other than in accordance with generally accepted accounting principles; they can omit items which they feel it would not be cost-beneficial to report to the users of the accounts; and they can measure the items which they recognize in the accounts in ways which they think are more appropriate to their business. As an alternative to an audit, non-public companies can choose either to have a 'review' of their accounts or, if a public accountant prepares the statements and does no other work on them, he can issue a 'compilation report' which states that no audit or review has been carried out (AIPCA, 1979).

Thus in the UK, the concession in the 1981 Act fails to simplify reporting by small companies, as it does not give them the freedom of reporting enjoyed by similar companies in the USA (and many other countries). This is because UK small companies are still required to produce true and fair accounts and to have them audited; they cannot produce accounts which do not comply with the recognition, measurement and disclosure criteria of the generally accepted accounting conventions, the disclosure requirements of the Companies Acts, and accounting standards, which are the ingredients of the true and fair view. There have been some moves to exempt small companies from the more onerous requirements of some accounting standards, but not from the whole framework of reporting. See Carsberg *et al.* (1985) and Arthur Young (1989, pp. 11–14) for a discussion of accounting, as opposed to auditing, questions about small companies.

Whether audits should be necessary for small companies must depend upon the nature of the companies and the uses and users of their accounts. The company – a corporate person with a separate legal identity – is a much more popular form of business vehicle in Britain than in other countries and the number of companies has been growing steadily. At 31 March 1989 there were 1,133,200 registered companies (Department of Trade and Industry, 1989a). Not all these companies are active and independent; many are subsidiaries of other companies, dormant companies or too recently formed to have filed accounts. Probably about 40 per cent of unlisted companies can be thought of as active, independent and subject to reporting regulations at any time. This estimate and some of those which follow are taken from Page (1984). Of these companies, a very large proportion will be regarded as small under any reasonable definition. Analysis of filed accounts of companies suggests that over 90 per cent of active independent companies are likely to come within the terms of the 1981 Companies Act definition. Adoption of a different basis of definition, or different thresholds, might alter the companies falling into the category at the margin, but the bulk of companies would continue to be regarded as small under any definition which is likely to be widely acceptable.

Similarly, analysis of the filed accounts of small companies shows that directors control the majority of shares in over 90 per cent of companies; in two-thirds of small companies the directors own all the shares. These statistics give little support to the formal view of financial reporting for small companies in which directors report to shareholders and auditors check that the shareholders are not being misled.

The origin of the current position was more historical accident than design. The Companies Act 1900 demanded an audit for all companies (including unlimited companies), a provision which has remained in force ever since. However, this requirement predated the development of detailed requirements about the contents of accounts and the distinction between public and private limited companies. Subsequent development of detailed requirements for the contents of accounts seems to have been designed mainly for public companies, but was applied to the information reported to private company shareholders without much consideration of the cost or need for audit. The Companies Act 1967, however, abolished the exemption from public filing enjoyed by most private companies, and so left the small private company exposed to the full rigour of reporting requirements.

The promulgation of the EC Fourth Directive on Company Law provided an opportunity to reassess the position. The Directive enforces minimum disclosure standards on companies in all countries of the EC; it also makes an audit compulsory for large and medium-sized companies, but not for small companies. The EC Council of Ministers adopted the Fourth Directive in July 1978 and in September 1979 the Department of Trade issued a Green Paper, *Company Accounting and Disclosure – A Consultative Document*, seeking comment on the implementation of the Directive and, in particular, to what extent an audit should be required of small companies.

Parallel with the developments ensuing from the Fourth Directive, the Auditing Practices Committee (APC) of the Consultative Committee of Accountancy Bodies was developing a series of auditing standards and guidelines designed to codify best auditing practice. The main feature of the auditing standards programme is to ensure that auditors create a network of evidence to support their opinion on whether the audited accounts present a true and fair view. It soon became clear to the APC and others that, if the same standards of verification were to apply to both large and small companies, the costs borne by small companies in having their accounts audited would be much greater, relatively, than the costs for large companies.

On the subject of small company audits the Green Paper had put forward three possibilities for discussion:

1. small companies should continue to be audited;
2. instead of an audit, a lower level of attestation called a 'review' should be introduced;
3. there should be no audit requirement.

The Green Paper clearly favoured the first possibility, but offered the suggestion that

> the adoption of the three-tier classification of companies in law might be used as a basis for developing further standards setting out the different approach and methods appropriate to the circumstances of smaller companies.
>
> (Department of Trade, 1979, Ch. 2, para. 14)

This passed the buck neatly to the accountancy profession.

The APC responded by issuing its own discussion document *Small Companies: The Need For Audit* (APC, 1979), in which it was explicitly recognized that, unless there were some concession in law or auditing standards, many small companies would receive qualified audit reports. The concern about small company audits was mirrored by an extensive debate in the professional press. The logically prior question of what small companies' accounts should contain received much less attention, and it is possible that the outcome of legislation would have been different if this had not been the case.

The government decided, after receiving responses to the Green Paper, to retain the audit because there was no strong consensus for its abolition. The debate did not die down, however, and has continued throughout the ensuing decade in response to various government reports and white papers and the Companies Bill 1989.

In 1985 the Department of Trade and Industry (DTI) published a scrutiny (DTI, 1985a) of the main burdens imposed on small businesses by central and local government. The scrutiny team suggested, *inter alia*, considering whether to 'eliminate the present statutory audit of accounts for "shareholder-managed" small businesses', together with simplification of reporting requirements (DTI, 1985a, p. 7). In response, the DTI published a further discussion paper (DTI, 1985b) setting out what it saw as the main arguments for and against the small company audit and requesting comment about whether the audit requirement should be abolished for small companies, all of whose shareholders were directors; a subset of very small companies; or for all small companies at the option of shareholders. The discussion paper was clearly more favourable towards abolition than the Green Paper had been. There followed a vigorous debate in which the various accountancy bodies were unable to present a united front. The Association of Certified Accountants came down in favour of retention of the audit, but the Institute of Chartered Accountants in England and Wales (ICAEW) reversed the view it held in 1979 and argued for allowing small companies to opt out of audits provided all shareholders agreed. The ICAEW also wanted a simplified set of accounts for the use of shareholders and for filing at the Companies Registry (ICAEW, 1985). The 1989 Companies Act has introduced provisions which allow listed public companies to send summary financial statements to shareholders who wish to receive them.

At first sight the ICAEW position seems surprising, given that its members were responsible for the majority of small company audits. However, the difficulty of framing appropriate auditing standards for large companies within the constraint that they needed to be applied to small companies was hindering the work of the APC. Further, such evidence as was available showed that the ICAEW's smaller practitioner members had no shortage of work and that a majority felt that they could spend time more profitably in advising clients rather than auditing their accounts.

Within the accounting profession, commentators on various proposals have divided among the three possibilities put forward in the Green Paper: those favouring abolition of the audit requirement; proponents of review; and retentionists.

Abolition

The case made for abolition rests on three points. First, the audit report of small companies should generally be qualified. This is 'not because there is a lack of controls, but because of a lack of independent evidence as to their operation and the completeness of the records' (Davison, 1980, p. 42).

Second, the economic benefits of the audit are not held to justify the cost. For example, Briston and Perks (1977) estimated (very much on a rule of thumb basis) the annual cost of auditing unlisted companies at £90 million and concluded that the possible benefits of the audit could not merit such a cost. Barker (1985, p. 14) suggested that the value of one of the benefits – information for suppliers – was low because of filing delays: 'normal trade creditors . . . would be ill-advised to rely on accounts likely to be at least nine months out of date'. And as Rutteman (1985, p. 12) points out, creditors may have access only to modified accounts which contain little information. Creditors have found other ways to protect themselves. He concludes: 'The crux of the issue is whether the cost of the audit, albeit small in itself, is disproportionate to the benefits it brings as far as small companies are concerned.'

Third, comparison with other countries where audit (and frequently disclosure) is not required suggests that no real harm will result if the requirement is abolished. Within the EC only the UK, Eire and Denmark require audits for small companies. There is no audit requirement in the USA, and Canada and South Africa allow small companies to opt out of audits.

Review

The case for review accepts most of the abolitionist argument, but makes the observation that a small company's accounts are almost invariably prepared by the professional accountant who subsequently audits them. In the process of preparation the accountant gains considerable insight into the state of the business, and does much to update and correct the company's records. The argument runs that the insight thus gained should enable the accountant to 'review' the accounts and attest to their 'reasonableness' without going on to obtain independent evidence of the truth and fairness of the final accounts. Gemell (1977) develops a framework for the review, consisting primarily of 'enquiry, comparison and discussion of (the) financial statements, and of the information and explanations supplied' by analogy with existing procedures in the USA and Canada. *Small Companies: the Need for Audit* (APC, 1979) provides a similar formulation.

The advantages of a review are its relative cheapness, since it involves little, if any, extra work by the accountant, and its avoidance of the problem of auditing businesses with rudimentary systems of internal control. In addition, those who take a monolithic approach to unified auditing standards for all businesses hold that progress in improving the audit function for listed companies is retarded by the need to have similar standards for small companies (e.g. Davison, 1978). Opponents of review, starting from the same premise of monolithic auditing standards, however, argue that the review would not be sufficiently distanced from the audit to avoid danger of confusion. Shaw (1978) argues,

Because a significant part of the total work of the accountancy profession in the UK has been involved in audit and the expression of opinion there has developed an expectation that the public accountant validates by association.

And, further, that attempts to remedy this are futile:

The proposed review procedure requires the reviewer to make manifestly clear by unambiguous disclaimer that his review was to all intents and purposes worthless.

Retention

The argument for retention is based either on the premise that the audit is 'the price of limited liability', that is, that only by offering reliable accounts to the public may potential creditors be safeguarded (e.g. White, 1985), or on grounds of equity – because many small companies would continue to have their accounts audited to satisfy the requirements of banks or to facilitate acceptance of tax computations, they should all do so.

A compromise between the retention of the audit and a review is the suggestion made in the Green Paper (Department of Trade, 1979, pp. 3–4) that the accounting profession should develop separate auditing standards for small companies. This suggestion was opposed in a number of articles in the accounting press and elsewhere, mainly on the grounds that the audit of large companies to existing standards might thereby be jeopardized, at least in the opinion of the public.

Of the respondents to *Small Companies: the Need for Audit*, opinion was divided equally between those who thought 'that the audit in its present form should continue to be mandatory for all small companies' and those who did not (APC, 1980a). The majority of respondents who wanted to retain an audit thought it would be acceptable if many companies received a qualified audit report. The majority of respondents who did not wish to retain the audit wanted small companies to have their accounts reviewed instead.

Of those who wanted to retain the audit, a two-to-one majority found it acceptable that a significant number of companies would receive audit reports containing a small company qualification (see below). Of those who did not want to retain the audit, or who found the prospect of a large number of small company qualifications unacceptable, most wanted a review as an alternative to audit. A majority of respondents thought the review option should apply to a narrower selection of companies than those eventually defined as such by the Companies Act 1981.

There was no joint submission by the Consultative Committee of Accountancy Bodies (CCAB) to the Department of Trade in response to the question in the Green Paper as to whether audits should remain compulsory for small companies. However, the English Institute in a memorandum to the Department of Trade (ICAEW, 1980) recommended that audits should remain compulsory, on the grounds that there was 'lack of desire or pressure for change on the part of most users of accounts'. ICAEW rejected a review as an alternative because of the danger of confusion with an audit and because it would not save a worthwhile amount of money.

It is therefore not surprising that, without a strong lead from the profession, and with evidence of strongly divided opinion, the inclination shown in the Green Paper to retain the audit was not changed, and the Companies Act 1981 retained the audit as a compulsory feature of small company accounts.

Despite the more favourable stance towards abolition adopted from 1985 by the ICAEW and the Institute of Chartered Accountants of Scotland, the DTI has continued to favour compulsory audits for small companies. Commenting on the decision not to abolish the audit requirement in the Companies Bill (now Act) 1989, *Accountancy* (December, 1988, p. 6) suggested that 'the DTI is believed to have bowed to pressure from the Treasury and the Inland Revenue, both of which wanted the audit retained as an additional protection against malpractice'. This echoes the reasons given in 1986 for retaining the audit, following the consultative document (DTI, 1985b) – the audit was considered to be the first defence against fraud.

The retention of the small company audit in the 1989 Act might seem to have settled the matter once and for all. However, the EC Commission is proposing an extension to the Fourth Directive on Company Accounts, which would oblige member states to abolish the compulsory audit and to allow small companies to produce much less information than currently, while still requiring their accounts to show a true and fair view (DTI, 1989b). A possible compromise, retention of the audit but less disclosure in the main accounts, would present auditors with a tricky dilemma: can abbreviated accounts show a true and fair view?

WHAT PROBLEMS DO AUDITORS OF A SMALL COMPANY FACE, AND HOW SHOULD THEY RESOLVE THEM?

The previous section suggested that there may be inherent contradictions in requiring directors of small companies to pay for an audit of information which in most cases is addressed, at least formally, to themselves. Nevertheless, in the UK the accounts of small companies must be audited. This section deals with the way in which the auditor can go about the task, and what advice auditing standards and guidelines give. There are two essential problems which face the auditor.

First, there are economies of scale in auditing; it does not cost twice as much to audit a company which is twice as big as another. This means that it is relatively more expensive to carry out similar audit procedures on small companies than on large ones. The reasons for the existence of economies of scale are numerous, but two important reasons are that the sizes of samples for use in statistical tests do not depend to any great extent on the size of the population being sampled, and that there is an element of fixed cost in many audit procedures (such as checking compliance with the Companies Acts and accounting standards, audit planning, audit review).

Second, auditing is more difficult in small companies, because they neither possess nor require the elaborate systems of internal control upon which the auditor can rely when auditing a large company.

There seem to be three possible reactions by auditors to these problems:

1. they can audit small companies in the same way as they audit big companies, adapting procedures as necessary;
2. they can adopt different auditing standards of evidential support;
3. they can qualify their audit reports.

Audit in the same way as big companies

Treating small companies in the same way as large companies enables an auditor to take a purist view of the nature of the audit, but it involves placing a very heavy burden on the companies concerned. Auditors have often expressed this by saying that an audit is 'the price of limited liability' (and ignoring the fact that unlimited companies must have an audit as well). Implicitly, to adopt this attitude is to say that most small limited companies should never have been incorporated in the first place. Indeed, making disincorporation easier, or introducing a new business vehicle for small companies, is often suggested as a means of alleviating burdens on small companies (e.g. Barker, 1985). See, for example, Page (1982) for a discussion of this proposed solution.

To say that small companies should be audited in the same way as large companies is not to say that audit procedures should be identical. Because there is little evidence of the operation of controls in small companies, and because of the danger of management override, auditors tend not to rely on controls and to do much more substantive testing, but these sorts of tests are also used in large company audits. A report of the Canadian Institute of Chartered Accountants (CICA, 1988) concluded that substantive testing of balances and analytical review were the most useful techniques in auditing small businesses. Similar conclusions were reached by Raiborn, Guy and Zulinski (1983).

Level of evidential support

The second possible strategy for auditors is to adopt lower standards of evidential support for their opinion. Auditors may be willing to give a true and fair opinion on small companies' accounts at less cost, if they are willing to countenance a higher relative degree of inaccuracy in the numbers in small companies' accounts, i.e. if they are willing to use a wider confidence limit for the figures in the accounts. Two ways in which the auditor can justify such a position are by looking to the nature of the 'true and fair view', and to the nature of the auditor's concept of 'materiality'.

When the Companies Acts require companies to prepare accounts showing a true and fair view, no mention is made of the costs of obtaining that view; on the face of it the requirement is absolute. However, it has long been recognized that practical considerations must temper the degree of accuracy which is required. A 'true and fair' accounting statement does not purport to be exact.

Can the cost of attaining a true and fair view be explicitly considered by preparers and auditors of accounts? An analogous question has confronted the Accounting Standards Committee, who took counsel's opinion (ASC, 1983) on the nature of the true and fair view and whether the ratio of costs to benefit could be considered in framing requirements for accounting compliance with the true and fair view.

Counsel's view was that cost–benefit considerations were a factor in defining the true and fair view. Auditors who accept this position could decide that the cost of forming an opinion on the truth and fairness of accounts should be limited by the potential benefits which users of the small companies' accounts are likely to be able to obtain. Recognizing the cost–benefit consideration would allow auditors to reduce the scope of their audits, and to simplify auditing procedures. However, this might well conflict with auditing standards and guidelines, which make no explicit concessions to a simplification of audit procedures for small companies.

As an alternative to cost–benefit considerations, auditors can look to the meaning of materiality in small companies' accounts in order to reduce the cost of their procedures. Like 'a true a fair view', 'materiality' is an undefined term in accounting and auditing. Its meaning does not seem to be susceptible to definition without introducing new, undefined terms, although it is possible to discuss its meaning using generally understood concepts. Perhaps the most widely used characterization of the meaning of 'material' is the idea that something is material if knowledge of it is 'big enough to make a difference' to decisions made by the users of a company's accounts. In analysing the potential materiality of items in a small company's accounts, then, auditors can look to the probable use of those accounts and determine how great they believe an error in the accounts would need to be to make a difference to potential users. Such considerations can give auditors good reason to increase the percentage of error which they would be prepared to accept in the financial statements under review. For example, an auditor might well be prepared to accept an error of 10 per cent in the value of stock in a small company where the total value was only, say, £2,000, and the principal users of the accounts were the directors; but he might find an error of 5 per cent too high if the company were listed on the Stock Exchange, there was a substantial body of investors relying on the accounts and the total value was, say, £2 million.

In analysing audit risks in small company audit engagements, CICA (1988) suggests that auditors should focus on the combination of the risks that material errors may not be discovered (discovery risk) and the expected value of the loss that may result (loss risk). Where the combined risk is low, for example because the amount of probable losses is low, only moderate audit assurance is required.

Small companies' qualification

Another option for the auditor in auditing small companies' accounts is to qualify the audit report. At first sight, qualification of the audit report would not seem an attractive route to adopt: because the Companies Acts require the auditor to form an opinion, there is a professional bias toward using qualification of the audit report sparingly to preserve its effectiveness, and clients would be expected to resist it. Nevertheless, a special form of audit report was the solution preferred by the APC between 1980 and 1989.

Auditing Guideline 501 gave the following suggested wording for an audit report on appropriate small companies.

> We have audited the financial statements on pages ... to ... Our audit was conducted in accordance with approved Auditing Standards having regard to the matters referred to in the following paragraph.
>
> In common with many businesses of similar size and organization the company's system of control is dependent upon the close involvement of the directors/ managing director, who are major shareholders. Where independent confirmation of the completeness of the accounting records was therefore not available we have accepted assurances from the directors/managing director that all the company's transactions have been reflected in the records.

Subject to the foregoing, in our opinion the financial statements, which have been prepared under the historical cost convention, give a true and fair view of the state of the company's affairs at 31st December 19 . . and of its profit and source and application of funds for the year then ended and comply with the Companies Acts 1948 and 1967.

(APC, 1980b)

In deciding in what circumstances such a qualification should be used, Auditing Standard 103, Qualifications in Audit Reports stated:

Small enterprises

The auditor needs to obtain the same degree of assurance in order to give an unqualified opinion on the financial statements of both small and large enterprises. However, the operating procedures and methods of recording and processing transactions used by small enterprises often differ significantly from those of large enterprises. Indeed, many of the controls which would be relevant to the large enterprise are not practical, appropriate or necessary in the small enterprise. The most effective form of internal control for small enterprises is generally the close involvement of the directors or proprietors. This involvement will, however, enable them to override controls and purposely to exclude transactions from the records. This possibility can give rise to difficulties for the auditor not because there is a lack of controls but because of insufficient evidence as to their operation and the completeness of the records.

In many situations it may be possible to reach a conclusion that will support an unqualified opinion on the financial statements by combining the evidence obtained from extensive substantive testing of transactions with a careful review of costs and margins. However, in some businesses such as those where most transactions are for cash and there is no regular pattern of costs and margins, the available evidence may be inadequate to support an opinion on the financial statements.

There will be other situations where the evidence available to the auditor is insufficient to give him the confidence necessary for him to express an unqualified opinion but this uncertainty is not so great as to justify a total disclaimer of opinion. In such situations the most helpful form of report may be one which indicates the need to accept the assurances of management as to the completeness or accuracy of the accounting records. Such a report should contain a 'subject to . . .' opinion. It would only be appropriate to use this form of report if the auditor has taken steps to obtain all the evidence which can reasonably be obtained and is satisfied that:

(a)   the system of accounting and control is reasonable having regard to the size and type of the enterprise's operations; and is sufficient to enable management to give the auditor the assurances which he requires;

(b)   there is no evidence to suggest that the assurances may be inaccurate.

(APC, 1980b, p. 4)

A similar recommendation is made by the Union Européenne des Experts Comptables Economiques et Financiers (UEC, 1985).

While the reasoning behind the use of the small business qualification is persuasive, what is the reader of an individual set of accounts to make of such an audit report? Does the report just mean that the company is a small company without much internal control? Does the report mean that even if he or she had no counter-evidence the auditor had some doubt about the explanations? Does the auditor think the directors have actively misled him or her? All these interpretations seem possible, despite subparagraph (b) quoted above. Which explanation is most likely would seem to depend on the prevalence of use of suggested wording, both by auditors generally and among the clients of the auditor giving the report. However, the frequency of use of the report probably varies quite a lot among auditors; some probably use it frequently, perhaps for the majority of their reports, some auditors may hardly ever use it. The user of accounts is therefore unable to interpret the report.

Keasey, Watson and Wynarczyk (1988) found that in the period from 1980 to 1982 about a quarter of small company reports had the small company qualification and that the proportion was rising. The companies most likely to receive the qualification were those which had been audited by a large firm of accountants, had few directors and non-director shareholders, had secured loans or had a long lag between the end of the financial year and signing of the audited accounts.

The APC has now changed its mind about the small company qualification and has withdrawn the example 6 report, despite its widespread acceptance. The APC's stated reasons for withdrawal were: the wording was inconsistent – if the auditors believed the directors' assurances a 'subject to' qualification should be unnecessary; the report was too general – it did not specify in which areas management assurances had been relied upon; and that its use had become so widespread that it was being used where it was not needed, so that its meaning had become impaired (APC, 1989).

In withdrawing the example report, the APC encourages auditors either to give an unqualified report or to specify the areas of uncertainty. If uncertainty is so pervasive of the accounts that particular areas cannot be specified, a general disclaimer of opinion may be appropriate. The strategy of a general 'subject to' opinion is treated as the option of last resort and, in the APC's revised view, it should be used so rarely that no example of the report is given. The new standard does not even have a separate section for small enterprises, referring only to the need to obtain management assurances in 'owner-dominated' enterprises. Only experience will tell whether the new standard will be taken up by smaller firms of accountants or whether the small company report, now that it has been accepted by clients, is too convenient to discontinue.

CONCLUSIONS

The special problems which arise in auditing small companies have their origin, as do many other auditing problems, in an accounting problem: the requirement for small companies to produce full, 'true and fair' accounts complying with the Companies Acts and accounting standards. Once this decision was taken the government had the option of requiring an audit, a review or having no requirement. In the Green Paper, the government suggested an audit, but with relaxed auditing standards. The profession made a divided response to the question whether an audit should be compulsory, but it has not considered in depth the possibility of dual auditing standards. The only apparent response by the APC to the problems of small audits has been to provide a suggested form of audit qualification for small companies.

Doubts about the varying circumstances in which the qualification is used in practice mean that users of accounts may have difficulty in interpreting it.

REFERENCES

AICPA (American Institute of Certified Public Accountants) (1979) *Compilation and Review of Financial Statements*, AICPA, New York.
APC (Auditing Practices Committee) (1979) *Small Companies: The Need for Audit*, APC, London.
APC (1980a) *Analysis of Public Comment on 'Small Companies: The Need for Audit'*, TR 382, ICAEW, London.
APC (1980b) *Auditing Standards and Guidelines*, ICAEW, London.
APC (1989) The old 'example 6' form of audit report and the new reporting standard, *Accountancy*, May, p. 163.
Arthur Young (1989) *UK GAAP*, Longman, London.
ASC (Accounting Standards Committee) (1983) Legal opinion on 'true and fair', *Accountancy*, November, pp. 154–6.
Barker, B. (1985) Why small businesses need no audit, *The Accountant*, 30 November, pp. 14–15.
Briston, R.J. and Perks, R. (1977) The external auditor: his role and cost to society, *Accountancy*, November, pp. 48–52.
Carsberg, B.V., Page, M.J., Sindall, A.J. and Waring, I.D. (1985) *Small Company Financial Reporting*, Prentice-Hall International/ICAEW, London.
CICA (1988) *Audit of Small Business*, CICA, Toronto.
Davison, I.H. (1978) Do auditors give value for money?, *Accountancy*, January, pp. 91–4.
Davison, I.H. (1980) Small companies – why a review is not the answer, *Accountancy*, March, pp. 42–6.
Department of Trade (1979) *Company Accounting and Disclosure*, Cmnd 7654, HMSO, London.
Department of Trade and Industry (1985a) *Burdens on Business*, HMSO, London.
Department of Trade and Industry (1985b) *Accountancy and Audit Requirements for Small Firms*, DTI, London.
Department of Trade and Industry (1989a) *Companies in 1988–89*, HMSO, London.
Department of Trade and Industry (1989b) *EC Directive Amending the Fourth Company Law Directive . . . : A Consultative Document*, February, DTI, London.
Gemell, J. (1977) Audit problems ahead with small companies, *Accountancy*, July, pp. 48–50.
ICAEW (Institute of Chartered Accountants in England and Wales) (1980) *Small Companies – The Need for Audit?: Memorandum to the Department of Trade*, TR377, ICAEW, London.
ICAEW (1985) *Response to 'Accounting and Audit Requirements of Small Firms'*, TR592, ICAEW, London.
Keasey, K., Watson, R. and Wynarczyk, P. (1988) The small company audit qualification: a preliminary investigation, *Accounting and Business Research*, Winter, pp. 323–33.
Page, M.J. (1982) Will a new form of incorporation really aid small business?, *Accountancy*, April, pp. 91–2.
Page, M.J. (1984) Corporate financial reporting and the small independent company, *Accounting and Business Research*, Summer, pp. 271–82.
Raiborn, D.D., Guy, D.M. and Zulinski, M. (1983) Solving audit problems in small business engagements, *Journal of Accountancy*, April, pp. 50–8.
Rutteman, P. (1985) Abolishing small audits: the pros (of change), *Accountancy*, June, p. 12.

Shaw, J. (1978) Why a review simply won't do, *Accountancy*, March, pp. 79–81.

UEC (Union Européene des Experts Comptables Economiques et Financiers) (1985) *Special Considerations Regarding the Audit of Financial Statements of a Small Enterprise*, UEC, Munich.

White, R. (1985) (Abolishing small audits) the cons of change, *Accountancy*, June, p. 13.

FURTHER READING

Recommended for further reading are APC (1979), Carsberg *et al.* (1985), Davison (1980) and Raiborn, Guy and Zulinski (1983). Also:

Pratt, M.J. (1983) *Auditing*, 2nd edn, Longman, London, Chap. 18 (which book reproduces APC (1979)).

DISCUSSION QUESTIONS

1. Why audit small companies? Why not?
2. The characteristics of the users of the accounts of a large, listed company are different from those of the users of the accounts of a small, private company. Discuss the implications of this observation for the individual auditor.
3. Is the law asking for the impossible by requiring the auditor to form an opinion on the truth and fairness of the accounts of a small company?
4. Why can auditors not put much reliance on the system of internal control in many small companies?
5. Draft a letter from a director of a small company questioning the need for a small business qualification on its accounts. Draft the auditor's reply.
6. 'The audit is the price of limited liability.' Discuss.
7. Why not have dual auditing standards for large public companies and small private companies?

16

Modern Internal Auditing

Gerald Vinten

INTRODUCTION AND LEGAL BACKGROUND

Not only has internal audit come of age, it is now firmly established as a regular part of organizational life in those organizations which can justify and afford it. Although many would prefer to see it as a voluntary activity being justified on its merits, it does receive a limited amount of statutory support. Local government and the National Health Service are the prime examples of direct legislation. The Local Government Act 1972 required under section 151 that a local authority shall 'manitain proper arrangements for the administration of its affairs, including an officer responsible for the administration of its financial affairs'. Section 166 permits the Secretary of State to issue recommendations regarding those arrangements, and this was done in the Accounts and Audit Regulations 1974, which required the responsible financial officer to maintain a current internal audit. Regulation 4 of the Accounts and Audit Regulations 1983 (Statutory Instrument 1791) made under sections 23 and 25 of the Local Government Finance Act 1982, has added extra weight to this:

> The responsible financial officer of a body to which these regulations apply shall maintain an adequate and effective internal audit of the accounts of the body, and . . . shall have a right of access at all times to such documents of the body which relate to the accounts of the body as appear to him to be necessary for the purpose of the audit and shall be entitled to require from any officer of the body such information and explanation as he thinks necessary for that purpose.

In the National Health Service, according to the two-volume *NHS Internal Audit Manual*, which itself was a major step forward when it was published in 1987, internal audit is required under a health circular. It therefore enjoys direct ministerial authority under legislation empowering the minister so to act. Health Circular (82) 3 states: 'The Treasurer shall be responsible for ensuring there are arrangements to measure, evaluate and report on the effectiveness of internal control and efficient use of resources – i.e. that there is an adequate internal audit function headed by a Chief Internal Auditor of sufficient status.'

Professor Gerald Vinten, B.A., M.A. (Leeds), M.Sc. (City), Dip. Ed. (Oxford), D.P.A. (London) I.P.F.A., F.R.S.A., F.R.G.S., F.R.S.H., is Visiting Professor of Managerial Auditing at the International Management Centres, Europe, and Director of the M.Sc. in Internal Audit and Management at the City University Business School.

Following on from the April 1987 government White Paper on Higher Education the respective funding councils for polytechnics and colleges and for universities are ' . . . to ensure that all institutions either establish their own internal audit arrangements or have access to internal audit capability on an agreed basis. It is possible, for example, that groups of institutions may wish to consider the possibility of establishing a joint internal audit service.' Previously only half the universities maintained internal audit. Now this is required as a condition of funding, as is the setting up of an audit committee (Vinten, 1988a).

In other cases there is legislation which is highly persuasive as to introducing or maintaining internal audit, but which does not explicitly require it. An influential example is the Foreign Corrupt Practice Act 1977 in the USA. Although overtly to halt the corrupt activities of US companies in their dealings with foreign countries, the Act also made it illegal, with possible criminal sanctions, knowingly or unknowingly to fail to maintain adequate systems of internal accounting control. Companies in the UK with a US listing also need to comply, and to specify the means of compliance in the annual report and accounts. In the USA this Act is frequently referred to as the 'internal auditors' charter', and led to an upsurge in internal audit activity.

In the wake of the Financial Services Act 1986, and not unrelated legislation such as the Building Societies Act 1986 and the Banking Act 1987, internal audit is a natural way to comply with requirements as to internal control, and is virtually ubiquitous. In July 1989 the Housing Corporation issued an audit code of practice which encouraged housing associations to employ internal auditors to complement the work of external auditors. Within the public sector, as in major financial services organizations, internal audit is virtually universal. We do not have any reliable statistics on the company sector, but a 1985 survey suggested that 52 per cent of UK companies with turnover in excess of £35 million had internal audit, whereas only 11 per cent of UK companies with turnover from £7.4 to £35 million had it (Institute of Internal Auditors, 1985). Charities are also taking an interest in internal audit (Vinten, 1989).

PUBLICATIONS, JOURNALS AND VIDEOS

Another token of the growing popularity of internal audit is the abundance of publications, journals and videos now available. The main professional body publishers are the Institute of Internal Auditors Inc. (IIA) in Florida and the Chartered Institute of Public Finance and Accountancy in London. The first has published on virtually every conceivable area, from quality assurance, audit and control of distributed data processing systems, risk assessment and quantitative techniques, to coverage of most operational audit areas such as production, purchasing, marketing, customer satisfaction and energy con-servation. The second has made a worthy contribution in the otherwise relatively neglected area of contract audit, but has also published on topics concerning audit management and practice. Commercial publishers are also showing a marked degree of interest in this subject.

The first journal to appear was *Internal Auditor*, the journal of the IIA, in late 1944. It has graduated from a brief broadsheet to a journal particularly impressive for its artwork and presentation, which have been awarded prizes. Next was the IIA UK journal *Internal Auditing*, which started in 1977, replacing the former newsletter. The American journal *Internal Auditing* aims to be primarily practice-orientated and to interest directors of internal auditing and their staff, mainly in a US context. The *Managerial Auditing Journal*, first published in 1986, has a worldwide focus and audience and aims to be of interest not only to internal auditors but also to functional managers, external auditors, directors, management consultants, and all those concerned with review and evaluation of organizations and their activities. Videos have now been produced by the professional bodies on topics such as contract audit, interviewing skills and computer audit.

THE NATURE OF INTERNAL AUDIT

What is this activity which is the subject of so much contemporary interest? There are three main official definitions. One is for the use of government departments: 'Internal audit is an independent appraisal within a department which operates as a service to management by measuring and evaluating the effectiveness of the internal control system, (HM Treasury, 1988, Section A1). Another is intended for the membership of the major accountancy bodies of the UK and Eire:

> Internal audit is an independent appraisal function within an organization for the internal control system as a service to the organization. It objectively examines, evaluates and reports on the adequacy of internal control as a contribution to the proper, economic, efficient, and effective use of resources.
> (Auditing Practices Committee, 1990)

The third is the only one that claims universal application, worldwide and spanning both public and private sectors:

> Internal auditing is an independent appraisal function established within an organization to examine and evaluate its activities as a service to the organization. The objective of internal auditing is to assist members of the organization in the effective discharge of their responsibilities. To this end, internal auditing furnishes them with analyses, appraisals, recommendations, counsel, and information concerning the activities reviewed.
> (Institute of Internal Auditors, 1988)

The Institute of Internal Auditors, the only body that specializes in internal audit, was founded in America in 1941, and founded a chapter in London in 1948. It has in excess of 32,000 members in over 100 countries. Its 1979 standards were derived from four preceding brief statements of responsibilities. The first, in 1947, spoke of a protective and constructive service to management, but that the main concern was with accounting and financial matters, although matters of an operating nature might also be dealt with. In the second edition, of 1957, it reviews 'accounting, financial and other questions', and the qualification is now missing, so each is considered of equal significance. In the 1971 version it simply states 'for the review of operations', and the 1976 version made no changes of substance. The 1981 statement was to bring the statements in line with the standards and the emphasis on serving the organization as a whole. This could include the board of directors, the audit committee (if any), employees, shareholders, trade unionists and any other related parties, and demonstrates the total service scope of internal audit. It was clear, however, that the drafting committee intended only the board of directors and management to be included.

If the internal auditor is to serve the organization as a whole, it is important that independence is upheld, and this independence is empnasized in each of the three definitions. The government definition, in speaking of serving management, runs the risk of alienating trade unions, and this has happened in certain instances (Vinten, 1985a). If auditors become identified as the eyes and ears of management, or as head office spies, they will not achieve the co-operation so essential for successful audit work. The IIA standards distinguish two aspects of auditors being independent of the activities they audit. The first is the need for sufficient organizational status to permit the accomplishment of audit responsibilities. The second is in part a mental attitude, and would be compromised if staff assumed any direct operating responsibilities or audited an area for which they had been immediately responsible before joining audit.

This leads to an interesting conundrum. The acid test of the auditor's independence is that the organization should not come to an abrupt halt if the auditor were no longer present. Quality might suffer, and the organization would be deprived of a helpful adviser, the long-term effects of which could be considerable. Nevertheless, the organization should not become functionally inoperable. The conundrum is that it is an easy step to argue that audit is therefore dispensable, and to reduce its staff as soon as there are economic pressures on the organization. This issue was demonstrated in a survey on computer fraud in both public and private sectors which discussed the method of discovery (Audit Commission, 1987), the results of which are shown in Table 16.1. We can see immediately that in only 10 per cent of the cases was discovery due to direct internal audit activity, and if we take the percentage of amounts of money involved then it was substantially less.

Auditors are frequently criticized for failing to detect frauds. This, however, betrays a fundamental misconception of the role of internal auditors, for their primary duty is to encourage management to install and maintain effective internal control measures. Management is responsible for preventing and detecting fraud, and the auditor is a staff officer and adviser, not involved in line management, except within the audit division itself. The Treadway Commission considered the issues in detail, including the collaborative role of internal and external audit, the audit committee and management (National Commission on Fraudulent Financial Reporting, 1987.) The survey evidence suggests that internal control mechanisms were generally adequate, if not immediately at least over time. What is worrying is the large number of 'other means' – voluntary confession, anonymous tip-offs and accidental discovery by other staff.

The IIA standards suggest five components of internal control:

1. the reliability and integrity of information;
2. compliance with policies, plans, procedures, laws and regulations;
3. the safeguarding of assets;
4. the economical and efficient use of resources;

5. the accomplishment of established objectives and goals for operations or programmes.

HISTORY, DEVELOPMENT AND SCOPE OF INTERNAL AUDIT

It is difficult to chart the history of what is an internal activity of a company, with documentation that is confidential and probably destroyed eventually. Business history generally has not been well researched by historians, who are least happy working in such an area. Since only the top of the iceberg is revealed in company external audit, in the true and fair certification and the rare qualification of accounts, there is not much history of interest here either. There is much more on public sector external audit, which is well documented in official publications going back to the eighteenth and nineteenth centuries. There is also a dearth of surveys that would allow one to record changes over time. An extensive research programme would be frustrated by a lack of available evidence. It is therefore necessary to concentrate on development and scope, which is the nearest one is likely to come to the history. Although impressionistic, conceptual and qualitative, it may not do serious injustice to the facts.

In his formative work on external company audit Professor Thomas Lee (1986) charted the historical primacy of the three British company audit objectives, from 1840. Figure 16.1 shows the developments in diagrammatic form.

Fraud and error detection is displaced to a secondary objective by verification of accuracy, which remains a primary objective but is eventually displaced by attestation to credibility. The trend is to widen the scope and concentrate on matters of interest and concern to the public at large, rather than just the shareholder. Fraud and error detection is again achieving a higher profile and may be moving back towards being a primary objective. As external auditors seek to stem a flood of litigation and out-of-court settlements, the courts and the public appear to have higher expectations than external auditors can or should be expected to meet.

Internal audit displays a similar process of widening scope, but whereas the external audit's ultimate development is blocked by statutory limitations, there is no such limitation on how far internal audit may develop, and it

Table 16.1   Method of discovery of computer frauds

Method	1987	Number 1984	1981	Total
Internal control	48	40	28	116
Internal audit	13	9	4	26
External audit	—	—	1	1
Other means	10			
Information received	29	23	34	109
Claimant/customer	13			
Not disclosed	5	5	—	10
Totals	118	77	67	262

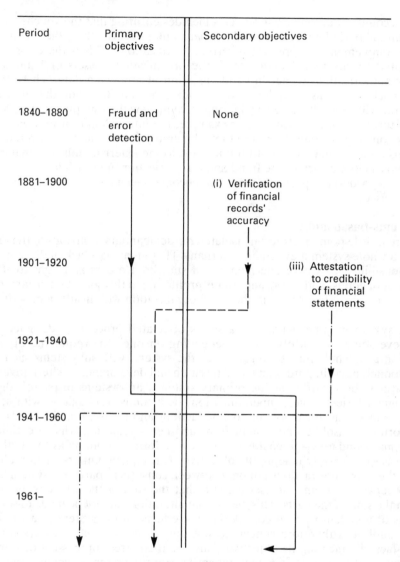

Figure 16.1 British company external audit objectives from 1840

already shows signs of having developed as far as its logical limits will permit. It is convenient to consider four overlapping stages of development.

Financial audit
Financial audit is often called, in less complimentary terms, 'tick and turn' audit, which refers to the auditor's habit of examining vouchers and the corresponding accounting entries, then ticking the voucher that has been checked and turning to the next voucher. Vouching provides documentary evidence, information, and explanations to substantiate the transactions in

the accounts of an organization. This includes ensuring that the voucher falls within the period under audit and has been entered correctly in the accounts. The complementary approach is termed 'verification'. This is the technique adopted to ensure the existence of the organization's assets or liabilities, their authorization, ownership and valuation at any given date. These two approaches are also employed by the external auditor, but the internal auditor will generally have a wider objective in view than simply the 'true and fair' certification of accounts. For example, the internal auditor may wish to verify one type of asset to ensure that all members of the class are covered by an insurance policy; this is of little interest to the external auditor. Financial audit is a close cousin of the fraud and error selection approach noted above. It is an arduous approach that can become mechanical if not properly supervised.

Systems-based audit
There is little point in criticizing isolated misdemeanours, oblivious to the fact that a whole system may require overhaul. There may be a lack of division of responsibility, as where one member of staff both orders and signs for the receipt of goods, and errors and frauds proliferate in this sort of environment, which may be a fact of life in the small organization with insufficient staff to divide.

A system may be defined as a series of related procedures designed to achieve some overall objective. Depending on one's viewpoint the organization as a whole may be regarded as the system, with subsystems such as personnel, payroll, purchasing, and research and development. Alternatively, these may be regarded as the primary systems. Subsystems of payroll then become salaries, wages, superannuation, deductions from salary (with separate subsystems for union and tax deductions and the like), and so on. It is important to isolate one system from another – imposing what are called systems boundaries – to enable the auditor to form an opinion as to whether each is satisfactorily meeting its objective. It is equally important to realize that there are interractions not only between constituent parts of a system but also between systems themselves, and that the sum of the whole is greater than the sum of the parts. This means that alterations cannot be made to some parts of a system without considering the effects on the system as a whole. The auditor is therefore concerned not only to ensure that each system is satisfactorily meeting its objectives, such as the correct processing of transactions, but that there is a comprehensive control system, encompassing all aspects of an organization's operations and systems in a linked and co-ordinated way.

This matter was highlighted in the case of the New Cross Building Society, which was forced to close by the Registrar of Friendly Societies. Although it had a 'systems manual', this was inadequate since it did not comprehensively identify and define all the controls, identify the persons responsible for their performance or provide for evidencing of their performance. Rather, it provided a dispersed specification of controls at various stages, in operating manuals for particular areas such as computers. Yet these were in no way integrated into the total control system, and there were formidable gaps in overall control, the right hand not knowing what the left hand was doing (Registrar of Friendly Societies, 1984).

The three crucial questions for any auditor to ask about systems are:

1. What is the officially determined system?
2. Is it functioning properly?
3. Is it adequate to achieve satisfactory internal control?

If the auditor is satisfied with how the system appears on paper and through interviewing staff, the next step is to perform system tests, also called compliance, transaction and walk-through tests. A small number of trans-actions, perhaps a dozen, are tested through the system from beginning to end. If these suggest inadequacies, the next step is to undertake weakness tests, also called substantive tests. These use larger samples and concentrate upon those specific control points that appear to deserve attention, using statistical sampling techniques as appropriate.

Both internal and external auditors perform systems-based audit. The internal auditor's role is to provide the organization with the assurance that its systems are adequate to perform the tasks for which they were designed. If the compliance test suggests firm controls, there is no need to proceed further. The company external auditor has a different aim – examining and reporting on the financial statements – and has little interest in other types of organizational control, such as control of overtime working. The interest in systems-based testing is not so much an interest in systems of internal control for their own sake, but purely to reduce the amount of detailed audit testing that is necessary. Even if compliance tests are satisfactory it will be necessary to perform substantive tests – this time across the board, rather than con-centrating, as did the internal auditor, on the specified weak control spots. It is the output of the system that concerns the external auditor, and everything else is just a means to the end represented by the final accounts. Where it would be cumbersome and expensive to examine a system, or only a few transactions are processed by it, or it is already known that controls are weak or non-existent, the external auditor will revert to the financial audit approach and ignore systems-based audit. The internal auditor, however, will wish to examine the system and sort out the control weaknesses.

Management audit

The two previous approaches ignore questions of economy and efficiency – whether the resources of land and buildings, employees and money have been used economically and efficiently. Furthermore, they ignore questions of effectiveness because it is argued that these are concerned with policy and objectives. The distinction between these three crucial concepts – the three Es – can be seen in the following popular definitions:

Economy – doing things cheap
Efficiency – doing things right
Effectiveness – doing the right things.

The British Institute of Management has offered a definition suggesting that the management audit will be an external review. The definition is based on the research of Jan Santocki (1974, 1983). Since it is no part of the require-ment for company external audit this would be performed by the manage-ment consultancy wing of an accountancy firm or by some other appropriate agency.

The definition is:

> A systematic, comprehensive and constructive examination and appraisal of the organization structure, management practices and methods conducted by an external independent person. It involves a review of each and every facet of management activity and its object is to ascertain whether or not the resources of an organization are used by its management in the most economic way to produce the maximum possible result in the shortest possible time in accordance with its goals. Management audit must contain the management auditor's findings and specific recommendations – its primary object is to motivate management to take action which will lead to increased efficiency and so profitability of an organization.
>
> (British Institute of Management, 1973, p. 3)

Examples of management audits by management consultants include the CBI review of Cheshire County Council (Confederation of British Industry, 1979), the management audit of the Library Association (Touche Ross, 1982; Vinten, 1982b) and the series of reports submitted to the District Auditor by Alex Henney criticizing the level of expenditure in the London Borough of Camden at the turn of the decade (Henney, 1984). Innes (1984) issued questionnaires to the head office and branch managers of three Scottish banks. There was widespread support for the use of a management audit as a helpful extension to the financial audit, and which would deal with the efficiency and effectiveness of management in achieving company objectives, the budgetary control system, and the performance of the management of the finance, accounting, marketing and production functions (Innes, 1984, 1987).

Others believe that a management audit is an activity sufficiently intimate to an organization that it is most satisfactorily carried out by auditors internal to the organization's workings. External reviews have sometimes been criticized for being superficial, trite, costly and uninformative for this reason. We return to the subject later, but Table 16.2 summarizes the differences of emphasis between financial and management audit.

There is no reason why one should not have a management audit approach to a financial area or function. The finance function merits more than just a financial audit approach, as much as any other function (Vinten, 1986).

Table 16.2   A comparison of financial audit and management audit

Financial audit	Management audit
Past orientation	Future orientation
Based on historic cost	Based on opportunity cost
Verification of profit/surplus	Improvement of profit/surplus and achievement of other corporate objectives
Protective	Constructive
Adequate controls and procedures	Efficient and effective use of corporate resources
Financial data primary source of evidence	Both financial and operational data used

Social audit

In the view of the US economist Milton Friedman (1963) there would be no need for a social audit, which he would regard as fundamentally subversive, undermining the very foundations of our free society. To him the only social responsibility of a corporation is to make a profit. Whether as a matter of enlightened self-interest or of pure philanthropy many would consider Friedman to have a dogmatic and restricted view of the wider environment in which the organization functions. Neglect could lead to poor industrial relations and lowered productivity, or poor consumer relations and reduced sales. Recklessly to pollute the atmosphere, exploit the Third World, or manipulate one's labour force will eventually precipitate a negative public reaction and possibly legislation that may occasion more expense than had the organization exercised voluntary restraint.

Some prefer the term 'social responsibility audit'; others dislike the term 'audit' if it suggests exact quantification but they approve of it because of its rich associations with objectivity, independence, comprehensive analysis and regularity (Humble, 1973). The following definition of a social audit is suggested:

> A review to ensure that an organization gives due consideration to its wider and social responsibilities toward those both directly and indirectly affected by its decisions, and that a balance is achieved in its corporate planning between these aspects and the more traditional business-related objectives.

Such a review may be carried out by an external agency either at the behest of organizations, or in opposition to them, as in the publications of Social Audit Ltd (Medawar, 1979). The external auditor has no statutory role to perform here. The internal auditor will have the standing to become involved in a way similar to the way he performs management audits. If the corporate plan expresses such concerns the auditor has a right to question and evaluate the way these concerns are met. This is part of the auditor's assistance to management and the organization (Vinten, 1985b, 1986).

BEHAVIOURAL ASPECTS

With what the Americans call 'broadened scope audit', the contemporary auditor is fully stretched to master all the necessary skills if audit credibility is to be maintained. The IIA standards suggest that the internal audit staff, supplemented as necessary by consultants, need to be trained in disciplines such as accounting, economics, finance, statistics, computing, engineering, taxation and law. This training should therefore not only make auditing a satisfactory career in its own right but also provide excellent preparation for top management posts. Unfortunately, what little evidence there is tends to suggest that, compared with middle-level managers, and external auditors from both larger and smaller firms, the internal auditor achieves the lowest job satisfaction (Chambers, Selim and Vinten, 1987). There is also what has been called the 'short-stay syndrome', whereby most staff stay no more than about three years in audit (Chambers, 1977). With the move to more creative auditing, increasing use of audit charters (Morris, 1983) and support from top management, and the underlining of the unrestricted scope of audit activity, matters may improve. With increasing investment in audit training, especially in computer auditing, and with central government taking a lead, morale may improve. If internal audit does not respond to increasing pressures for improvements in accountability, 'there is a danger that external agencies will step into the gap' (CIPFA, 1976).

Several studies have investigated the extent to which the auditor experiences role conflict. Delaney (1971) found that 79 per cent of those interviewed were allowed to define their jobs either to a considerable extent or completely and that auditors apparently experience no more stress or pressure in the performance of their roles than others at the same level in their organizations. Yet 64 per cent felt some trouble with their role requirements, and some felt a conflict between their informal working relationships with auditees in solving their control problems, and the demands of upper management as expressed by the auditing manager.

Mints (1972) formulated three working models. The first, the traditional audit approach, identifies the auditor's primary mission as protecting employers against possible loss. The auditor is an outsider, sent in to review and appraise the operations and to report unsatisfactory conditions to higher levels of management. The second, the current moderate approach, is a mixture of protective and constructive, with as friendly an attitude as is possible without risking sacrificing objectivity through excessive intimacy. The third, the participative teamwork approach, means that the auditor sees the primary objective to be assisting operating management to achieve overall organizational goals. This is reckoned to be most suitably achieved through gaining the interest and assistance of the auditees to establish a teamwork relationship.

The results of an audit manager survey, a laboratory experiment and field studies led Mints (1972) to champion the participative teamwork approach. His results were not without ambiguity, however, and more research is needed to unravel an extremely complex set of behavioural components. One suggestion was to divide auditors into 'group auditors' and 'management consultants' or 'analysts', the latter to adopt the teamwork approach.

Morgan and Pattinson (1975) found that in the UK auditors and auditees tend to have different frames of reference of the role and objectives of the internal auditor. Auditees view the auditor as an inspector, seeking out errors and possibly frauds, maintaining a fairly distant relationship, and assisting auditees only so far as the auditor's professional frame of reference permits. The auditor likes the adviser image in which close working relationships are established. Yet when forced to state the relative importance of the different aspects of the role, the auditor opts for the inspecting role as paramount.

OPERATIONAL AUDIT

Operational audit has considerable topical and political significance, and so justifies treatment apart from that provided in the previous section on the development of audit. It is required by law for the external audit of local and central government and the National Health Service, and this in turn influences internal audit practice. It is also becoming increasingly common in the private sector, but is by no means as universal as in the public sector, from whose experience many lessons can be learnt. The scant evidence that exists suggests a steady increase in operational audit activity. International surveys suggested that in 1968 only one-fifth of internal audits pursued financial audits only; by 1975 this was down to 2 per cent, with 52 per cent of the audit time spent on operational audit (Institute of Internal Auditors, 1969, 1976b). The 1983 US survey found 63 per cent of respondents claiming to provide a comprehensive audit service (Institute of Internal Auditors, 1983), whereas in the UK the figure was 65 per cent (Institute of Internal Auditors, 1985). All these surveys are subject to considerable error, including conceptual confusion, and results should be interpreted with caution. These figures fail to distinguish between compliance audits and efficiency and effectiveness audits, but a Harvard study suggests 44 per cent of available audit time is spent on operational audit, with just under a third of total audit effort spent on efficiency and effectiveness, which had doubled over a five-year period (Miguel, Shank and Govindarajan, 1976). Santocki (1983) found an increase from 37 per cent in 1974 to 48 per cent in 1982 in organizations that had been subject to management audit, and from 23 to 60 per cent of those not already so subject but who believed they would be in the next ten years.

There is unfortunately no uniformity of terminology, and one survey found nineteen different terms to describe non-financial audits, often used interchangeably, which does not help communication with auditees. These include value for money audit, programme effectiveness audit, performance review, operational review, and cost reduction. Dismissing the term 'performance auditing' as an undesirable synonym for operational audit, since more is audited than simply performance, the report argues for a standardization of terminology and recommends the use of just three terms: financial, operational and management audit.

Management audit is a comprehensive term which contains operational audit. It includes the audit of management decisions themselves in relation to the organizational objectives and the quality of management – the resultant report both identifies problems and recommends solutions. The internal auditor was considered the appropriate party for such audits by both location and expertise, with the external auditor playing only a marginal role. To avoid confusion a term such as 'management advisory services' was recommended to apply to the external auditor (Institute of Internal Auditors, 1975). The alternative preferred by this author is to confine operational audit to the three Es audit of individual operational areas, such as marketing, production, finance, and research and development (thus contravening one standard definition that excludes finance). Management audit is then reserved for across the board audits at the corporate level spanning several departments. Examples would be energy conservation, utilization of vehicle fleet, the corporate planning strategy and control over overtime. With no sanctions to compel standardization the multiplicity of terms will continue. The production of a CIPFA glossary of audit terms has not helped, since it carries little authority beyond that of the author of the report (CIPFA, 1988).

Two possible complementary approaches are suggested in a publication on cost reduction (CIPFA, 1979b). The first is the pragmatic approach. This seeks to attack waste without waiting for the development of systems that provide for this automatically. It would be expected that such matters could be acted upon quickly. Matters that could be investigated include employee expenses, premises expenses, supplies and services, transport and plant expenses, establishment expenses, agency services, debt charge and capital expenditure. The second is the systematic approach. This involves extending budgets and budgetary control into the areas of target-setting to include measures of physical performance and a management information system that enables achievements to be compared with standards. This approach is inevitably costly, time consuming and complex, but it is so central to the survival and prosperity of any organization that it is ignored at its peril. The vital role that the auditor has to play in auditing management information systems has been emphasized in an IIA publication and accompanying workbook (Smith, 1980). Such systems are audited by 67 per cent of organizations which responded to the UK and Eire survey (Institute of Internal Auditors, 1985).

Another text (Norbeck, 1969) distinguishes the *ad hoc* and the *ex natura rerum* approaches. The former is a special-purpose audit in reaction to a problem of which top management has become aware. The latter makes the operational audit a natural exercise in business management. It reviews both problem and non-problem areas, and may therefore uncover grey areas that would otherwise go unnoticed. There are also behavioural advantages, since it provides a balanced appraisal in which both strengths and weaknesses are mentioned.

ORGANIZATION FORM FOR MANAGEMENT AUDIT

It remains to discuss the most appropriate audit structure to achieve overall audit objectives, including that of management audit. Since computer audit and contract audit could be regarded as operational audit the arguments that follow for employing a specialist team apply equally to them.

1. A different sort of expertise is required from that of traditional financial audit.
2. A specialist team may be more cost effective.
3. Inter-departmental issues, such as utilization of vehicles, or water charges, may be most adequately dealt with.
4. Time scales for projects will be different, and also a different style of approach and management of projects may be appropriate.
5. In order to maintain credibility, especially when dealing with multi-disciplinary groups and with staff from a wide variety of professional backgrounds, it is advisable to employ specialists who have the time and energy to become proficient in all the necessary areas (Vinten, 1982a).
6. The techniques involved, being related more to general management than simply financial management, are different, and suggest a separate unit (Vinten, 1982c).
7. Fire-fighting, such as dealing with frauds, could reduce the time and emphasis that should be devoted to management audit.

The disadvantages are:

1. Planning and co-ordination may be a problem, especially if the two sections work to different time scales.
2. Duplication of work may occur.
3. Management audits sometimes develop naturally out of financial audits,

or, conversely, management audit may give rise to financial audit aspects. A comprehensive investigation by a unified team may have distinct advantages.

4. Job dissatisfaction and lowered morale may result if all the interesting and constructive work is allotted to management auditors.
5. Management audit may slip imperceptibly into management consultancy and have a tenuous link with audit.
6. The management auditor may lose contact with other areas of audit, and find promotion a problem.
7. Some management audits produce an information overload that departments find hard to cope with.
8. Management auditors, with across-the-board responsibilities, may lack the network of contacts available to the financial audit, especially if the latter is based on a specific subsidiary or operating area.
9. Overlap and duplication could occur with related agencies, such as management services, corporate planners or marketing staff.
10. Management audit should be an attitude of mind or emphasis on all audits.

CONCLUSION

Over the past fifty years internal audit has displayed a steady and consistent evolution, which over the later period has almost amounted to a silent revolution. Although it is only rarely a legal requirement, it is becoming an increasing part of the international scene. As audit committees are established to marshall and co-ordinate both external and internal audit resources, internal audit will increasingly come into its own. Public recognition and acknowledgement will lead to increased responsibilities, the challenge of which internal auditors need to be prepared to face. Truly, internal audit has come of age.

REFERENCES

Audit Commission for Local Authorities in England and Wales (1987) *Survey of Computer Fraud and Abuse*, HMSO, London.
Auditing Practices Committee (1990) *Guidance for Internal Auditors*, Auditing Guideline, APC, London.
British Institute of Management (1973) *Quarterly Review*, Vol. 3, no. 3.
Chambers, A.D. (1977) *Employment in Internal Auditing – With Special Reference to the Graduate*, Report No. 23, Institute of Internal Auditors (UK), London.
Chambers, A.D., Selim, G.M. and Vinten, G. (1987) *Internal Auditing: Theory and Practice*, Pitman, London.
Chartered Institute of Public Finance and Accountancy (1976) *Internal Audit Management in the 1980s*, CIPFA, London.
Chartered Institute of Public Finance and Accountancy (1979a) *Internal Audit in the Eighties*, CIPFA, London.
Chartered Institute of Public Finance and Accountancy (1979b) *Cost Reduction in Public Authorities*, CIPFA, London.
Chartered Institute of Public Finance and Accountancy (1988) *Glossary of Audit Terms*, CIPFA, London.
Confederation of British Industry (1979) *Value for Money*, PA Management Consultants' Report on Cheshire County Council, CBI, London.

Delaney, P.R. (1971) A field study concerning the role of internal auditors, Ph.D. thesis, University of Illinois.

Friedman, M. (1963) *Capitalism and Freedom*, University of Chicago Press.

Henney, A. (1984) *Inside Local Government. A Case for Radical Reform*, Sinclair Browne, London.

HM Treasury (1988) *Government Internal Audit Manual*, HMSO, London.

Humble, J. (1973) *Social Responsibility Audit. A Management Tool for Survival*, Foundation for Business Responsibilities, London.

Innes, J. (1984) External management auditing of companies – a survey of bankers, Ph.D. thesis, University of Edinburgh.

Innes, J. (1987) External management auditing of companies – a survey of credit managers, *Managerial Auditing Journal*, Vol. 2, no. 1, pp. 26–31.

Institute of Internal Auditors (1969) *Survey of Internal Auditing 1968*, Research Committee Report No. 15, IIA, Florida.

Institute of Internal Auditors (1975) *An Evaluation of Selected Current Internal Auditing Terms*, Research Report No. 19, IIA Inc., Florida.

Institute of Internal Auditors (1976a) *A Survey of Internal Auditing in the United Kingdom*, IIA, London.

Institute of Internal Auditors (1976b) *Survey of Internal Auditing, 1975*, IIA, Florida.

Institute of Internal Auditors (1988) *Standards for the Professional Practice of Internal Auditing*, IIA, London.

Institute of Internal Auditors (1983) *Survey of Internal Auditing, 1983*, IIA Inc., Florida.

Institute of Internal Auditors (1985) *Survey of Internal Auditing in the United Kingdom and Eire*, IIA, London.

Lee, T.A. (1986) *Company Auditing*, Van Nostrand Reinhold, Wokingham.

Medawar, C. (1979) *Insult or Injury? An Enquiry into the Marketing and Advertising of British Food and Drug Products in the Third World*, Social Audit Ltd, London.

Miguel, J.G., Shank, J.S. and Govindarajan, V. (1976) Extending the audit function, *Harvard Business Review*, November, pp. 5, 6, 10.

Mints, F.E. (1972) *Behavioural Patterns in Internal Audit Relationships*, Research Report No. 17, IIA Inc., Florida.

Morgan, G. and Pattinson, B. (1975) *The Role and Objectives of an Internal Audit – A Behavioural Approach*, CIPFA, London.

Morris, R.M. (1983) *Developing a Charter for an Internal Audit Function*, Institute of Internal Auditors, Florida.

National Commission on Fraudulent Financial Reporting (Treadway Commission) (1987) *Report*, AICPA, New York (available through IIA, Florida).

Norbeck, E.F. (1969) *Operational Auditing for Management Control*, American Management Association, New York.

Registrar of Friendly Societies (1984) *New Cross Building Society*, Cmnd 9033, HMSO, London.

Santocki, J. (1974) *Management Audit Survey*, Institute of Cost and Management Accountants/City of Birmingham Polytechnic.

Santocki, J. (1983) *Report on Management Audit Survey*, City of Birmingham Polytechnic.

Smith, B.E. (1980) *Managing the Information Systems Audit: A Case Study*, 2 Vols., Institute of Internal Auditors, Florida.

Touche Ross and Co. (1982) *Management Audit of the Library Association*, Touche Ross, London.

Vinten, G. (1982a) Efficiency techniques for the public sector, *Public Finance and Accountancy*, April, pp. 27–9.

Vinten, G. (1982b) The management audit in perspective, *New Library World*, August, pp. 109–10.

Vinten, G. (1982c) A critical outline of auditing techniques, *Public Finance and Accountancy*, September, pp. 10–12.

Vinten, G. (1985a) The internal auditor and the trade union, *Internal Auditing*, Vol. 8, Pt. 6, June, pp. 196–204.

Vinten, G. (1985b) Social audit: fact or fad?, *Public Finance and Accountancy*, November, pp. 7–8.

Vinten, G. (1986) The social auditor, *Internal Auditing*, Vol. 9, Pt. 4, April, pp. 128–37.

Vinten, G. (1988a) All change in further and higher education – audit in a period of transition, *Managerial Auditing Journal*, Vol. 3, no. 1, p. i.

Vinten, G. (1988b) Internal auditing in relation to financial control, in P.R. Garner, G.M. Dickinson, J.E. Lewis and J. Wooller (eds.) *Financial Management Handbook*, Kluwer, London.

Vinten, G. (1989) Charities: regulation, accountability and audit, Working Paper No. 95, City University Business School.

FURTHER READING

There has been a recent and rapid upsurge in the volume of books and articles devoted to internal audit. The following books provide leads to be followed up. The subjects of management and computer audit are particularly fertile areas for publication.

Brink, V.Z. and Witt, H. (1982) *Modern Internal Auditing: Appraising Operations and Controls*, Wiley, Chichester and New York.

Buckley, R. (1979) *Audit Committees: Their Role in UK Companies*, ICAEW, London.

Chambers, A.D. and Court, J.M. (1986) *Computer Auditing*, Pitman, London.

Chambers, A.D., Selim, G.M. and Vinten, G. (1987) *Internal Auditing: Theory and Practice*, Pitman, London.

Sawyer, L.B. and Summers, G.E. (1988) *Sawyer's Internal Auditing. The Practice of Modern Internal Auditing*, Institute of Internal Auditors, Florida.

Sherer, M. and Kent, D. (1983) *Auditing and Accountability*, Pitman, London. (Reprinted 1988 Paul Chapman, London.)

DISCUSSION QUESTIONS

1. To what extent should internal audit be universally present in the private sector as it is in the public sector?
2. Discuss the importance of fraud investigations to the role of (1) the internal auditor and (2) the external auditor.
3. Why are so few computer frauds detected directly by internal auditors?
4. What are the problems of introducing management or social audit for the first time in an organization?
5. Is management audit the sole preserve of the internal auditor? If not, what role might the external auditor perform?
6. Why does the internal auditor experience role conflict? Can it be resolved?
7. Should the internal auditor be accountable to (1) senior management, (2) the organization as a whole, (3) the consumer, (4) the public as a whole? What problems do you see for widened accountability?
8. Outline the similarities and differences between management audit and management accounting.

17
The Audit Commission

John Greenough

INTRODUCTION

The Local Government Finance Act 1982 can now be seen to have been one of the most important Acts ever passed in terms of local government audit. It introduced two major changes: first, the formation of the Audit Commission; and, second, to embody in statute for the first time an obligation on an external auditor to 'satisfy himself that the body whose accounts are being audited has made proper arrangements for securing economy, efficiency and effectiveness in its use of resources' (1982 Act, s. 15).

In this chapter we examine the origins of the Audit Commission, we review the way in which the Audit Commission has helped auditors to carry out their new duties and we assess the successes of the Audit Commission in helping local authorities improve value for money in the use of their resources.

ORIGINS OF VALUE FOR MONEY AUDITING AND THE AUDIT COMMISSION

In 1974 local authorities were allowed to choose whether they were audited by the District Audit Service, a public service under the wing of the Department of the Environment (DoE) or by a private sector firm. Both sets of auditors were given guidelines by the DoE in 1973 which emphasized, *inter alia*, that the auditor must be concerned not only with the form and regularity of the accounts, but also with issues of substance arising from them, such as the possibility of loss due to waste, extravagance, inefficient financial administration, poor value for money, mistake or other cause. The District Audit Service devoted up to 20 per cent of its audit effort to value for money (VFM) auditing as opposed to conventional legality and regularity work.

The origins of VFM audit lie in public concern about the use of money raised by compulsory levy and a strong climate of opinion in favour of more evaluation. It was no longer enough for auditors to confirm that sums voted by members had been spent as authorized; they should also examine the way the funds had been used and satisfy themselves that the authority had achieved value for money. There was, and still is, an expectation that public authorities should be striving to improve their efficiency and, in particular, to cut out waste and extravagance; they have an obligation to spend as little as

John Greenough is a partner in KPMG Peat Marwick McLintock, Manchester. The views and opinions expressed in this chapter are those of the author, and do not necessarily reflect those of KPMG Peat Marwick McLintock.

necessary to provide the services to the standard required by the electorate. This line of argument is often confused with simple cost-cutting exercises, and critics of value for money reviews have thought that they were concerned more with cutting services than the cost of performing services.

The Local Government Finance Act 1982 was passed in order to improve and co-ordinate the activities of all auditors in their efforts to ensure that all local authorities were making proper arrangements to secure economy, efficiency and effectiveness in the use of their resources. This Act established the Audit Commission and gave auditors a statutory duty in respect of VFM audit.

Before proceeding further it is appropriate to consider the definition of the terms used in the Statute. These have become known as the 'three Es'.

1. *Economy* is defined as the terms under which the authority acquires human and material resources. An economical operation acquires them in the appropriate quality and quantity at the lowest cost.

    Thus, authorities with excessive manning levels of overgraded staff would not be economic.
2. *Efficiency* is a relationship between goods or services produced and resources used to produce them. An efficient operation produces a maximum output for any given set of resource inputs or it has the minimum input for a given quality and quantity of service provided.

    If a vehicle workshop can be reorganized so that costs are reduced without affecting service to customers there will be an efficiency gain.
3. *Effectiveness* may be defined as how well a programme or activity is achieving its established goals or intended effects.

    It is often in local government, however, that clear statements of objectives do not exist and, therefore, it is not always possible to assess effectiveness.

The Act has thus widened considerably the auditor's duties in respect of value for money. They now cover the whole operation of the authority, including not just tangible losses through poor purchasing or stock control but less easily identifiable matters such as operational methods of performing a service so that greater benefits can be achieved. They even extend to the structure of the authority itself, to ensure that the authority is in a position to review its own value for money controls.

The auditor has therefore entered new and extremely difficult territory and the Audit Commission was charged with the task of guiding both the District Audit Service and private sector firms successfully through these new challenges. The task facing the Commission in the early days should not be understated. There was a belief that the private sector was much more economical, efficient and effective than the public sector and therefore that the private sector audit firms had much to offer in transferring examples of best practice from private to public sector. However, only a handful of firms had experience of VFM audit and few had enough experience of existing local authority audits to contribute actively in this field without becoming totally submerged in bureaucracy and politics. The District Audit Service, meanwhile, had suffered in the run-up to the introduction of the Audit Commission, when it was believed that a large proportion of the work would be transferred to the private sector. It was therefore understaffed and staff morale was low.

If this were not enough the Commission was seen by local authorities as an agent of central government, which would be used as a tool to extract information which could then be used to criticize local authorities.

RELEVANT FEATURES OF LOCAL AUTHORITIES

In order to assess the task facing the Commission it is first necessary to look at the features of a local authority and identify the difficulties facing the auditor. The audit of a local authority is quite different from the audit of a limited company, and audit firms who approached local authority audit with the belief that all management and financial problems are common have had to modify their views or leave the market. The whole concept of audit is different and the first statement in the Code of Local Government Audit Practice for England and Wales acknowledges this difference. The basic approach requires the auditor 'to recognize that the requirements for audit of public funds financed by compulsory levy are different from those applicable to the audit of commercial undertakings' (Audit Commission, *Code of Audit Practice*, para. 8a). It is not simply that the approach to the audit is different, however; local authorities themselves are very different from the typical commercial company. Some of the principal differences which are relevant to public sector audit are that:

1. Local authorities are service organizations with limited resources trying to meet a vast range of social and practical needs. Their success in meeting these needs depends on a mix of policy decisions and management operations.
2. Each authority is in practice a consolidation of separate service organizations; the cost structure of the various services depends on a range of factors including some which are uncontrollable such as weather, geography and the social/economic mix of the population. This means that unit costs alone are not an accurate indicator of economy or effectiveness.
3. The locus of decision-making is not always clear. Although in theory the members set policy and the officers implement it, practice differs widely between authorities. At one extreme, members may be happy to approve policy guidelines developed by influential chief officers and, at the other, members may wish to involve themselves in the minutiae of operational decisions.
4. The operational style of most local authorities is more participative than in the private sector. Newcomers have found the delays that this can introduce frustrating and have not appreciated the relationship it has to local democracy and sensitivity to public needs.

These distinctive features of local authorities mean that simple cost indicators have to be interpreted with great care and in many areas no real performance measures have been identified, e.g. social services and education. In addition, some authorities measured their success by the amount of money they could spend. The greatest danger faced by the auditor, however, was the accusation of interfering in policy matters. Almost without fail auditors presenting their first value for money report were faced by a hostile authority which accused the auditor of interfering in policy.

STRUCTURE OF THE AUDIT COMMISSION

The task which faced the Audit Commission in 1983 was enormous. To take on these challenges it established the structure set out below, which has remained largely unchanged until today.

1. Directorate of Special Studies – to carry out the research into areas of known poor value for money and to develop audit methodology so that auditors would have a framework for tackling the issues.
2. Chief Inspector of Audit – to control and co-ordinate the activities of the District Audit Service.
3. Directorate of Accounting Practice – to research technical auditing and accounting issues and to co-ordinate and control the activities of the firms.
4. Directorate of Management Practice – to develop an approach to improve management in local government which could be used both by the auditors and the auditee.

The Commission immediately decided to play an active part in interpreting and developing the concept and practice of VFM auditing. It could have chosen to allow its own staff and private sector firms to develop their own methods and audit programmes independently. Instead it sought to steer the value for money work centrally and to sponsor research studies to develop methodologies. Sensing some of the risks and dangers in naive or insensitive application of value for money questioning it decided to control the initial work carefully. The Commission's approach had the following features.

1. A clear statement in the code of audit practice of what VFM auditing involves.
2. A programme of special studies designed to prepare the ground for audit practice in following years. This programme was to prove one of the most successsful aspects of the Commission's work. It aimed to examine a limited number of local authority activities or services each year. In each study good practice was identified and ways of improving economy, efficiency and effectiveness explored. The early studies concentrated on economy and efficiency. However, later studies were to pay equal attention to effectiveness.
3. A recommendation that VFM auditing should consist of between 40 and 50 per cent of the total audit resources.
4. A range of documents and analytical aids for both auditors and local authorities. These include notes with practical guidance for auditors as well as self-assessment questionnaires.

The Commission took a proactive role from the start. It was aware that its performance would be measured by a range of criteria: to satisfy those who seek cost economies; to demonstrate that it is capable of tackling the effectiveness issues; to overcome the problems of comparability; and not least to demonstrate its independence from central government. One of the Commission's first difficulties was to train its auditors to think in considerably larger sums than they had previously been accustomed to. In early VFM audits the target for cost savings were up to 10 per cent of the revenue budget of the authority over the expected five-year life of the audit. To achieve savings of this magnitude major issues of management had to be tackled; this was an area where very few auditors had any experience and a considerable amount of research and training was obviously necessary.

The Commission also has the power to conduct studies on the effect of central government policy upon the economy, efficiency and effectiveness of local government. Under this heading, the first two studies carried out were into the Rate Support Grant arrangements and the effects of imposed capital controls. The reports on these studies demonstrated that the Commission was not afraid to criticize central government actions. This, more than any other activity of the Commission, demonstrated its independence and helped to secure the co-operation of the local authorities, which began to believe that the Commission was less an agent of central government and more an ally in defence of local government.

CONFLICTING APPROACHES TO VFM AUDITING

Before the formation of the Audit Commission VFM auditing in local authorities had been confined almost exclusively to the District Audit Service. It was carried out on a very small scale and concentrated on economy and efficiency with little attention paid to effectiveness. The Commission encouraged auditors to think in larger terms and interpreted the statute to mean that auditors should look at the general management arrangements of the authority to ensure that they were capable of securing value for money in the use of their resources.

This, as stated earlier, thrust auditors into the areas of management and effectiveness, for which they had received little training and had almost no experience. The resources for this additional audit effort obviously had to be found from somewhere and although extra days were paid for by the authorities it was still difficult to carry out the normal regularity audit within the resources available. This raised doubts in the minds of some firms whether they could carry out an adequate audit in terms of the systems and accounts of the authority and also meet the Audit Commission's requirements in terms of value for money.

The private sector firms found that they had difficulty in complying with their own in-house requirements for the audit of accounts within the time available. One answer was the concept of cyclical auditing, whereby there was a rotation of emphasis on items in the accounts so that in a particular year of account certain items were looked at in depth but considerably less time was spent on others. The decision on which items to test in depth was taken after the analytical review. This had been a practice adopted by the District Audit Service over a great many years but was quite new to the culture of the firms. Some of the firms have been able to adopt cyclical auditing on the grounds that there is considerably less exposure to risk in the final accounts of a local authority, little public interest in the accounts and no local authority has gone into liquidation or been taken over. Other firms have been unable to accept this argument and continue to audit less material items of accounts each year. In contrast, the District Audit Service paid less attention to the accounts of the authority, relying on the inherent stability and comfort to be gained from analytical review and believing that it was a more productive use of scarce audit time to carry out value for money work than to examine systems and final accounts.

This lack of interest in the accounts of local authorities by both the authority and the auditor, and the absence of precise rules for their preparation and presentation, led to serious problems of comparability between sets of accounts of different authorities, and may also have contributed to the growth in creative accounting in the mid-1980s.

Obviously, the Commission had to optimize the benefits of the two different approaches. It had to improve the opinion work of the District Audit Service and the value for money performance of the firms. The District Audit Service also had to be persuaded to think on a larger scale in terms of its VFM audit approach.

Changing the audit approach of district auditors to provide an effective final accounts audit was relatively easy once the practitioners had accepted that the change was necessary. Encouraging the firms to spend up to 50 per cent of their time on VFM audit work has not been quite so easy. Encouraging all auditors to tackle effectiveness and general management issues has been even more difficult. In general, auditors have coped well with the project-style VFM audit but less well on the management aspects of the audit.

In both areas auditors have been accused of interfering in policy and the general management of the authority. The duty of the auditor in respect of policy is to ensure that when the members made the policy decision they had all the relevant information and did not consider anything which was not relevant to the decision to be taken. If satisfied on those aspects the auditor could not question the decision of the authority. He or she could, however, comment on the effects of policy. In some circumstances the dividing line has been very fine and has varied depending on which side of the fence the adjudicator is sitting. It is not surprising that the issue has been one of the most difficult faced by the auditor.

ACHIEVEMENTS OF THE COMMISSION

Without doubt the Commission has achieved a great deal in its relatively short life. It has demonstrated its independence and it has made major contributions both to local government accountancy and local government affairs in general. It has significantly improved value for money throughout local authorities and it has maintained and in many areas enhanced the quality of regularity audit.

The independence of the Audit Commission was seriously questioned when it was first formed in 1983. There was a strong suspicion that it would be used as an agent of central government. Seven years later the Commission's independence is no longer questioned. Indeed it has taken the side of local authorities on many issues and is generally seen to be supportive of the efforts of local authorities.

The Commission is seen as an acknowledged authority on most local authority affairs, and its views are frequently sought on a wide variety of topics. Its occasional papers on topical subjects are well received by local authorities and there has been a complete change from the old reactive role of the auditor to a far more proactive approach where the Commission often leads the debate on such issues.

For many years management in local authorities has been criticized as poor and the many mitigating factors such as size, diversity and local democracy have been conveniently ignored. The Commission has now joined this debate and taken positive steps to improve management and to prepare local authorities for the changes being imposed on them by the current legislative programme of the government. Here, again, the Commission is probably the UK's acknowledged expert.

In accounting matters the Commission is seen to make major contributions and is represented on most working parties concerned with local authority accounting.

It is, however, in the area of VFM auditing that the Commission's work is most appreciated. The suspicious and defensive approach initially adopted by many local authorities has now disappeared and considerable savings are being achieved. There is also considerable evidence that these savings are being achieved at an earlier stage.

The Commission's *Report and Accounts: Year Ended 31 March 1989* shows that 5,800 projects had been undertaken up to March 1989. These projects had identified opportunities to the value of £992 million, and £372 million had been achieved. This represents an achievement of 40 per cent, an increase from 29 per cent for the corresponding period last year. This clearly demonstrates an improvement in the Commission's approach to value for money studies and also the greater willingness of local authorities to co-operate.

With all this attention paid to VFM audits it would not be surprising if the regularity aspects of the audit had suffered, but this has not been the case. The integrity of British local authorities continues to be the envy of the world and this must be due in some part to the existence of an effective regularity audit.

A further area where the Commission has made useful contributions has been where it has promoted studies designed to enable it to prepare reports on the impact of legislation or guidance from ministers on the economy, efficiency and effectiveness in local authorities. A number of these studies have now been carried out and the Commission has made extremely useful contributions to the debate, but it is not always clear whether the actions of the Commission have had a major impact in Whitehall.

THE EFFECT ON LOCAL AUTHORITIES

The Commission has had a major impact on local authorities. There is no doubt that local authorities now achieve better value for money as a result of their co-operation with the Audit Commission. There is no doubt that the standard of audit within local authorities has been improved considerably by the Commission and that this improvement has enhanced confidence in the local authorities. The Commission's proactive approach to the problems of local authorities has also helped authorities to prepare for those changes in attitude which will clearly be necessary as a result of central government's view of the role of local authorities in the future.

The success of the Commission is now accepted throughout the local authority world and it is extremely pleasing to note that the success has recently been acknowledged by central government – when it asked the Commission to take on responsibility for the audit of health authorities within the UK, pursuant to the National Health Service and Community Care Act 1990.

DISCUSSION QUESTIONS

1. What is the role of the auditor in respect of policy decisions reached by democratically elected members of a public authority?
2. Discuss the statement 'value for money is the responsibility of management and the external auditor has no part to play'.
3. Is the Audit Commission an unnecessary 'quango' which simply confuses proper relationships between auditor and auditee?
4. Does the rise in creative accounting in local authorities demonstrate that the auditor should concentrate on the regularity aspects of the audit rather than value for money audit?
5. Is value for money auditing transferable to the private sector or is it relevant only where there is no profit measure?

18

The Audit of Central Government

David Dewar

Accountability and audit in central government, as elsewhere in the public sector, are in a period of change and opportunity. This is the result of three main pressures: first, the determination to cut back the public sector and to reduce the proportion of gross domestic product taken up by public expenditure – the so-called 'rolling back the boundaries of the state'; second, developments being introduced in the organization and management of governmental and quasi-governmental programmes and activities; third, initiatives being taken by auditors themselves to revise their objectives, approach and methods.

At the same time the fundamental verities remain: high standards of accountability for public funds; a concern for propriety, regularity and authority in expenditure; the importance of sound financial accounting and management systems; and arrangements to promote the economic, efficient and – above all – effective use of resources. These are all continuing responsibilities; Parliament and the public expect nothing less.

ROLE OF THE NATIONAL AUDIT OFFICE

The National Audit Office (NAO) was established in 1984 to take over the responsibilities of the Exchequer and Audit Department following the passing of the National Audit Act 1983. Under the Act the conduct of the NAO's work is independent of both the executive and Parliament; its budget is controlled directly by Parliament rather than the Treasury; and the head of the NAO, the Comptroller and Auditor General (C&AG), is an officer of the House of Commons, is appointed by the Queen, and can be removed from office only upon an address presented to the Queen by both Houses of Parliament. This independence extends also to such matters as staffing, pay and conditions of service. A crucial part of the NAO's powers is that it reports directly to the House of Commons on the results of its work; and when presented, its reports are followed up by the Committee of Public Accounts (PAC).

The NAO's responsibilities encompass both certification audit and value for money examinations.

CERTIFICATION

The C&AG is the appointed external auditor for all government departments and a wide range of other bodies. He provides an audit opinion on some 500

David Dewar is Assistant Auditor General, National Audit Office. The views and opinions expressed in this chapter are those of the author and do not necessarily reflect those of the National Audit Office.

annual accounts, covering a total expenditure of nearly £190 billion, some 60 per cent of public expenditure. These include the main departmental appropriation accounts, cash accounts for a number of other bodies of differing sizes, and a range of commercial and other accounts prepared on an accruals basis. There are also a significant number of international accounts. The C&AG also examines, but does not formally certify, the annual revenue accounts of the Inland Revenue, Customs and Excise and other bodies, involving the collection of some £180 billion a year.

Certification audit is conducted mainly under the Exchequer and Audit Departments Acts 1866 and 1921 but also under a number of other statutes and by agreement. The scope of the work covers financial audit to ensure that the accounts are accurate or present a true and fair view, and regularity audit to check the propriety of expenditure and conformity with statutory provisions and parliamentary and other authority. The work is carried out in accordance with accepted professional standards and practice.

VALUE FOR MONEY

The National Audit Act gave statutory authority for examinations of economy, efficiency and effectiveness in the use of resources, with direct access to documents and other information and the power to report results to the House of Commons regularly throughout the year. Such examinations are carried out not only in those government departments and other bodies for which the C&AG is the appointed auditor but also in hundreds of other bodies receiving public funds to which the C&AG has rights of access. The only significant exclusions are expenditure by local authorities and the nationalized industries (though even here the NAO may examine the relationships between such bodies and their 'sponsor' government departments). The total expenditure and revenue subject to the NAO's value for money audit is approaching £400 billion a year, together with incalculable capital assets and other resources.

The 1983 Act is framed in powerful terms, particularly in the provision for direct examinations of effectiveness, which is limited only to the extent that it does not entitle the C&AG 'to question the merits of policy objectives'. (This is not, as is sometimes assumed, a barrier to examining and reporting on the implementation of policy and the results achieved.) The Act, in fact, goes significantly further than equivalent statutes in Canada, Australia and a number of other countries, which, in one way or another, restrict the power to carry out direct audit examinations of effectiveness or prohibit them entirely as getting too close to the heart of government.

Despite the strength of such provisions, the 1983 Act did not mark the introduction of economy, efficiency and effectiveness examinations within the NAO. It was not a watershed, but a consolidation of the extensive value for money work carried out by the former Exchequer and Audit Department over many years. Value for money examinations, in one form or another, have been part of public sector audit almost from the start, and they developed extensively in the period between 1946 and 1983 as a consequence of the massive growth in public expenditure.

During that period the Exchequer and Audit Department published more than 1,000 reports on a wide range of value for money issues, to be followed up by the PAC. Major subjects pursued included defence procurement; contract control and pricing; project management in such areas as weapons systems, civil works, roads and hospitals; a wide range of grants and subsidies; National Health Service programmes; agricultural schemes; and assistance to industry. Indeed, value for money work became a dominant feature of the Department's audit, with well-developed methods and techniques. It was the success of this work, and the results achieved, that prompted a chairman of the PAC during this period to note that the Committee's effectiveness 'depended on the fact that it had the C&AG's reports as a starting point.'

The extension of certification audit into value for money issues, and later the pursuit of such issues in their own right, were obvious and logical developments, at least in the public sector. A concern that expenditure accords with Parliament's intentions when voting funds leads naturally into a concern that taxpayers' money is spent wisely and well, and certainly not wastefully. There was some fuss when such work started a hundred years ago but, with the firm support of the PAC, this was quickly overcome. It became accepted that an audit which verified thorough and accurate accounting for unnecessary or extravagant expenditure had a hollow and unsatisifactory ring.

The 1983 Act provided the statutory basis to secure and further develop value for money work.[1] It gave examinations the strength of express statutory authority instead of relying upon the encouragement and support of successive PACs. And – a particularly important point – it enabled separate and more in-depth reports to be presented at the time examinations were finalized rather than findings being published only once a year with the annual appropriation and other accounts. This added depth and immediacy and stimulated further improvements. The Act also fitted in well with strategic planning developments and improved audit methods which had been set in hand a few years before.

The NAO now publishes more than forty reports a year on the results of its main value for money examinations, and intends in the next few years to increase this to over fifty. The balance and thrust of the programme of examinations vary from year to year; the aim is to pursue cycles of coverage based on the materiality of the expenditures and resources involved, the assessed risks to value for money, the demands of parliamentary accountability, and the opportunities to secure improvements in systems, controls and results. The pattern of reports includes:

1. a concentration on systems designed to secure good value for money rather than reporting examples of bad value for money – i.e. a 'top-down' approach, but without allowing this to become too rarefied;
2. examinations of departmental accountability in determining aims, objectives, targets, etc. and monitoring progress and results;
3. more examinations dealing specifically with effectiveness in achieving objectives, and with efficiency rather than economy in expenditure – i.e. spending well on the right things rather than simply spending less;
4. continuing efforts in familiar areas where massive resources are still involved; for example, defence procurement, major capital programmes,

computers, the National Health Service, social security, employment, grants and subsidies, assistance to industry;
5. early coverage of emerging issues from such developments as the Financial Management Initiative and 'Next Steps' agencies;
6. privatizations;
7. 'across the board' examinations. Although central government offers fewer opportunities for comparative examinations than, say, local government or the National Health Service, examinations are carried out across departments into the provision of common services or similar activities such as estate management, publicity services, and staffing and manpower.

The basic purpose of this work is not simply to produce reports but to encourage better value for money and secure beneficial change. Following through reports and monitoring implementation of recommendations are therefore standard practice, not only through the subsequent examination by the PAC but also with audited bodies directly. Results are also pursued in considering subsequent strategic plans, with follow-up examinations at appropriate intervals.

This, then, is the framework of the National Audit Office's responsibilities on both certification and value for money work, within which current developments, and potential opportunities and threats, fall to be considered. Some of these issues can already be identified in reasonably clear terms; others are only starting to emerge; and others are no doubt in the pipeline. What is certain is that the 1990s will be a period of continuing change to which both auditors and audited will need to adapt.

ROLLING BACK THE BOUNDARIES OF THE STATE

It can be argued that reducing the public sector by eliminating services and functions, or completely privatizing them, does not in principle raise problems for public accountability. The theory goes that once the necessary decisions have been taken, and approved by Parliament, such services and functions are by definition no longer part of the public sector, ministers are not accountable for them, and no public funds are involved – so the need for public accountability itself disappears. The appointed auditors of privatized functions – like those of commercial companies – should not normally have any responsibility for carrying out examinations of economy, efficiency and effectiveness and publishing reports on the results. Bodies must be left free to manage.

This line of argument has the merit of apparent simplicity and logic but matters are in practice not always so clear cut. There are a number of half-way houses, privatization may be only partial, and unless accountability is clearly defined there is the risk of a messy and uncertain situation. The idea that accountability is inimical to effective management is false.

For example, some services – whoever is delivering them – may be perceived by the public and Parliament as activities in which there remains an inherent public interest, and where what is done and how it is done are matters for legitimate public inquiry. Other activities, though themselves privatized, may remain closely associated with or directly affect services still in the public sector. Again, there may be a need in the public interest to retain some overall control over certain aspects of the functions being privatized.

Accountability is most obviously put to the 'public interest' test at the more extreme end of the possible privatization spectrum: if, for example, there were privatization of prisons or perhaps police services, the operation of a major 'private' roads network, even – who knows? – defence or other security services. Such boundaries are being extended progressively and there is certainly less of a consensus than before as to the inherent distinctions – if indeed there are any – between what should remain public and what could be private sector provision. There will be continuing debate over what functions ministers should remain answerable for and what they can legitimately avoid. Nevertheless, probably few would argue that in the type of examples cited above the most appropriate level and form of continuing public accountability are not important issues.

Lower down the list are those activities where, although privatization of the direct service itself has been accepted, there are still associated matters of public interest and concern for which some degree of accountability should be retained. Perhaps the most obvious examples are in such fields as environmental protection, control of pollution, nuclear safety and public health; and less obviously perhaps in such matters as fair trading, consumer protection, and monopolies and mergers. It is a sensible principle that, particularly when there are commercial pressures, controlling such matters should be subject to independent oversight. An organization's own operating responsibilities need to be backed up by powerful outside scrutiny. Environment, health and safety will always be public concerns.

Here the way forward in maintaining public accountability, whilst avoiding direct government involvement in managing a service, has typically been to establish inspection or regulatory agencies, operating to statutory standards and/or within ministerial control and direction, and with a recognized line of answerability to Parliament. Such bodies are often financed, directly or indirectly, from public funds and this further underpins public accountability for their activities and performance. Some are set up within departments but separately identified and with independent powers, including public reporting powers. Examples include the national inspectorates for education, police, prisons, pollution and the probation service. Other regulatory bodies are established as free-standing organizations, such as the Office of Telecommunications, the Office of Fair Trading and the National Rivers Authority.

Where does audit stand within this spectrum and what is its contribution? It is not of course for the National Audit Office to say where privatization is desirable and where it is not, or where the boundaries between public and private management and accountability should lie, or how direct such accountability should be. These are constitutional matters for Parliament. Where it is decided, however, that some level of public accountability should be retained, and what form it should take, Parliament normally expects the National Audit Office to be given the necessary rights of access to examine and report on performance and results, not only within the body concerned but also as regards its wider effectiveness and impact.

In the case of certain regulatory bodies, the C&AG will in some cases be the appointed auditor – for example where the body is within a department and thus falls automatically within his or her audit, or where other direct public funding is involved. In other circumstances the C&AG will have statutory or other rights of access. Thus the C&AG is the appointed auditor for the bodies regulating such activities as telecommunications, electricity, gas, water and fair trading; and has rights of access to the National Rivers Authority.

In considering the auditor's remit it is important to recognize the differences in accountability requirements between more or less complete removal of activities from the public sector – as outlined above – and those current developments which retain a service within the public sector, with an agreed level of ministerial responsibility, but have aspects of delivery or day-to-day management contracted out on an agency basis. The latter arrangements normally remain firmly within the NAO's remit, as discussed in the next section.

The process of privatization itself, and nationalized industries' relationships with 'sponsor' departments, are also part of the NAO's remit. The C&AG has so far presented nearly twenty reports to Parliament on such matters; and others are under current examination.

DEVELOPMENTS IN ORGANIZATION AND MANAGEMENT

Services in government have for many years been delivered not only by front-line departments but also by an increasingly wide range of quasi-governmental bodies. Some of these bodies perpetuate historical developments which it has not been thought necessary or expedient to change. Others reflect a concern that, mainly because of the nature of the service and the freedom it should enjoy, government responsibility for overall policy and direction should be distanced from day-to-day management (as, for example, in areas of law and order and the probation service). And in more recent years some bodies have been set up to introduce new activities or consciously to change the way in which existing functions are carried out.

Within this last category there is a greater chance of finding defined operating objectives, agreed targets and yardsticks of performance, and appropriate staffing and funding arrangements. Often such bodies are conceived as being more commercial in character and are organized accordingly. But the picture is mixed, with some bodies still operating virtually as 'departments in exile'. Others, though nominally free to operate commercially or well placed to do so, are constrained by rules devised for government departments.[2] The growth in the number of 'quangos' has not always been accompanied by a clear view of their purpose, objectives and desirable operating characteristics.

Given this background, there have in recent years been a number of significant developments in organization, management and accountability. This reflects a perception – true or false – that civil service operations are not well managed and would benefit from the application of more direct and robust managerial objectives and techniques. The 'ethos and culture' of public sector operations is held to be old fashioned and inimical to prompt and forthright action and to value for money; or it is thought to need sharpening up by more businesslike or entrepreneurial approach.

Such views are often too sweeping or exaggerated. Nevertheless, calls for clearer objectives, better planning and improved management are not new. They were an important part of such developments as programme planning and budgeting, and programme analysis and review which arose and submerged in the 1960s and were ultimately replaced by simpler and more brutal control techniques like cash limits. Financial control, rather than being based on identifying need and levels of service and providing funds accordingly, swung over to the requirement that departments should do only as much as they could as well as they could within a predetermined and firmly enforced cash budget.

Current organizational and management initiatives operate still within the framework and priorities of cash limits. The main lines of development are the following.

The Fulton Report 1968[3]   This conveniently marks the start of real concern over performance, impact and results rather than systems, rules and procedures. Better management was to be structured around clear quantified objectives, and performance measured against defined targets. Changing the operational culture does not happen overnight, however, and it was to be some time before the stone rocked into motion by Fulton started to rumble firmly on its way.

Rayner scrutinies   Examinations under the direction of Sir Derek (later Lord) Rayner in the early 1980s reviewed not only the detailed operation of a large number of departmental programmes but also sought to identify 'lasting reforms' to strengthen management by improving systems and changing the existing approach. A significant example of a more management-orientated system was the introduction in 1980 of MINIS (Management Information for Ministers) in the Department of the Environment and later extended, with mixed results, to other departments. Programmes of work were broken down into allocated responsibilities of designated management units which were then held directly accountable for their performance in meeting defined objectives and priorities and for the resources used in doing so.

Financial Management Initiative   Set in hand in 1982 in response to the report of the Treasury and Civil Service Committee, *Efficiency and Effectiveness in the Civil Service*,[4] the FMI repeated the familiar refrain for clearer and more quantified objectives, and better performance and output measures, allocated responsibility for making the best use of resources, and improved systems, skills and training. There were to be organizational changes to decentralize operating responsibilities to smaller, more self-contained units or cost centres, with individually allocated line-management responsibilities. The FMI led directly to the current 'Next Steps' developments.

'Next Steps'   Set in motion in early 1988 by the Ibbs report, *Improving Management in Government: The Next Steps*,[5] this development is currently being pressed forward vigorously by the creation of 'executive agencies' with appropriate management objectives, structures, and systems. To date nearly seventy agencies have been created or announced, to a variety of patterns. A number are being created by redefining areas of existing departmental functions and giving them a semi-independent operating role – for example the Vehicle Inspectorate within the Department of Transport. Others are organizations which in many respects are already well-established entities in their

own right, for example the Stationery Office and the Central Office of Information. Few so far are perhaps genuinely being created from scratch as free-standing organizations.

Developments such as 'Next Steps' present both risks and opportunities for accountability and for auditors. They will not work if they are shackled by the approach and attitude of the past, or if management remains concerned with organizing inputs rather than maximizing outputs and getting results. On the other hand, the creation of agencies and the pursuit of 'commercial' patterns should not become ends in themselves; they should be a considered response to circumstances and operating parameters to which their attributes are well fitted. Agencies are not the organizational panacea to every area of service delivery. Nor are they a way of hiving off responsibility, so an essential framework of accountability needs to be retained. Indeed, accountability for results and use of resources should be enhanced by taking advantage of the greater relevance of the information that should be available on performance, and from improved reporting arrangements. Properly managed they should have a great deal to offer.

The main audit and accountability issues so far emerging include:[6]

1. *Forms of account* The standard arrangement will be for agencies to produce 'commercial' accounts prepared on an accruals basis, as being in principle better suited to presenting use of resources and financial performance. But in many cases this will mean converting from a departmental cash accounting system, and identifying and valuing agency assets from among a much larger volume of unvalued and undepreciated departmental resources. Financial arrangements with parent departments, and charging regimes, will need to be set up. Accounting and management information systems may have to be specially developed and tested. Reporting arrangements – including reports to parent departments and to Parliament – have to be considered and accounting officer relationships clarified. Staff skills and training will need early attention.

    All such matters require audit examination from the outset. Consultation should start well before an agency is set up, and continue through the development and implementation phases. A considered view of the financial control and accounting readiness of the operating agency will then underpin the normal annual audit and opinion. Advice and assistance by the auditor will often be needed, without compromising audit independence and reporting freedoms.

2. *Setting objectives and measuring performance* For many public sector activities, setting quantified objectives and measuring performance are not easy. There may be no reliable 'bottom line' of profit or loss; and 'soft' issues and judgements may bulk larger than they do elsewhere. It is simple enough to identify the desirability of moving towards such aids to effective management but more difficult to do so sensibly. A determination to measure more has to be tempered by the recognition that not everything of value and importance can reliably be measured. In delivering services of a more social kind, the requirements of the 'three Es' (economy, efficiency and effectiveness) may need to be accompanied

by such further 'Es' as equality (in terms of consistency of treatment) and equity (in terms of fairness and justice).

Auditors with experience in value for money examinations are, of course, familiar with all of this. But the issues involved need to be watched especially carefully when dealing with organizations specifically set up to break away from the past and pursue different objectives, better management and more quantified performance. The auditor has to stand back and consider wider aspects of performance, not just those chosen by the organization as the basis for its own reports. Reports – particularly annual reports presented to Parliament with accounts – containing performance measures will need to be independently examined, without necessarily moving to the stage of regarding this as part of an audit opinion. Matters here are at an early stage and there are a number of open questions.

3. *Attitudes and approach*   One of the purposes of the 'Next Steps' developments is to encourage a more adventurous and entrepreneurial approach and 'can do it' attitude. But such an approach may not sit well with traditional civil service or departmental procedures, and the latter will have to be modified. Public expectations, too, must adapt to the idea that a responsibility to make things happen and to drive forward must be accompanied by the right to make some mistakes. This is not, however, an acknowledged feature of present public accountability whose concerns include conformity with rules and regulations. But expecting managers to run fast whilst looking too often over their shoulders will produce the inevitable pile-up.

Auditors examining the agencies will need to acknowledge such changes in reaching their conclusions and framing their reports. They also have a part to play in the wider education process. Such considerations will place a premium on audit judgement and the ability to identify and focus on those actions and those occasions where risks have not been carefully enough assessed, planning has been insufficient, and poor results could have been avoided. The criteria for good management, and not just the application of rules and procedures, will have an increasing part to play in audit examinations.

Changes in the pattern and distribution of public accountability are also arising from developments other than those associated with 'Next Steps'. Some activities are being moved away from direct departmental control or existing methods of provision. Contractors and other agents are being introduced more widely to carry out activities or deliver services on the government's behalf.

As noted previously, however, such changes do not normally remove all existing rights of access for public sector auditors where ultimate accountability remains with the departments concerned. For example, the policy of increasing the extent to which funds for the provision of housing are channelled through the Housing Corporation and the housing association movement does not diminish the National Audit Office's powers to examine and report on the economy, efficiency and effectiveness of the relevant programmes. Similarly, the use of private sector managing agents to deliver employment training, and the introduction of contractors to manage the Royal Dockyards, still leave such areas of activity open for NAO examination and report.[7] There is firm PAC support for ensuring that organizational changes do not significantly curtail the C&AG's audit remit and his ability to review the full range of departmental responsibilities, direct and indirect.

AUDIT INITIATIVES

Developments such as those outlined above, and the natural processes of professional change and advance, mean that audit objectives, approach, methods and techniques are under continuing review by the public sector audit bodies themselves. In the case of the National Audit Office there are also developmental pressures from Parliament – not only as part of the regular exchanges with the PAC but coming also from other Select Committees. The NAO's direct rights of access to departmental documents and other sources of information are attractive to a wide range of parliamentary and other interests – but these rights are granted for the purposes of audit only, and the NAO is not a conduit of information other than as a result of its examinations and published opinions and reports. Though the C&AG reports to the House of Commons as a whole, by long-standing convention and practice the reports are considered only by the PAC and not by other Select Committees.

The impact of current and prospective developments on the main features of the NAO's approach, and on the pattern and thrust of published reports, has already been identified in the earlier part of this chapter. Other impacts of a more general kind include:

1. selecting subjects for examination where the NAO's findings, conclusions and recommendations are most likely to achieve results and provide a significant 'added value' in improving departmental performance and accountability;
2. pursuing wider issues but retaining the solid audit base which characterizes NAO examinations, with accurate, fair and balanced reports based on that firm evidence;
3. analysing and identifying at the outset the key features of good management, and yardsticks for performance, in the organizations, programmes and projects to be examined;
4. bringing together a wider range of professional skills and experience relevant to the issues to be examined, by associating consultants and specialist advisers with the audit teams;
5. varying the output so as to increase the value of the NAO's work to the bodies it audits – for example by developing good practice guides, by producing a wider range of unpublished reports and other advice, by encouraging consultation, by assisting in developing and establishing new forms of accounts and other reports: in short, to maximize the potential benefits from the resources already being invested in audit work.

The nature of some of the developments taking place, however, means that as well as developing and realizing opportunities the NAO increasingly has to recognize and avoid potential threats. For example, there are continuing pressures on independence and on the boundaries of the C&AG's remit. The greater politicization of debate on public sector issues and on accountability means that the NAO has more than ever to be seen to be unbiased in the selection and conduct of examinations and in its published reports.

A greater concentration on effectiveness issues inevitably brings the auditor into policy matters – inherently ill-defined and shifting ground – and underlines the importance of avoiding criticism of the merits of policy objectives whilst firmly pursuing the relevance and reliability of data on which policy decisions are based, the implementation of policy, the results achieved and the economy, efficiency and effectiveness with which resources have been used. Ministerial involvement – often a red herring as a guide to the boundaries of the NAO's remit – is an increasing complication, since it now extends well beyond the formulation of policy and into management and implementation. Maintaining the right relationships with audited bodies – cordial but not cosy – requires constant attention.

CONCLUSION

Any examination of current issues and developments, and their consequences for audit and accountability, can only be a snapshot at a particular point in time. Whilst there are already enough challenges and changes in hand or in prospect to make matters interesting, there are inevitably further opportunities and threats round the corner. In some respects therefore the only plan for a public sector audit body is not to have a rigid plan but to remain flexible, look forward not back, be ready to change, anticipate problems and remain light on its feet. Its work must remain relevant, and make a genuine contribution, to current issues and concerns. Findings, conclusions and recommendations must command the respect of the departments and other bodies audited; but at the same time independence in action and in reporting is crucial. Current developments within the National Audit Office stand four square at the heart of these issues.

NOTES

1. See *A Framework for Value for Money Audits*, published by the National Audit Office, February 1988 (revised November 1990).
2. The NAO has reported in recent years on two cases where organizations, though operating in potentially favourable circumstances, were inhibited from securing the full benefits by imposed departmental constraints: *Review of the Operations of HM Land Registry* (HC 39, 1987–8); *Objectives and Management of Ordnance Survey* (HC 177, 1987–8).
3. *The Civil Service*, Report of the Committee 1966–8 (Chairman: Lord Fulton), Cmnd 3638.
4. *Efficiency and Effectiveness in the Civil Service: Government Observations on the Third Report from the Treasury and Civil Service Committee, Session 1981–82*, HC 236, Cmnd 8616.
5. Efficiency Unit (1988) *Improving Management in Government: The Next Steps*, Report to the Prime Minister by Sir Robin Ibbs, HMSO.
6. For an early NAO report on executive agencies, see *The Next Steps Initiative*. HC 410, 1988–9.
7. See, for example, NAO reports: *Provision of Training through Managing Agents* (HC 569, 1988–9); *Transfer of the Royal Dockyards to Commercial Management* (HC 359, 1987–8).

DISCUSSION QUESTIONS

1. What are the key features of the C&AG's role in making government departments and agencies accountable to Parliament?
2. How will the nature of accountability change as departmental functions are increasingly devolved to 'Next Steps' agencies and other bodies?
3. What are the future opportunities and risks the auditor will face as a result of greater devolution?
4. How far and in what directions will value for money auditing need to develop to meet such challenges?
5. Does 'traditional' certification audit have an increasing or diminishing role to play in the public sector of the future?

List of cases

Author Index

Subject Index